Bridging the Gap between
Strategy & Valuation
A Real Option Approach to R&D Valuation

Philip Skjødt

WP 8/2001

June 2001

MPP Working Paper No. 8/2001 ©
June 2001
ISBN-13:   978-87-90403-95-9
ISBN-10:   87-90403-95-9
ISSN: 1396-2817

This working paper is published as a part of the REMAP Research Project

Research Management Processes under rapid change

Department of Management, Politics and Philosophy
Copenhagen Business School
Blaagaardsgade 23B
DK-2200 Copenhagen N
Denmark
Phone: +45 38 15 36 30
Fax: +45 38 15 36 35
E-mail: as.mpp@cbs.dk

http://www.cbs.dk/en/research/departments-and-centres/
department-of-management-politics-and-philosophy

Bridging the Gap between Strategy & Valuation

A Real Option Approach to R&D Valuation

by

Philip Skjødt

MASTER'S THESIS

A Master's Thesis submitted in partial fulfillment of the Cand.Merc. degree; the Master of Science Degree in Economics and Business Administration at the Copenhagen Business School.

Date of submission: March 1, 2001

Executive Summary

This paper analyzes the real option framework's capacity for bridging the gap between strategic theory and financial theory. Through a theoretical discussion of the interface between them, it is shown that they have an obvious point of contact, since strategic theory aims at identifying the path to the highest value creation, while the financial discipline of valuation contains tools for appraising the value creation. Nevertheless, it is argued that differences in foci and prerequisites cause a gap. The real option framework is put forward as holding potential for bridging this gap by being applicable to both strategic analysis and financial valuation. Correspondingly, it is suggested that the real option framework contains a strategic and a financial perspective. The paper then moves forward to investigate the perspectives individually in the light of a case analysis in order to be able to conclude on their alignment at the end of the paper.

First, the strategic perspective on real options is positioned within strategic theory. Through a theoretical discussion, it is shown that the strategic perspective is in excellent concord with the capabilities view. This is a generic perspective containing various strategic positions unified. It is shown that the capabilities view combined with the strategic perspective on real options is relevant for the strategic analysis of R&D. The case company, NKT Research Center is presented and a brief but illustrative discussion of the applicability of the strategic perspective on real options in combination with the capabilities view shows its appropriateness.

On the other side of the gap, the financial perspective on real options is investigated through a complete real option valuation of one of NRC's new research-based start-ups - Scandinavian Micro Biodevices (abbr. SMB). Following a theoretical presentation of the fundamentals behind real option valuation, positioned relative to conventional valuation techniques, the practical application is carried out.

This begins with an introduction to the business case of SMB, which is a venture into biochips. In three years, it is argued, management effectively holds a real option to initiate production of biochips, to the extent that proof-of-concept has been achieved and the market potential is considered satisfactory. The Black & Scholes option pricing formula is chosen as the mathematical solution, and the required numerical inputs are estimated with special attention being paid to the most extraordinary variable introduced by the real option framework, namely the volatility. The main result of the real option valuation is the appraisal of the value of SMB, which is found to be DKK 58 millions, compared with an estimate at DKK 9 millions calculated using the Discounted Cash Flow method (abbr. DCF).

The real option valuation of SMB is found to uncover significant value compared with conventional valuation techniques, such as DCF. Though the quality of some of the numerical inputs that enter into the valuation are wanting, most of these issues appear to be general difficulties related to the activity of valuation per se. Still, real option valuation is concluded to suffer from some of the rigidities of conventional valuation, as well as newly introduced ones, which all-in-all counteract its capacity to capture the complexities of strategic analysis and thus bridge the gap. Nevertheless, the gap is narrowed through the application of real option valuation. Finally, it is argued that corporate practitioners may come even closer to bridging the gap, by utilizing their hands-on feel of the company-specific uncertainties and strategic complexities to better quantify the framework and capture option value.

Table of Contents

List of Figures

List of Tables

Preface

The beforehand paper is my Master's thesis, which is submitted in partial fulfillment of the Cand.Merc.-degree, or translated into English the Master of Science Degree in Economics and Business Administration. Of the different Master programmes at the Copenhagen Business School, I have followed the line called International Business. This line aims at providing a generalist approach to business administration by covering a wide variety of economics and business administrational disciplines. Emphasis however, is on strategy in the face of the internationalization, which has had a growing influence on the business enterprise sector in recent years, and is expected to have so increasingly.

Though my specialization is strategy, I have been very interested in financial tools, and perceive strategy and finance as a very powerful combination. For this reason, I have chosen in my elective courses in the Master's programme to look into financial valuation as a support for strategy formulation. My elective courses were taken at Università Bocconi in Milan in the Fall semester of 1999, where I, among other things, conducted a Discounted Cash Flow valuation. It was during my time at Bocconi that I first got acquainted with the real option framework, and its potential for aligning financial valuation with strategic analysis and strategic planning.

Throughout my studies, I have worked part-time as a Student Assistant in the Ministry of Research, which has given me an interest in research management and the dynamics of corporate research, as well as public research. Hence, it was concurrently my intention to write my Master's thesis within the field of research management.

The combination of real option valuation and strategic research management obviously targets relevant, but challenging issues. Two of the main issues are whether research can be strategically planned, given its unforeseeable nature, and if so, whether this research can be appraised to come up with a quantitative estimate of its value. In short the ambition has been to determine whether the real option framework can be applied to analyze and evaluate the uncertainties of research management meaningfully per se, while concurrently testing the real option framework's potential for aligning financial valuation with strategic theory.

Given my intention to test the applicability of the real option framework, I was fortunate enough to establish contact with the Danish company NKT Holding (abbr. NKT). They gave me permission to use their R&D subsidiary, NKT Research Center as the case company in my analysis. The initiation of my project coincided with NKT's sale of GIGA to Intel in the spring of 2000, which is the most significant success of NKT research to date in terms of value creation. Preceding this event, NKT Research Center had worked some time to implement an ambitious research-based corporate venturing business model. With a target of establishing three to five start-ups a year, based on research results, the foundation for carrying out my analysis appeared as good as imaginable.

As my business case, I chose a start-up established in March 2000 called Scandinavian Micro Biodevices. This start-up is NKT's first venture into the field of medico-technology, targeted at the development and the commercial introduction of biochips. One of the main drivers behind the development of the biochip product technology is to be found within the field of genetics, where major steps have been taken in recent years, and the future development is expected to cause a substantial impact on health care research and practice.

Since neither the real option framework, nor the recent advances within genetics are among the standard curriculum at the Copenhagen Business School, I have put efforts into explaining and communicating the fundamentals behind these fields, in the paper, while maintaining the academic level. It has been my ambition to demonstrate the application of the real option framework in an intelligible way for people unfamiliar with the framework, but with a basic understanding of corporate finance principles. In my own acquisition of insights into genetics, I started out from scratch. I have put my best efforts into communicating the fundamentals and the exciting perspectives of this field of research in a way that is intelligible for economists.

The explorative nature of the thesis statement has offered many interesting side tracks in its exploration, as has the ambition to bridge the two vast theoretical fields of strategy and finance. In order to stick to the thesis statement, extensive use of notes and appendices have been made to incorporate relevant aspects that nevertheless deviated from the academic intentions of the paper and the level of insight assumed for the evaluation. Furthermore, the substantial amounts of empirical sources, data and theoretical positions have added to the use of notes and appendices for the purpose of documentation. Hence, endnotes have been chosen, which can be found at the end of this volume. For easier reference, these have also been attached as an appendix in the accompanying booklet, which contains the appendices.

Ultimately, the applicability and the value of the real option framework is determined by its usefulness to practitioners. With a view to that I hope with this paper to have returned something useful to NKT Holding and NKT Research with thanks. Within the organization, I would especially like to thank personally Søren Isaksen, CTO, NKT Holding, for opening the door, and Dorte Thulstrup, Business Developer, NKT Innovation, for helping me with the fundamentals of genetics and the dynamics of the biochip industry.

I would like to thank my academic advisor Kenneth Husted, and my friends Jeppe Bregenov-Pedersen, Jens Laugesen and Sune Andersen for comments and critique on select parts of the paper. All misconceptions and errors are of course my own.

Copenhagen, February 2001

1. Introduction

The concept of real options has been around since the 1980's and has surfaced in the financial and academic debate from time to time[1]. With alluring promises of improved financial valuation, the notion of a more sophisticated and flexible alternative to conventional valuation techniques is very appealing. Despite of the substantial research efforts put into developing the real option framework, it has yet to make its breakthrough into the standard corporate finance curriculum, and to become a tool widely used among practitioners. The reasons for this may be manifold, but the mathematical complexity associated with option pricing techniques, and the way that complicated formulas tend to obscure intuition, are definitely two of main obstacles.

The activity of valuation is particularly relevant, whenever quantitative estimates are required as a foundation for some sort of ownership transfer of entire companies or parts hereof. Prominent examples are companies undergoing initial public offering of stock and subsequent offerings, mergers and acquisitions of companies to determine respectively post-merger equity shares or sales price, and companies left as inheritance by entrepreneurs to their heirs, where the ownership must be divided somehow. The financial discipline of valuation provides models for appraising such assets as companies with complex going concern cost and revenue profiles, where pricing is not as straightforward as in the transfer and pricing of simple goods. Valuation is also utilized within companies for evaluating and prioritizing among investment projects in the face of scarce resources, thus aiming at portfolio efficiency.

This paper tests the applicability of the real option framework. This is done in the light of the real option framework's proposed potential for better aligning financial valuation with strategic theory. It is argued that financial theory and strategic theory have hitherto been so disparate that a gap exists between them, in spite of the fact that strategic planning aims at outlining the path to the highest value creation, and financial theory contains valuation techniques to measure this value creation quantitatively. The proposition is that the real option framework provides for a more sophisticated financial analysis, which is capable of better capturing the complexity of strategic analysis and strategic planning. This proposition becomes the main thesis of the paper, and the test of the applicability of real option valuation thus becomes one of the most critical aspects in the investigation of this thesis.

The test of the applicability is undertaken by conducting a real option valuation of a research investment project of NKT Research Center (abbr. NRC). The research investment project is a recently established start-up called Scandinavian Micro Biodevices (abbr. SMB), which develops biochips. Biochips are functional microstructures targeted at the analysis - i.e. measuring and screening - of biological cells and molecules.

The advances that have been made within genetics over the last decade in terms of mapping the human genome and identifying all human genes[2] will greatly improve research on gene-related and genetic diseases and drug development with huge impact on the pharmaceutical and biotechnology industries. Biochips has the potential of becoming one of the most important tools in this development by allowing for quicker and cheaper gene and DNA sequencing and analysis of gene expression. Furthermore, by taking genetic diagnosis from the laboratory to the private medical practices, and thus facilitating more personalized diagnosis and customized treatment, the biochips are foreseen to be a critical piece in this predicted revolution of health care research and practice[3].

After this brief introduction to the main topics of the paper, the next step is to formulate the thesis statement, along which I will delve into these topics in a more detailed analysis.

1.1 Thesis Statement

> The main thesis investigated is the real option framework's capacity to bridge the gap between strategic theory and financial theory.

Figure 1.1 The Gap between Financial Theory and Strategic Theory

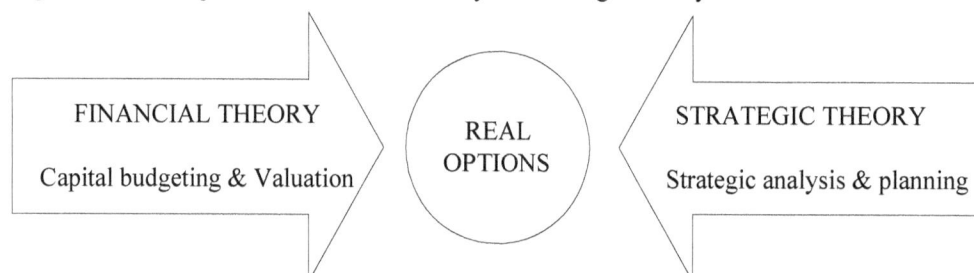

Source: Own construction.

Though the gap may be intuitively recognizable, the thesis is not as such based on empirical observation and identification of the phenomenon. Rather the analysis takes its point of departure in a theoretical discussion of the interface between financial theory and strategic theory, which has been wanting to the extent that a gap can be identified.

The analysis begins on the strategic side of the gap. First the strategic perspective on real options will be presented and positioned relative to strategic theory. The themes looked into in the analysis hereof, and thus the questions answered, are:
- What is the contribution of the strategic perspective on real options to strategic theory?
- Is the strategic perspective on real options compatible with predominant strategic perspectives, or is it merely an alternative perspective?
- How relevant is the strategic perspective on real options for the analysis of research investments, and what lessons can be learned in this regard from the literature?

The investigation of the strategic perspective does not lead to a full-blown strategic analysis of the case company. Rather the ambition is to outline its potential theoretically. Following the presentation of the case company however, the strategic perspective on real options will be discussed in the light of the reality of the case company.

2

The analysis then moves on to the financial side of the gap, which makes up the largest part of the analysis. The investigation of the financial perspective has two intertwined purposes.

> First of all, to determine how well-aligned the financial perspective on real options is with the strategic perspective.

This is related to the thesis on the gap.

> The second purpose is to test the applicability of real option valuation.

Of course, this is an integrated part of evaluating the financial perspective relative to the gap. But it can also be perceived as a more separate test of real option valuation as a tool for financial valuation. Therefore, the applicability of real option valuation will also be compared with conventional valuation techniques.

The analysis of the financial perspective on real options begins by placing it relative to financial theory. The analysis uncovers the answers to the following questions:
- What are the similarities between conventional valuation techniques and real option valuation?
- What are the distinctive features of real option valuation?

Hereafter, the analysis undertakes the empirical preparation, which includes the configuration of the real option in the case company - i.e. interpreting the reality of the case company as a real option, and operationalizing the variables. These analytic steps are relatively straightforward in terms of what must be uncovered, but do contain an explorative element in the sense that few applications have been carried out and little operational guidelines exist in the literature. Hence, a suitable empirical focus will be chosen within NRC in order to conduct the analysis on a feasible business case. The empirical application leads to a valuation estimate.

> Based on the application of the financial perspective on real options to the case company, the analysis will appraise the value of the business case investigated.

The evaluation of the applicability of real option valuation will touch upon the following aspects:
- How well can the reality of the business case be interpreted as a real option?
- What is the quality of the numerical inputs of the variables that enter into the valuation?
- How suitable are research investments for real option valuation?
- How does the real option valuation compare with conventional valuation techniques?
- What are the major shortcomings and the major benefits of applying real option valuation?

After having tested the applicability of real option valuation, and thus investigated the financial perspective on real options through this, the paper concludes with a discussion of the main thesis; namely

> the real option framework's capacity to bridge the gap between strategic theory and financial theory.

The aspects of this are:
- To what extent can strategic complexities be captured by real option valuation?
- How easily and adequately are the financial implications - i.e. valuation aspects - integrated into strategic analysis and strategic planning?
- Where does the real option framework hold the most potential for bridging the gap?
- What are the main shortcomings of the real option framework with regard to bridging the gap?

The analysis behind the investigation of the thesis statement will be structured in the order presented in this section. As illustrated below, the strategic perspective is presented first. Following this, the financial perspective is rolled out in a complete real option valuation. Thereafter, the conclusions on the financial perspective / real option valuation follow, with the conclusions on the gap at the end.

Figure 1.2 Composition of the Paper

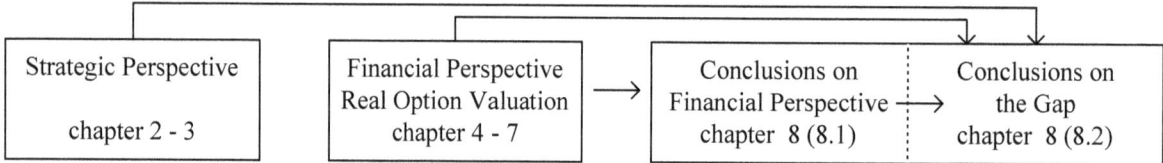

| Strategic Perspective chapter 2 - 3 | Financial Perspective Real Option Valuation chapter 4 - 7 | → | Conclusions on Financial Perspective chapter 8 (8.1) | → | Conclusions on the Gap chapter 8 (8.2) |

Source: Own construction.

The real option valuation takes up the main part of the analysis. If the reader is only interested in its application by itself, chapter 4 to 8.1 can be read as a complete and independent example of real option valuation applied to a case. In order to facilitate this, a few points on the mathematical principles and the value-impact of option valuation are refreshed in chapter 4, which are already introduced in chapter 2 to establish a basic and shared understanding, before rolling out the strategic perspective.

On a final note to the terms that have been in play in the formulation of the thesis statement and will be used repeatedly hereafter, the term *the real option framework* refers to the theoretical complex of contributions that rely on the theory and the mathematical principles behind financial options to apply these by analogy in the corporate setting. As such the term covers both the application for financial valuation, as well as for strategic analysis. In this perception, the main distinction in the real option framework is between the financial perspective on real options and the strategic perspective on real options, which is respectively related to financial valuation and strategic analysis. Whereas the term real option framework contains both perspectives on real options, the terms *real option valuation* and *the real option approach to valuation* only relate to the financial perspective on real options; i.e. the financial side of the gap.

1.2 Theoretical Perspective and Delimitations

Since the main focus of this paper is to test the applicability of real option valuation, and the broader framework's capacity for bridging the gap between strategic theory and financial theory, the choice of theoretical perspective is inherent in the purpose of the paper itself.

It should be mentioned though, that

> one central theoretical principle pervades the financial analysis, namely that the value of a company or an investment project is fundamentally determined by its capability of generating future income, and the assumption that this income must take into account the time-value of money and be duly adjusted to the uncertainty profile.

This is in contrast to principles such as intrinsic book value, historic performance and other valuation principles. The chosen perspective on valuation is known as a Net Present Value approach. Besides the real option approach, the primary approach that explicitly does likewise is the Discounted Cash Flow approach (abbr. DCF). Hence, the evaluation of real option valuation is held up against the DCF approach, which is sometimes referred to in the paper as the conventional valuation technique, due to its widespread acceptance and use[4]. Other approaches may indirectly take this criteria into account, but for the lack of explicitness, these are not considered. An example hereof is the use of multiples, where ratios are taken from a transaction involving the sale of a comparable company, thereby providing a market value to relate the valuation to. The ratios could be turnover-to-market value, book-to-market value, net-income-to-market value, and many more. Also the stock market capitalization value of comparable companies could be applied proportionately through ratios, but since all the mentioned approaches surpass the explicit forecast of future income-generating potential, they are theoretically flawed and too indirect for a detailed treatment, and thus understanding, of the subject matter. If the reader is unfamiliar with the range of valuation approaches presented, appendix 2 positions real option valuation relative to those.

1.2.1 Theoretical Delimitations

The two theoretical disciplines, which this paper draws on, are financial theory and strategic theory.

Within the field of financial theory, I have refrained from looking into the issue of derivation; i.e. deriving and proving the formulas. Furthermore, I have abstained from delving deep into the complex mathematics, which are readily available within the real option framework and option theory in general. This is not to say that the use of mathematics has been unduly simplified, but rather that the subtleties and complexities are quite substantial. An emphasis hereon would have changed the focus and the character of the paper. From the onset, the emphasis has been on exploring and testing the application and applicability in *lieu* of exploring and sophisticating the theoretical foundation.

The field of strategic theory contains a vast number of diverse contributions. In this paper's placement of the strategic perspective on real options *vis-à-vis* strategic theory, a number of positions have been unified into one generic perspective. This generic perspective is labeled the capabilities view and represents certain predominant lines of thinking in current strategic theory. This perspective has been chosen due to its compatibility with the strategic perspective on real options. Still this approach bypasses many other important contributions and positions. This simplification has been a necessity in order to limit the extent of the presentation and the complexity of positioning the real option framework. This choice effectively places the focus on competitive advantage and ignores other aspects of a strategic theory of the firm, such as issues of optimal organization and boundaries, and the existence of firms. Interested readers may find a more thorough presentation and positioning of the strategic perspective on real options relative to strategic theory in appendix 1.

1.2.2 Empirical Delimitations

Additionally, the use of strategic theory has primarily been kept at a theoretical level in the determination of the real option framework's consistency and applicability. Though a full-fledged analysis of the case company through the strategic perspective on real options would have been very relevant and enlightening for the thesis, this delimitation has been necessary, due to size constraints. However, a brief and illustrative analysis following the presentation of the case company demonstrates and discusses a potential application of the strategic perspective on real options to NRC.

Finally, the expectations and projections of NRC with regard to the aspects of the business plan that are used in the estimation of the variables, such as market potential, expected revenues, chances of achieving the required research results, etc. have scarcely been questioned in the paper and discussed with NRC. Though, the estimates could be biased, it is impossible for layman to evaluate this, and for reasons of confidentiality, it has not been possible to have data verified by independent experts. Nevertheless, it is reasonable to rely on the NRC estimates.

1.3 Methodology

The methodical approach is fundamentally dependent on the purpose and the context of the study[5]. Though the methodical approach must be adjusted to the characteristics of the study, there are typically more ways to achieve this fit. This choice of methodical approach conversely influences the study too. To better analyze the methodical approach, a model of the process for the production of knowledge, and the factors influencing this process, has been used. This is shown in the figure below.

The framework conditions influence the process for the production of knowledge. The production of knowledge evolves from the interactions between four fundamental aspects; the research question - in this paper known as the thesis statement, the theory, the empiricism, and the conclusions. The process for the production of knowledge must be based on an integrated methical approach. Conversely, the methical approach must be adapted to the nature of the framework conditions and the process for the production of knowledge itself. Thus, the process for the production of knowledge follows the methical approach chosen, which in turn is also determined by the content of the four formerly mentioned aspects of the process. From this interdependence arises the need for an integrated approach that is both determined by the framework conditions and the four aspects, as well as directing the interplay of the four aspects of process for the production of knowledge.

Figure 1.3 The Control Factors and the Main Components in the Choice of Methical Approach

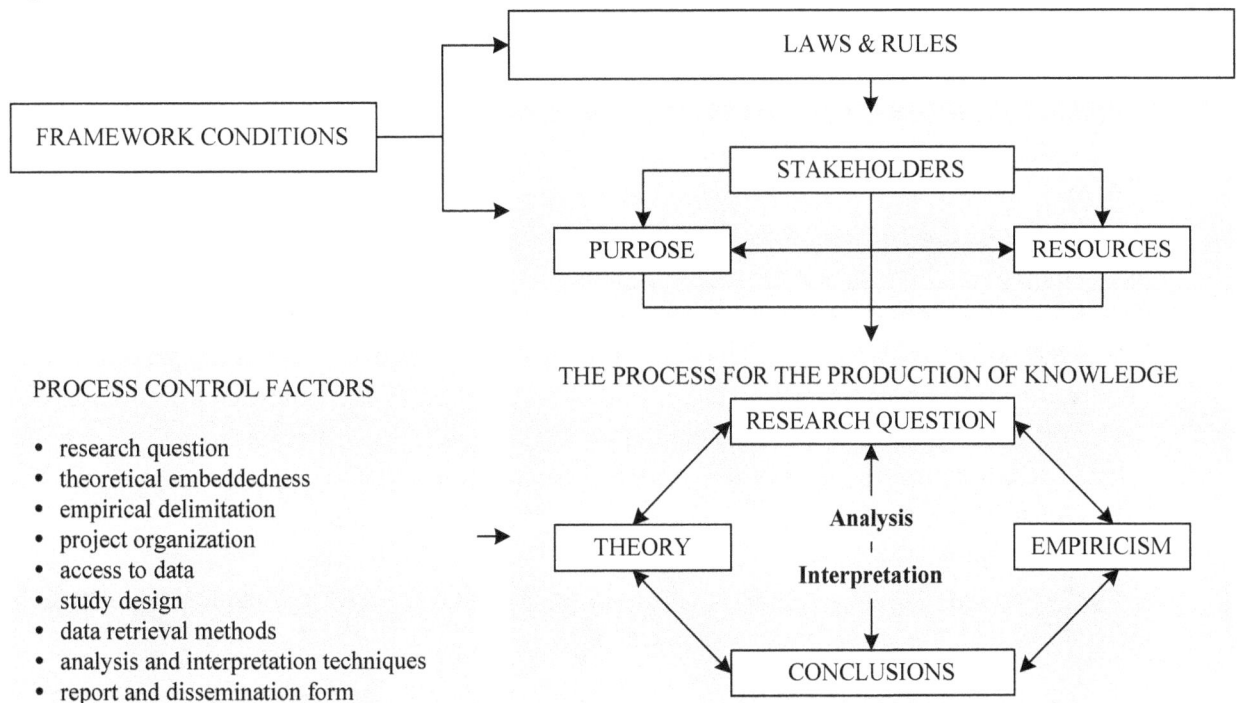

PROCESS CONTROL FACTORS

- research question
- theoretical embeddedness
- empirical delimitation
- project organization
- access to data
- study design
- data retrieval methods
- analysis and interpretation techniques
- report and dissemination form

Source: Andersen (1999) p. 51. Own translation.

The concrete and operational methical lines that the interplay - i.e. the process - follows, stem from a number of process controlling factors. Some are given, some are chosen, while some can be partially inferred from the given and chosen ones, once these have been laid down. The outlined interdependency between the process for the production of knowledge and the methical approach, and the relationships between the process control factors are depicted in the figure below.

Figure 1.4 The Interdependencies in the Process for the Production of Knowledge

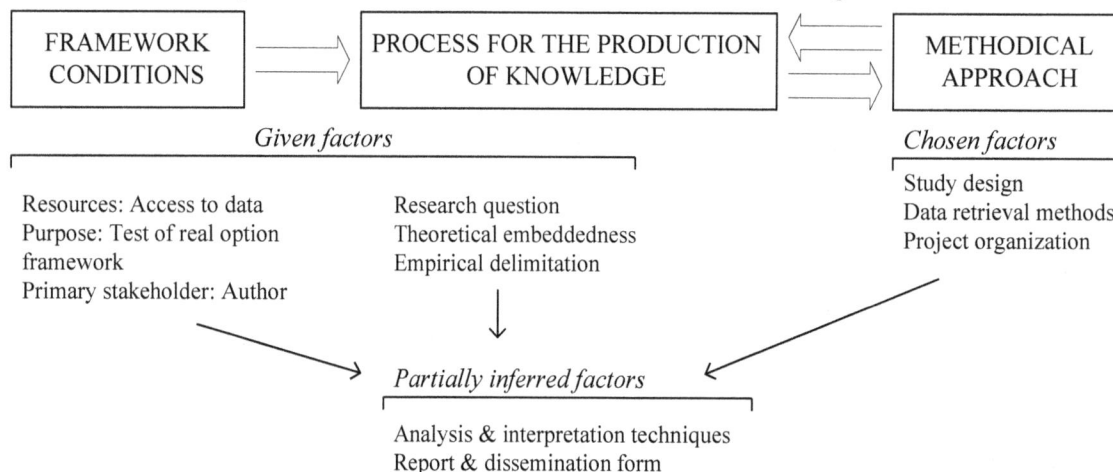

Source: Own construction, based on Andersen (1999).

The *given factors* are the research question, the theoretical embeddedness, the empirical delimitation, and the access to data. These are decided upon prior to the choice of methodical approach, though they are subsequently also influenced by the choice. The *chosen process control factors* must be chosen in accordance with the given ones. The chosen process control factors are project organization, study design and data retrieval methods. The study design and data retrieval methods constitute the concrete methodical approach to the empiricism. Finally, the given process control factors and the corresponding choice of methodical approach have implications for the interplay (i.e. the process for the production of knowledge) through their consequences for the analysis and interpretation techniques, and the report and dissemination form. These are the *partially inferred process control factors*, which are partially determined by the given and chosen ones.

After having outlined the concepts and interrelations behind the choice of methodical approach, this will be laid down with regard to the analysis.

1.3.1 Framework Conditions

For this study, the point of departure was the author's - in casu the primary *stakeholder* - desire to test the usability of the theories behind the real option framework for a business case. As such, the *purpose* - to follow the terminology of the above illustration - was the starting point, which was chosen by the author based on academic ambitions and experiences, as well as own preferences. Therefore, the other stakeholders, such as the management of the case company and the academic supervisor, have had a rather limited influence on the choice of purpose, field of study or study object. Nevertheless, the focus in the paper on the application and the applicability of the framework coincides with an ambition to return something usable to the company.

For the company, however, the potential value is not in the academic test of a theoretical framework. From a corporate and practical point of view, the challenge is to appraise the value of research investments. These investments are characterized as uncertain, long-term, and often involving sizable investments. Though conventional valuation techniques exist, the outlined characteristics accentuate these techniques' shortcomings and weaknesses in the face of projections related to a distant and uncertain future. Therefore, as seen from the company, the potential value added from this study, or the study's purpose, is the test of a new valuation technique on research investments.

For theoretically undeveloped or underdeveloped fields of study, explorative and inductive case studies are quite common and meaningful. In order to enhance the understanding of the field of study, thorough analyses of one or few study objects are conducted, which lead to general, but cautious statements[6]. The same approach is applied in this paper. Not because the field of study is theoretically undeveloped or underdeveloped, but rather because the theoretical framework has been transferred more or less directly from a financial context to the corporate setting. In other words, the real option framework does not, as is most common, originate from empiricism, but is deducted from a set of principles originally identified for another field of study; namely the study of financial derivatives and financial options. Therefore, in its lack of empirical testing and underpinnings, this field of study can be said to be undeveloped or underdeveloped, though not in a strictly theoretical sense. Hence, the explorative and inductive nature of this paper at the general level in terms of purpose, research question and conclusions. As Andersen points out: '(T)he less previous knowledge we possess about the field of study and the study object, the more explorative (inductive) we have to work'[7].

> Since the findings of this single-case study will be empirically based, it can be foreseen that the findings will be qualitative in nature. At the end, it will be necessary, as is the case for almost all kinds of inductive reasoning, to separate the findings that are generalizable and the ones that are particular, i.e. specific to research investment projects, specific to the case company, or even specific to the business case chosen; here the valuation unit[8].

The use of a single case study to come up with general statements is problematic, given the fact that this is basically one observation of numerous imaginable cases. However, as Flyvbjerg points out, one case is sufficient for reasonable falsification[9]. Thus,

> the single-case study provides for defensible testing of the limits of the real option framework,

both as regards the gap, as well as the real option valuation.

The case study is critical in the sense that it aims to scrutinize and test existing theory[10]. At the same time, the empirical focus will be chosen in terms of suitability to facilitate the application. This choice, Flyvbjerg labels '*the most-likely case*', which is particularly suitable for falsification[11]. This follows the line of reasoning that if the theory is not applicable or valid to a most-likely case, there are strong indications that it is generally not applicable. Another benefit of studying a most-likely case is that the findings might hint at verification or generate new theses in the sense that the indications as to aspects that are problematic and thus require further testing or entirely new theoretical development might be uncovered, due to the anticipated suitability. However, it should be emphasized that to the extent that certain aspects of the framework are falsified, it will be hard to pinpoint the causes, as it will be difficult to identify solutions to aspects that are problematic. Of course, this may lead to indications as to aspects that require further research, but it cannot be expected that new theoretical contributions, or indications hereof, will emerge from this single-case study.

In the other aspect of the framework conditions, the company has of course decided on the access and availability of critical *resources* to the study. The sensitive nature of the financial data analyzed[12] and the work pressure of the relevant people - particularly in the very busy business development department NKT Innovation - were the two most critical issues related to the resources at hand.

The sensitive nature of the data was quite simply handled with a confidentiality agreement, and access was given to the most detailed financial projections available. Though the confidentiality conflicts with the desire to let the Master's thesis be read by whomever would be interested herein, it had no practical implications for the methodical approach taken. In the interviews, however, it appeared that some respondents were cautious about their replies, despite of the confidentiality agreement and the read-through-for-prior-approval clause herein. Still, the most problematic data to get by in the application of the framework are not of such a kind that more interview time or better access to the organization would have helped. These data are related to the numerical depiction of uncertainty, known as the volatility. As will be explained in the theoretical presentation, volatility estimates are very specific to real option valuation, and are rarely produced in companies, unless they work very specifically with this valuation technique, which is not the case for NKT Research Center.

So all in all, there were some limitations in the resources provided for by the company, but these were not significant, due to the field of study. In the process, there has been no need for producing extensive primary data. These have been limited to interviews. External sources for certain data, e.g. stock price data on comparable companies for the estimation of the volatility, and internal reports in the shape of business plans, followed by a few clarifying questions, proved to be sufficient to fulfill the purpose of the paper, and to answer the research questions.

1.3.2 The Process for the Production of Knowledge and the Process Control Factors

From the above illustration, it is clear that the framework conditions influence the process for the production of knowledge. However, the framework conditions' direct influence on the four aspects has been limited with regard to the choice of methodical approach. More important is the direct influence of the research question, the theory and the empiricism on the methodical approach; in particular their influence on the study design and the data retrieval methods.

The *research questions* have a two-folded impact on the methodical approach. At the general level, the research questions reflect the earlier described purpose, which is inductive and explorative in nature leading to a qualitative approach to the data retrieval. But at the analytical level, where it is outlined which steps the analysis must take, the focus on operationalizing known variables leads to a quantitative approach and a schematic study design. Also the valuation focus which basically needs the analysis to come up with one figure that expresses the value, implies a quantitative focus and study design. The quantitative end-result of a valuation could imply that the validity of the framework could be determined very exactly and accurately. Though, the final figure on the value is very concrete and specific, this is unfortunately altogether not the case. Because the value of complex phenomena, such as companies or research projects, is often appraised under assumptions and looking to the future, and as such arbitrary, it is impossible to compare the quantitative value of the valuation with any known value of the valuation unit. A valuation is simply carried out under too many temporally and contextually delimiting assumptions for an exact benchmark to found. Nevertheless, the operationalization and application of the valuation technique all-in-all leads to a quantitative study design in the test of applicability.

The above quantitative implications for the methodical approach at the analytical level is further reinforced by the *theoretical embeddedness*. The fact that real option valuation is taken from the well-established framework of financial options makes the approach deductive, since the application is quite straightforwardly outlined, based on this. Furthermore, real option valuation is build around option pricing techniques, which, among other things, incorporate mathematically calculated volatilities. Both of these aspects of the theoretical embeddedness imply a quantitative methodical approach.

In the application, real option valuation meets the empiricism. In the corporate setting, the terms and concepts are applied to the realities of the company. Both the operationalization of research in all its complexity, and the estimation of the variables require a qualitative approach to both the data retrieval, and the interpretation of the findings. In the operationalization and the interpretation of the reality as a real option - a.k.a. the configuration, the approach does get explorative, due to the lack of previous applications in the literature to lean on for directions.

Figure 1.5 The Main Methodological Perspectives in the Paper

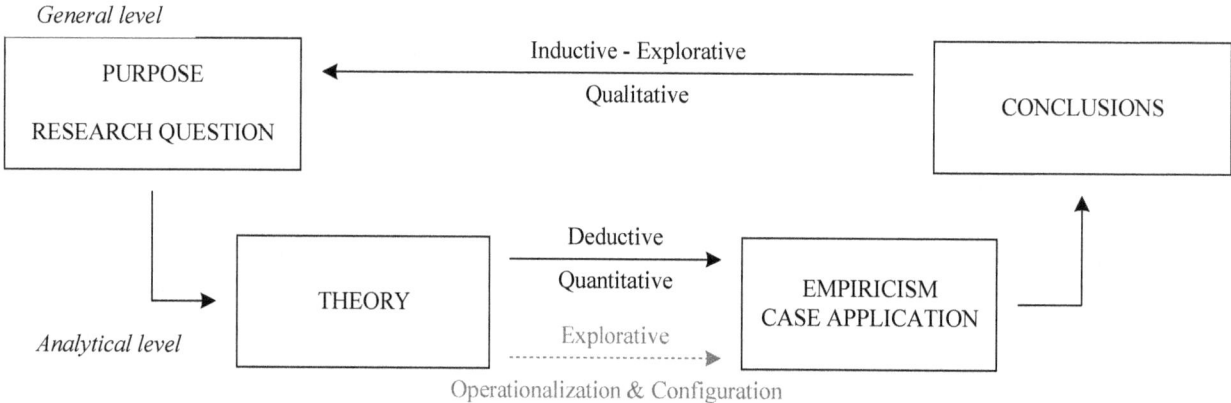

Source: Own construction.

In the above illustration, the methodical approach is presented as two-stringed. At the general level the findings will be qualitative, due to the nature of the study. But since the general level is more of a frame for the study, the qualitative nature is not reflected in the study design and the data retrieval methods. This is because the theoretical framework applied in the analysis is so established that a quantitative and factual study design can be applied. Thus the data that ultimately needs to be established are quantitative in nature. Yet, the application of real option valuation is in some aspects so untested that some elements of the analysis will be explorative in nature. Thus, the complexity of the *empiricism* requires qualitative data retrieval methods and reasoning, when interpretations are necessary in connection with the operationalization and configuration.

> The concurrent application of both the inductive and the deductive approach in the study is not unusual[13]. In this paper, it basically reflects the fact that, at the general level, the purpose is to conclude on the overall applicability and thus validity of the theory from one empirical case (induction). The general level is related to the main thesis on the real option framework's capacity for bridging the gap between strategic and financial theory. In order to do so, the directions of the theory have to be followed in the application (deduction). Consequently, large parts of the analysis become descriptive, explanatory and problem-solving (i.e. the capital budgeting and resource allocation function that valuation techniques fulfill) in a quantitative and deductive way. This is related to the financial perspective; i.e. real option valuation.

The conceptual framework and the formation of terms is in this study - as in all studies - very important to introduce clearly and concisely in order to avoid confusion and to improve the communication. Solid definitions maintained throughout the paper is the way to ensure this. The challenge is to secure that the theoretical definitions, the operationalized variables and the data gathered are in accordance with each other. The figure below illustrates the case in point.

12

Figure 1.6 The Relationship between Reliability and Validity

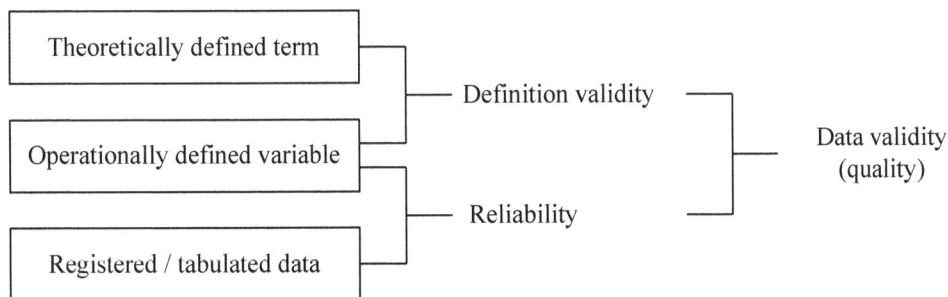

Source: Andersen (1999) p. 110. Own translation.

In this paper, it is particularly challenging to establish the two fits; definition validity and reliability. Especially, because the terms and their relations are conceptually given and well-established from option pricing theory. Yet, the terms have to be operationalized and their content interpreted from the corporate reality. Therefore, the challenge, when testing the application and the applicability of the framework, is closely related to the establishment of definition validity. Hence, a problem, which is usually methodological, is in this paper actually at the root of the research question. In other words,

> the test of the applicability of real options is a test of the terms and variables, when taken from the field of financial derivatives into the corporate setting.

Thus, it should be kept in mind that if the framework is questioned after the application, this could also reflect the fact that the theoretically defined terms and their relations are not that appropriate, possibly due to the underlying assumptions or the terms, which may not work in the corporate setting.

2. Strategic Perspective

This chapter serves four purposes. First of all, it gives a historical and conceptual introduction to the field of options. Secondly, it specifies the gap theoretically, while thirdly it positions the strategic perspective on real options with regard to strategic theory and scrutinizes its potential in this regard. Finally, it presents a literature overview of contributions to the field of real options and R&D. The number of purposes may seem large, but as will be clear their fulfillment are intertwined. The following presents an outline of the chapter-

At first, a distinction is introduced between the traditional options traded on various exchanges, labeled financial options in the paper, and real options in the corporate setting. Following this, another distinction is drawn between strategic real options and financial real options. The strategic perspective on real options - a.k.a. strategic real options - comprises the contributions that the real option framework puts forward with regard to strategic theory, and the financial perspective - a.k.a. financial real options - in parallel, the contributions made to financial theory. The emphasis in this chapter is on placing the strategic perspective on real options relative to the predominant perspectives in strategic theory. The financial perspective on real options is only presented to the extent necessary for the understanding and contextualization of the strategic perspective. The financial perspective will be treated in more detail later in the paper. The distinctions of the chapter and the progress of the presentation are illustrated below.

Figure 2.1 Distinctions and Progress in Chapter Two

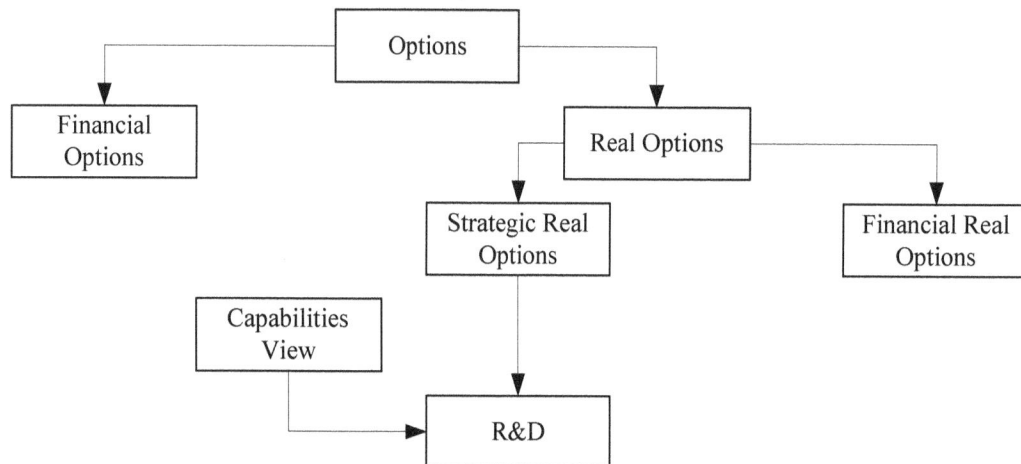

Source: Own construction.

In the placement of the strategic perspective on real options into the field of strategic theory, a generic perspective labeled the capabilities view is presented. The capabilities view comprises a range of similar theoretical contributions. For the analysis of competitive advantage, the strategic perspective on real options and the capabilities view are in excellent concord. The combination of these two perspectives is related to the analysis of R&D, because of the nature of the case company. The chapter concludes with a presentation of the contributions made specifically to real options and R&D.

2.1 The Emergence of Option Valuation

Options as practical financial tools have been traded in one form or another since the turn of the 20th century[14]. Due to options' usefulness for hedging undesired temporal risks for traders, options have fulfilled real needs. The pricing, however, was up until 1973 an arbitrary matter. Before that several attempts had been made at solving this problem, with most of these succeeding only in ad hoc, numerical solutions to specific analyses[15]. At that point, Fisher Black and Myron Scholes published their seminal article '*The Pricing of Options and Corporate Liabilities*'[16], which contained a closed-form analytical pricing solution[17]. This discovery boosted the use of financial options at several exchanges, which quickly implemented the Black & Scholes option pricing formula in their operations[18]. The use of options has since then been steadily increasing with stock- and commodity-based options as the most widely offered financial options. The popularity of the financial options is not only due to their hedging properties - i.e. the transfer of temporal risk in market transactions that enable business enterprises to off-set undesired risks, but also due to the highly geared speculation that the financial options enable.

2.2 Financial Options

At first Black & Scholes discovery initiated further research into the pricing of financial options. Throughout the 1970's, the option pricing techniques were developed further, most notably with Cox, Ross & Rubinstein's presentation of an option valuation technique that used a binomial approach[19], as opposed to Black & Scholes' solution, which was based on the normal distribution. The binomial approach towards the modeling of uncertainty in option valuation has the Black & Scholes option pricing formula as a special limiting case, when the binomial distribution, among other things, is approximated to the normal distribution[20]. The binomial approach enables more complex options to be modeled and appraised, due to its more flexible mathematics and use of discrete observations, as opposed to the continuous observations of the normal distribution. In other words, the analysis and design of more complex and exotic options was made possible through the easier development of both analytical and numerical solutions that the binomial approach facilitates. Until the mid-1980's, the focus was almost solely on the development of quantitative, theoretical solutions for the valuation of financial options.

2.3 Real Options

In 1984, Stewart Myers is acknowledged to be the first to coin the term 'real options'[21] in an article on the gap between strategic planning and financial theory[22]. Myers observed that:

> '*Strategic planning is many things, but it surely includes the process of deciding how to commit the firm's resources across lines of business. The financial side of*
> *strategic planning allocates a particular resource, capital. ... Yet finance theory*
> *has had scant impact on strategic planning.*' Myers (1984) p. 126.

This way, Myers perceives the most relevant part of financial theory for strategic planning to be in the area of capital budgeting, i.e. the firm's capital investment decisions[23,24]. One of the most functional[25] definitions of strategy points to the same similarity in focus. It was laid down by Alfred Chandler in 1962, and defines strategy as '*(t)he determination of the long-run goals and objectives of an enterprise, and the adoption of courses of action and the allocation of resources necessary for carrying out these goals*'[26]. Since real option valuation belongs to the corporate finance discipline labeled capital budgeting, which focuses on the '*allocation of resources among investment projects on a long-term basis*' [27], the shared focus is obvious by these definitions.

Myers is well aware that the strategic planning must take into consideration more than the financial implications, because '*capital budgeting is in practice a bottom-up process. ... Picking valuable pieces does not insure maximum value for the whole. Piecemeal, bottom-up capital budgeting is not strategic planning*'[28]. Nevertheless, Myers reasons, management does set out for a course that will increase the value of the firm in the formulation of strategy. In so doing, an implicit estimate of net present value is effectively made. Hence, the formulation and choice of strategy would benefit from the application of capital budgeting techniques to appraise the value of the strategy and the strategic alternatives explicitly. The recognition of the benefits from integrating strategy and financial theory, and a reconciliation of the two disciplines thus becomes the way to improve the process of strategic planning.

Myers identifies three reasons for the gap between strategic planning and financial theory. These are (1) differences in language and culture, (2) misuse of the most well-established capital budgeting tool - particularly Discounted Cash Flow valuation (abbr. DCF), and (3) the inadequacies of the DCF approach for certain applications. The two first-mentioned of the identified three reasons for the disparity between strategic planning and financial theory should obviously be surmountable. By consciously striving to unite the two disciplines, despite of cultural differences, and avoiding misuse of conventional valuation techniques (particularly DCF) by knowing the limits hereof, this could be ensured. The third reason is the important one for this paper; the inadequacies of the DCF technique and the potential of a real option approach to improve valuation within the field of capital budgeting, and thereby to bridge the gap between financial theory and strategic planning. In fact, the implementation of a real option approach is also likely to help overcome the two first reasons for the gap. This is so because the real option approach provides a mindset that more obviously integrates strategic considerations, while the approach also in effect delimits the appropriate use of the DCF, and thereby prevents some kinds of misuse of the DCF technique[29]. To better understand the reasons behind the gap, which in the above line of reasoning is particularly connected with the inadequacies of conventional valuation techniques, I will look further into the substance of strategy. Through this the critical differences between strategic analysis and strategic planning, and financial valuation will be clarified.

Strategic analysis and strategic planning are at the most holistic and aggregated level of corporate decision making in the sense that they aim to embrace all corporate activities into one shared perception of direction with implications for all other corporate activities. As such, valuation must be a tool supporting strategic analysis and strategic planning. By its encompassing nature however, strategic analysis is too complex to be captured by conventional valuation techniques[30]. Therefore, the choice between strategic alternatives is seldom guided by the application of quantitative valuation techniques and appraisal of their value-impact. This is due to the complexity of the strategic analysis, which frequently counteracts strategic planning that is consistent with the requirements of conventional valuation techniques, since these rely on explicit, linear, and fixed scenarios and precisely defined cash flow predictions to come up with a quantitative valuation. In other words, the main schism - the cause of the gap - between strategic planning and financial valuation stems from their divergent foci and prerequisites. Strategic planning exhibits a need for inherent flexibility in the face of the complexities and contingencies it must be able to cope with, which forfeits financial valuation's contrasting requirements in terms of simplicity and concrete forecasts.

Table 2.1 Differences in Focus and Prerequisites behind the Gap

Strategic Analysis & Planning	Financial Valuation
Inherent flexibility	Stable forecasts
Complexities & contingencies	Simplicity & linearity
Leeway & maneuverability	Explicitness & fixation

Source: Own construction.

Nevertheless, if the strategic analysis is to benefit from the incorporation of valuation by capturing the financial implications, they must be aligned somehow. Fundamentally, valuation must serve strategy. Therefore, there is no point in simplifying strategic analysis and strategic planning to accommodate the conventional valuation techniques. Rather, the valuation techniques must be adapted to the reality of strategic analysis.

In many ways, Myers set the agenda for the following research in the real option framework by high lighting the main schism; i.e. the gap between financial theory and strategic planning, and by identifying the option pricing techniques as holding potential for bridging this gap[31]. The misuse and the inadequacies of the DCF and the consequences hereof becomes a reoccurring theme in the real option literature in the motivation and exemplification of the improvements of valuation that the real option approach offers[32].

Before Myers' article, a few contributions had been made on the application of the option pricing technique to corporate cases, but these were specific explorative attempts outside any established framework. With Myers' article, a *raison d'être* and an incipient framework of this field of research was laid down. From here the research took two directions.

One is focused on the application of the option pricing technique to the corporate setting. In terms of the identified gap, this approach takes its point of departure in the financial theory and is directed at operationalizing the real option framework for quantitative uses. The focus is quantitative valuation and the results are 'estimates'. In the following, I shall refer to this side of the real option approach as the 'financial perspective on real options' and 'real option valuation'.

The other direction aims at using the mathematical principles from the option pricing techniques and the general framework to develop a strategic understanding of the firm. The line of reasoning is mathematically based and conceptually abstract like in traditional economics. In terms of the identified gap, this approach embarks from the field of strategy and facilitates the alignment of strategic theory with financial theory. The focus is strategic analysis and the results can be labeled 'insights', due to their qualitative nature. In the following, I shall refer to this side of the real option approach as the 'strategic perspective on real options'.

Summing up, the gap stems from the incompatibility between strategic theory and financial theory. This incompatibility is caused by divergent foci and different prerequisites. But the fundamental foci do in effect not deviate that much, since strategic analysis and strategic planning implicitly aim at creating the highest value. The gap lies in the difficulties related to explicitly analyzing the value-impact of strategic alternatives. Since financial valuation techniques must support, and not determine, the holistic and conceptual value-creation that is the target of strategic analysis and strategic planning, the challenge presented by the gap is to identify valuation techniques that capture the complexity of strategic analysis and strategic planning, while making the value implications explicit and quantitative. In other words, the gap causes a non-optimal basis for strategic decisions. If the financial valuation techniques could be aligned with strategic analysis and strategic planning, this could significantly improve the basis for strategic decisions by making the value implications of strategic alternatives explicit.

2.4 The Financial Perspective on Real Options

The concept of real options originates from options as financial derivatives. Financial derivatives are securities whose value is derived from the price of another underlying traded assets. The characteristic of a financial option is that for a certain purchase price, a right is bought to acquire or sell an underlying asset like a stock at a certain price, labeled the exercise price, up until a future point in time. The critical feature is that no obligation is attached to exercise the option to either buy or sell – it is only a right; i.e. an option. In this way the downside risk is limited to the initial investment, whereas the upside potential is unlimited.

Black and Scholes (1973) have shown in their seminal paper how to appraise the value of a financial option, i.e. the purchase price, C_0. The formula, as well as the derivation of the formula, is rather complex, but for the purpose of introducing the concept, suffice to say that the following variables enter into the formula, and influence the option value:

$$C_0 = f(E_x, S_0, \sigma, t, r)$$

where,

- C_0 is the purchase price,
- E_x is the exercise price,
- S_0 is the current stock price,
- σ is the volatility of the stock price,
- t is the time to maturation, and
- r is the risk-free interest rate.

Real options are investment projects in the corporate setting, which can be interpreted along these lines. When the formula is applied by analogy to real options in order to evaluate an investment project, the formula remains the same, but the content of the variables change, as follows.

Table 2.2 The Analogy between Financial and Real Options; Content of Variables and Notation

	Financial option (derivative)	Real option
C_0	Purchase price	Value of investment project
E_x	Exercise price	Required level of investment at the time of decision
S_0	Current stock price	Present value of expected cash flows derived from the project
σ	Volatility of the stock price	Volatility in the driver of project value
t	Time to maturation	Project duration
r	Risk-free interest rate	Risk-free interest rate

Source: Own construction.

The benefit of real option valuation is that it incorporates the value of the option for management to alter course, when uncertainty is gradually resolved in the course of time, and a contingent investment decision can be identified. The contingent decision can be the option to default on later investments, if developments have turned against the investment project, or otherwise change the commitment of resources along the way. The uncertainty is perceived as the price fluctuations of the underlying asset, expressed as the variance, and depicted as the volatility. The notion is that uncertainty is distributed with probabilities for positive and negative developments relative to a mean value. This means that uncertainty is not just perceived as possible losses (risk per se), but equally so as potential gains. Consequently, the higher the uncertainty is, the broader the spectrum of possible outcomes will be. Since the investment project is seen as an option in the sense that management may continue the project by investing, but are not obliged to do so, the downside can be limited to the investments prior to the contingent decision, if developments have been unfavorable to the project. On the other hand, the upside can be reaped, if developments have been supportive. That is, the higher the uncertainty and the longer the project duration, the better the chance is that the investment will be worthwhile at a given point-in-time in the future. The cone-shaped figure below illustrates the point.

Figure 2.2 The Cone of Uncertainty

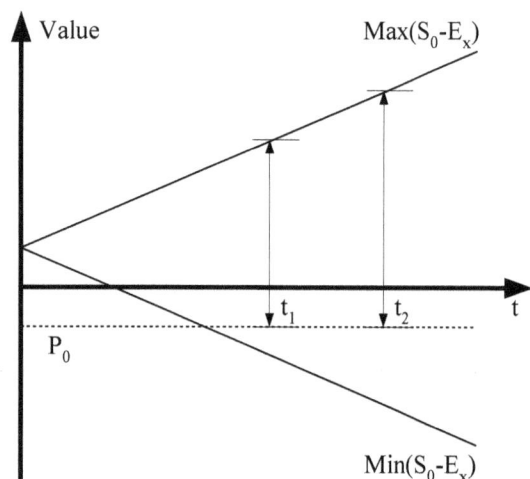

Source: Own construction, inspired by Amram & Kulatilaka (1999) pp. 15-17.

P_0 is the investment undertaken prior to the contingent decision, and thus represents the highest possible loss, if the option is not exercised. As it can be observed, the longer the project duration, and consequently the longer the investment project is exposed to the uncertainty, the wider the range of possible outcomes will be. Graphically, the higher the uncertainty in terms of volatility is, the wider the cone will be likewise. As illustrated, the downside is maximally P_0, whereas the upside changes notably from t_1 to t_2. The difference between Max (S_0-E_x) and P_0 is the range of outcomes.

The incorporation of the value of management's option to alter course in the face of uncertainty, and to await the development as the future unfolds, makes real option valuation particularly useful for long-term projects under high uncertainty involving sizable investments. Examples of such projects are natural resource extraction (e.g. mining and oil drilling), real-estate development, and R&D projects. The option might come in many shapes, as long as they share the same basic option characteristic; i.e. a contingent decision or more during the lifetime of an investment project. If for example, the investment outlays and progress of the project are staged, a sequence of decision points can be identified, each of which has an improved foundation for deciding whether to proceed with or abandon the project, or whether to contract or expand the scale or the range of the project.

Summing up, the benefits of real option valuation stem from the flexibility captured by seeing investments as projects that can be influenced by active management, when uncertainty is resolved through the course of time. This initial presentation of the quantitative applications of real option valuation was made as an introduction to the real option approach. Such an introduction naturally begins with the mathematical principles and quantitative applications. In the following, and most of this chapter, the focus will be on the strategic perspective on real options. Later in the paper, the financial perspective will be treated in more detail in connection with the application of real option valuation to the business case.

2.5 The Strategic Perspective on Real Options and the Capabilities View

In Foss (1998), a review of the potential impact of the real option approach on a strategic theory of the firm is put forward and evaluated. Through a comprehensive approach to the strategic theory of the firm, Foss presents a unification of numerous theoretical contributions to the field into generic perspectives, and looks into the strategic perspective on real options' positioning among them[33]. One of the generic perspectives is labeled the capabilities view. This perspective holds the highest potential for the integration of real options into strategic theory. Concurrently its focus on competitive advantage makes this perspective the most relevant for the analysis. Behind the capabilities view are such contributions as the evolutionary theory of the firm, the competence perspective, the capabilities perspective, the dynamic capabilities perspective, and the resource-based approach[34].

In the capabilities view on firms, the point of departure is distinctively internal.

> 'Each firm is a unique collection of highly differentiated resources and capabilities. Establishing competitive advantage is concerned with formulating and implementing a strategy that recognizes and exploits the unique features of each firm'. Grant (1996) p. 111.

Resources are at the most disaggregated level of analysis with focus on e.g. constituent skills, and physical or financial resources, whereas capabilities are teams of resources that work together[35]. The approach does not ignore the external environment, but primarily perceives it as the place where opportunities arise[36]. In this view, the keywords are 'invisible and intangible assets', 'knowledge', 'learning', 'capabilities', 'innovation', etc.[37] Much emphasis has been on the properties of knowledge-based capabilities, those being tacit and organizational in nature, and hard to transfer[38]. Knowledge-based capabilities come across as highly relevant in the various analytical frameworks of the capabilities view. The characteristics of knowledge-based capabilities make them very appropriate for the analysis of e.g.:

– Core competencies, since knowledge-based capabilities may be competitively unique and difficult to imitate *vis-à-vis* the competitors, widely applicable in terms of markets and products, and capable of making a '*disproportionate contribution to customer-perceived value*'[39].

– Competitive advantage, since knowledge-based capabilities are very relevant in many of today's knowledge-intensive emerging industries (the extent of the competitive advantage), hard to replicate by competitors or to otherwise transfer from the firm; e.g. to competitors (the sustainability of the competitive advantage) and strongly embedded in the firm, due to its organizational nature (the appropriability of the competitive advantage)[40].

In particular the ability to apply a capability repeatedly and in a broad range of contexts has received much attention in the analysis of competitive advantage. The notion is closely related to Hamel & Prahalad's (1996) concept of core competencies - the before-mentioned wide applicability, and they label this 'leveraging'[41].

The capabilities view provides a strong framework for analyzing the competitive advantage of the individual firm, and is as such at the heart of strategy. However, it has been criticized for a distinctively retrospective character in its analysis of path-dependent, unique resources and capabilities, and its focus on the current situation[42]. Additionally, it can be argued that the capabilities view is rather introverted in nature and ignores the firm's adaptation to external pressures and developments in the environment, among other things. Furthermore, the capabilities view neither presents any directions as to the establishment of new resources and capabilities, nor offers a dynamic and forward-looking perspective.

In the strategic perspective on real options, Foss argues that firms are perceived as options-providing institutions[43]. In other words, firms are '*governance structures whose primary rationale lies in their provision of options*'[44]. This perception of firms goes hand-in-hand with the capabilities view in the sense that a capability can be defined as '*a capacity to act in certain ways in a certain range of circumstances. Thus, the idea of real options is arguably inherent in the idea of capability (sic)*'[45]. This way, the real option approach adds a forward-looking and dynamic perspective to the capabilities view's analysis of competitive advantage. The forward orientation is very explicit in the point of origin of the real option approach; i.e. in the framework of financial options. The common denominator is the definition of a capability, which resembles the concept of a real option to the extent that exploiting (leveraging) and building capabilities could be seen as similar to exercising and creating real options[46]. Thereby, the unification of the two perspectives holds the potential for adding a dynamic perspective to the capabilities view's somewhat '*retrospective character*'[47] in terms of competitive advantage. In the following sections, the point of contact between the two perspectives will be elaborated both absolutely, as well as in the light of the business case.

The real option framework can be applied with different foci. Already in Black & Scholes (1973), it was suggested to apply option pricing techniques to the analysis of warrants and equity, both on the liabilities side[48]. Anyway, the analysis of real options has increasingly focused on corporate assets, which come in the shape of both tangible and intangible assets. In this integration of the real option approach and the capabilities view, the focus is on the real options related to assets, due to the capabilities view's focus on resources and capabilities.

The assets treated with the real option framework will broadly be labeled investment projects in this paper. Though assets in their widest sense range from acquisition of companies to operational business development and investment in e.g. production equipment, the discussion of capabilities will in this chapter be related to capabilities in existing business areas and the development of capabilities in new business areas and new technologies. These foci can be interpreted as broad capabilities, which constitute the two perspectives' point of contact.

The focus as seen from the capabilities view is on resources, capabilities, and core competencies. *'The resource-based view conceives of the firm as a unique bundle of heterogeneous resources and capabilities'*[49], and as earlier outlined, capabilities are in this view organized teams of resources. The more organizational and knowledge-based the capabilities are, the harder they are to imitate, the more valuable they are, and the more widely they can be utilized, the better they are competitively. The best capabilities fulfill the criteria of 'core competencies'.

Within the framework of real options, three categories of real options can be identified, each containing different types of managerial actions that might be taken during an investment project. These categories are flexibility, timing, and growth options[50]. The flexibility options include options to expand or contract the scale of the investment project, to abandon and / or to default on staged investments, and to switch use of the underlying asset. The timing options include the options to defer and to temporarily suspend operations, while growth options is a category of its own characterized by being broad in nature and vaguely defined.

The options to expand or contract the scale and the options to defer are not the most appropriate to integrate with the capabilities view, since the building of capabilities implies the development of not so clearly defined organizational capabilities. In order for these kinds of options to be looked into, more concrete predictions and knowledge of the underlying assets would be required, such as in the case of production facilities or oil drilling. In other words, the above types of options require exact estimates on e.g. a gradual (read percentage) expansion or contraction of the activity level, which capabilities in their broadness are usually too loosely defined to allow for.

Likewise, the options to switch and to temporarily suspend operations do not fit the focus on capabilities. These options are more related to production functionalities and optimal capacity utilization, such as switching to other energy sources, when relative world market prices on energy change, or temporarily shutting down mines, when world market prices are low.

As will be elaborated in the following, the most obvious types of real options to incorporate in an integration of the real option approach and the capabilities view are growth options and options to abandon [51].

More authors have pointed to the potential compatibility between the capabilities view and the real option approach[52]. Kogut & Kulatilaka (1994) were the first ones to suggest the integration of the capabilities view and the real option approach. They seek to bridge these perspectives and develop

'a set of heuristics that view an organization's capabilities as generating platforms to expand into new but uncertain markets. These capabilities are considered options because they are investments in opportunity'.
Kogut & Kulatilaka (1994) p. 53.

They focus on platform investments as the point of contact between organizational capabilities and real options. Platform investments provide the firm with both operating flexibility and growth options, and by their broad, organizational character, they hold the competitive edge potential of becoming a core competency[53], as earlier presented.

Foss (1998) also touches upon the compatibility between the two perspectives. Though he does not seek to develop the firm-level implications further, he is more specific on the point of contact between the capabilities view and the real option approach. He defines a capability as *'a capacity to act in certain ways in a certain range of circumstances'*[54], and points to the real option nature herein. Like Kogut & Kulatilaka (1994), he sees capabilities as a set of real options, but unlike Kogut & Kulatilaka (1994), Foss does not integrate the two perspectives as completely, but limits their concord with each other to a complementary extension, where the real option approach might facilitate *'a theory of building new capabilities through the creation of options'*[55].

Kulatilaka & Perotti (1998) establishes *'a strategic rationale for growth options under uncertainty and imperfect competition'*. In the analysis, they conclude that there are competitive advantages, when investments under high uncertainty lead to the establishment of growth options, which *'results in the acquisition of a 'capability' that allows the firm take (sic) better advantage of future growth opportunities'*[56].

From the above contributions, it is clear that the three terms constituting the conceptual triangle, around which the integration of the capabilities view and the real option approach must center, are as illustrated in the figure below.

Figure 2.3 Conceptual Triangle for the Integration of Perspectives

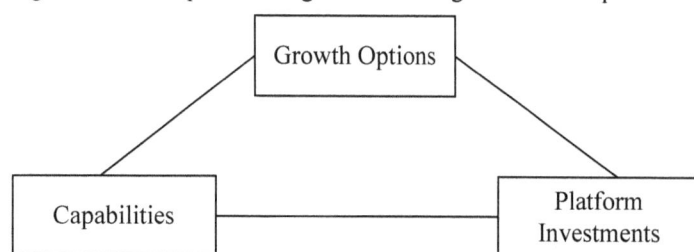

Source: Own construction.

Amram & Kulatilaka (1999) further emphasize the relationships in the figure by stating that *'a real options perspective complements traditional resource-based perspectives by identifying new capabilities needed'*[57], and by elaborating on the benefits of framing growth options as platform investments[58]. Amram & Kulatilaka may oversell the framework, when they point to its capacity for identification of capabilities needed. It is rather questionable how the framework may help specifically to identify desirable capabilities. More cautiously, it can be argued that the framework provides for a more encompassing approach to the assessment of capability needs, by not only looking at current needs and competitive value, but also incorporating the subsequent options that a capability may bring. Furthermore, the framework may enlighten the evaluation of desirable characteristics in a capability, e.g. by conceptually providing insights on aspects of uncertainty and the structuring of investment projects to capture option value. This issue will be considered in the proceeding chapter on the case company.

In agreement with Kogut & Kulatilaka (1994), one conclusion of this section is that the best focus for the integration of the capabilities view and the real option approach is knowledge-based, organizational capabilities: *'The value of platforms as options ultimately comes down to viewing organizational capabilities as investments in learning and acquiring broad-based expertise'*[59]. By looking into this kind of capabilities, the relevant investments can easily be related to the analysis of core competencies. In their broadness, they establish options of the growth kind, which is the most suitable integration point between the capabilities view and the real option approach. With this in mind, the R&D aspect, which is predominant in this paper, will be looked into in the following section.

2.6 Strategic Real Options, the Capabilities View and R&D

R&D investments in a real option perspective have mostly been seen as growth options or in the words of Kester (1984) *''call options' for growth'*[60]. Also Smit & Ankum (1993) observe that:

> *'Some investment projects can actually be seen as the first links in a chain of subsequent decisions. With projects of this type, the firm essentially acquires an option to invest in a potential follow-up project. For example, an R&D project, the development of a new technology, or entry into a new geographical market may create future investments opportunities. In strategy, these projects are often compared with options for future company growth'.* Smit & Ankum (1993) pp. 241-243.

With the conceptual triangle from the preceding section in mind, two contributions point to the integration of R&D investments into this set of relations. Amram & Kulatilaka (1999) point out that R&D investments are among the most obvious to perceive as platform investments generating growth options[61], while Kulatilaka & Perotti (1998) - among their examples of strategic investment that beneficially can be made as growth options - find that *'research into building a technological advantage'* is particularly relevant[62]. Following this, it is clear that R&D investments fit nicely with the conceptual triangle behind the integration of the capabilities view and the real option approach, as illustrated in the figure below.

Figure 2.4 Conceptual Diamond for the Integration of Perspectives

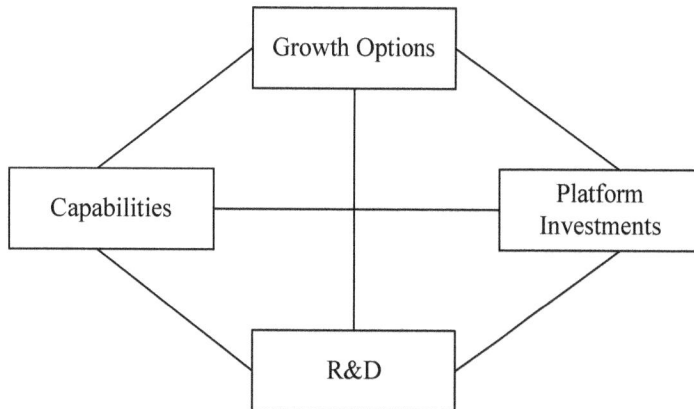

Source: Own construction.

2.7 Real Options and R&D

Many authors have hinted at the potential for applying the real option approach to R&D investments[63], but most have mentioned this focus area only in passing and few have made specific contributions. Herath & Park (1999) even calls the real option approach to R&D investments promising, but neglected in the literature[64]. Some of the specific contributions on R&D and real options have already been presented[65], while others will appear throughout the analysis, when called for. A few contributors deserve mentioning here though, since there contributions are quite central to one of the cornerstones of the real option framework, investigated throughout the chapter; namely the desirability of research-related uncertainty in the shape of volatility.

Myers (1984) was not only the one to coin the term real options and outline the real option framework's potential for bridging the gap between strategic planning and financial theory, but in his early article on real options he also emphasized R&D as an obvious focus for real options analysis. *'DCF is no help at all for pure research and development. The value of R&D is almost all option value.'*[66] Kester (1984), shortly after Myers (1984), specifies that the most appropriate approach is to see R&D investments as '*'call options' for growth'*[67]. He conducts the first conceptualization of the real option framework for R&D. Morris, Teisberg & Kolbe (1991) looks into the relationship between risk / uncertainty and R&D project value. By applying the option pricing technique and focusing on the volatility component, they argue that decision makers, when choosing among R&D projects, should go for the most risky ones.

Huchzermeier & Loch (1997) investigates the effect of volatility on the option value. Conventional option thinking says that the more volatility, the higher the value of the option is, due to the increased upside potential and the fixed downside. The authors model three kinds of uncertainty within the real option framework and show that the conventional relationship is valid for volatility on market payoffs. However, for the volatilities on technical uncertainty and on uncertainty in market performance requirements, the relationship is the opposite, when these uncertainties exceed the company's capacity to respond - i.e. to utilize the higher potential

26

outcomes. These kinds of uncertainty reduces the option value indirectly by affecting the volatility in market payoffs negatively. Huchzermeier & Loch this way open up for a more subtle discussion of the kinds of uncertainties, and their impact on value. This sophistication of the concept of uncertainty is a significant modification that will be taken up in the analysis.

Finally, four purely quantitative case applications have been found. Schwartz & Moon (2000) appraises R&D in the shape of drug development in the pharmaceutical industry. Herath & Park (1999) analyzes a long term product development within the razor blade industry (Gilette). Lint & Pennings (1999) look into operationalization and valuation of R&D projects at Philips, incorporating business shifts in the analysis, modeled as a Poisson distribution. Kemna (1993) conducts a number of explorative applications of different types of options in Shell with a view to the implications for practical, managerial decision making. A common weakness among these contributions with regard to drawing upon them in this analysis, is that they focus on the choice of mathematical models and the modeling of uncertainty at a theoretical level, without presenting the details of the configuration or estimation of inputs relative to the reality of their business cases. Two of the contributions specifically point to the confidential nature of the data, as the reason for this. Thus, the practical recommendations of these cases are of limited instrumentality with regard to this analysis. Where appropriate, they will be drawn upon in the analysis of the empiricism.

2.8 Concluding Remarks on the Strategic Perspective

This chapter started out by looking into the gap between strategic theory and financial theory. It was determined that they respectively target strategies that lead to the highest value creation and the measurement of this value creation. The point of contact is obvious and on financial side, the activity is valuation. It was argued that the reason they have not been better integrated is that they have different requirements for achieving this goals. The real option framework was put forward as holding potential for bridging this gap, by being applicable to both strategic analysis, strategic planning and financial valuation.

Throughout the chapter, it was shown that the strategic perspective on real options is relevant to strategic analysis, and especially so to R&D investments. Additionally, it was shown that the strategic perspective on real options is not just an isolated contribution to the theoretical field of strategy, which can be introduced to support the parallel use of real options required to bridge the gap from the strategic side. The strategic perspective on real options is also compatible with a prevailing strategic position, namely the capabilities view, and in particular so with focus on knowledge-based capabilities. Research capabilities can adequately be perceived as options, since initial investments that might lead to research results around which a business concept can be established, are inherent herein. The research capabilities come in the shape of general principles and knowledge that potentially can be combined and applied in a wide range of contexts, depending on the targets set. This kind of capabilities can be seen as an investment platform holding growth options. Concurrently, there is substantial uncertainty as to the achievement of the research targets and the value of the targeted results. By its incorporation of the value of flexibility in the face of uncertainty, the strategic perspective can therefore be seen as holding promising potential for a much required extension of the capabilities view in terms of a forward-looking and dynamic perspective that might provide directions as to valuable capabilities. The strategic perspective will be revisited at the end of the following chapter, where the case company will be briefly discussed in relation to this perspective for illustrative purposes.

3. Case Company

This chapter is dedicated to the presentation of the case company, NKT Research Center (abbr. NRC), and an illustrative presentation of the potential in applying the capabilities view and the strategic perspective on real options to a strategic analysis of the case company. The chapter first presents the history, the research areas and their backgrounds, and the newly established corporate venturing business model. Hereafter, the chapter goes on to look into the potential and suitability of applying the two before-mentioned strategic perspectives with regard to a strategic analysis. This treatment of the perspectives relative to the case company does not pretend to be a full-blown strategic analysis. Rather the intention is to outline and illustrate the capabilities view and the strategic perspective on real options' potential with regard to a strategic analysis of the case company. Their applicability is shown to be quite obvious. This indicative outline will later serve as foundation for an evaluation of the real option framework's ability to bridge the gap between financial theory and strategic theory seen from the strategic side of the gap.

3.1 Corporate History

NKT Research Center A/S is the research and development unit of the NKT Holding Group (abbr. NKT). NKT was originally established in 1891 in Copenhagen, Denmark, and made into a limited company in 1898 under the name *Nordiske Kabel og Traadfabrikker A/S* (Nordic Cable and Wire Factories Ltd. – own translation). The founder H.P. Prior built the company around the production of cables and wires for telecommunication and electricity. By taking NKT public at an early stage, he lost decisive control of the company to the investors that were invited to join. In 1947, the Danish FLS Industries Group began to acquire shares in NKT, and today the control of the company is in the hands of this group.

Through the years, NKT evolved into a conglomerate that was active in a number of different industries. The history of the company is characterized by a significant number of acquisitions and spin-offs. The two oil crises in the 1970's and the high interest rates of the 1980's had shown how dependent NKT's traditional cable business was to the level of activities in the construction industries that suffered in these periods, both due to the high interest rates and the high oil prices. To avoid the vulnerability, a diversification and internationalization strategy was carried out. Partly, due to professional investors' complaints about the intransparent economics of conglomerates and the following 'conglomerate discount' on the shares, NKT initiated in 1993 a restructuring strategy that aimed at focusing the company on a few core businesses. Up until 1998/1999, a radical strategy was carried out, and the companies that were outside the core businesses were spun off.

As a part of the focus strategy, an independent, centralized research and development subsidiary was established to strengthen the business development of the remaining core businesses. Until then, the R&D in NKT had been spread over a number of specialized laboratories attached to the different business areas. The various R&D efforts were then reorganized to establish one R&D unit with critical mass, occupied with the more fundamental and applied research, and a number of smaller laboratory units that served as product development departments in the respective companies. Thus, NRC was established in 1990 to provide research and development related to technologies of long-term and strategic importance to the focused NKT. Currently, NRC has some 50 employees, a turnover of approximately DKK 19 millions, and cost budget of DKK 50 millions.

3.2 NRC Research Areas

The first R&D efforts in the NKT Group stemmed from the traditional preoccupation with cables. It was quite obvious for the company to initiate research and development on the transmission potential of different materials with regard to cables, due to its cable manufacturing facilities and traditions. In 1980, NKT began the production of optical fibre cables, and in 1988, another cable related materials research area was initiated, namely superconductor technology. Whereas optical fibre technology has to do with high-speed and high-capacity transmission of signals which are less sensitive to electric distortion than traditional cable materials, superconductor technology is about the transmission of electricity without the loss of energy. Also related to the cable businesses, NRC has conducted research on polymers and surface technology. The research began with focus on plastics in the early 1950's in order to improve the properties of the plastics used for cable insulation and jacketing. The scientific advances achieved by NKT in these technologies have through the years led to a number of different inventions and applications, and in turn new business units, within the group.

The research in superconductor technology was begun in 1988, when this field of research was boosted by the discovery of high-temperature superconductors. Though superconducting materials have been known since the beginning of the century, the new discovery was a giant step towards commercial applications of this phenomenon[68]. In 1988, however, the technology was not ready for feasible commercial applications. NRC's position was to conduct research to the extent required to keep up with developments in international research; i.e. relatively little R&D efforts. There were two reasons behind NRC's decision to maintain ongoing investments, instead of just waiting completely for the breakthrough to happen. First of all, this was a prerequisite for being able to monitor the developments in terms of skills. Secondly, it was also a necessity to bring something to the table, when participating in international research networks, conferences, etc.[69] Nonetheless, it was considered feasible to maintain these efforts, in order for NRC to be able to enter at a later, more mature stage of the technology. In 1997, NRC established Nordic Superconductor Technologies, which produces tapes that are an important component if superconducting electricity cables are to become widely used. The cautious approach of maintaining small efforts in order to monitor and await the development is still being pursued with regard to other superconductor applications in NRC.

In comparison, optical fibre technology has already matured in terms of commercial applications. A number of research results within NRC have already been achieved and resulted in the establishment of several independent businesses. Some of these have been divested, and the major current efforts related to earlier NRC research take place in IONAS; a subsidiary involved in optical chip production.

In addition to the research areas mentioned, NRC has identified medico-technology as a future focus area. The idea is not to initiate research into something entirely different from the current portfolio, but to utilize existing research competencies complemented with new capabilities. As will be presented in more detail later, NRC has for example initiated research into biochips, which utilizes current competencies from the research areas of optical fibre technology, surface technology and materials chemistry. To complement these competencies, biotechnology know-how is being obtained through recruitment and research.

Summing up, NRC's research areas can primarily be traced down to either the preoccupation with developing new applications for cables, or the physical properties and environmental consequences of cables. Yet, the spill-over effects of having research facilities beyond a certain size have given rise to research into seemingly unrelated technologies.

3.3 Corporate Venturing

From the late 1980's and throughout the 1990's, a number of companies have been established based on research results from NRC[70]. Divestments of four of these have demonstrated NRC's value-creating capacity as significant[71]. Until 1999, the research-based start-ups were decided on an ad-hoc basis. The policy was to separate promising research results into independent businesses to improve efficiency and transparency, and to better test the competitiveness of the ventures. In 1999 the NKT Group embarked on a strategy labeled 'Vision 2005', which explicitly aims at utilizing the business potential of NRC's research capabilities in a systematic and structured approach to the establishment of new companies.

NRC's vision is to be an incubator for the development of new high-tech businesses. The focus is: '*businesses*
– *with the potential of creating added value to its owners*
– *having a global perspective; and*
– *which take their starting point at a technologically leading position of NKT Research Center*'[72]

As a consequence of the new corporate venturing focus, NKT Innovation was established as a department of NRC, initially with five employees. NKT Innovation refers directly to the executive committee of the NKT Group. However, NKT Innovation works in close cooperation with NRC in the identification of promising research results with regard to technological value, market potential and competitive situation. Based on these analyses, the target is to turn three to five of these research results a year into separate business units that have the commercial potential to become an independent company.

The research results need not be taken from NRC. Given the ambitious target of three to five new company establishments a year, external research results are also taken in. The notion behind this is to utilize NRC's research competencies and academic relations to spot interesting research results in the environment.

The business model behind this is set up with top-management involvement in the decision making. Thus Project Councils with members from the executive committee are consulted in an initial screening with regard to potential. At a later stage, the Project Councils have to approve the business plans - known as business maps - on the venture, before resources are allocated and the start-ups established. NRC has developed a so-called 'NKT Company Package', which offers the start-ups administrative services in order to let the management of the start-ups concentrate on R&D and market development in the early phases[73].

3.4 The Capabilities View on NRC

When evaluating the suitability of the capabilities perspective for a strategic analysis of NRC, a natural first step is to look into some of the distinctive resources and capabilities in NRC's business model. Some examples are given in the table below.

Table 3.1 Selected Examples of Distinctive NRC Resources

NRC's Resources	Resources from Parent Company
Specialized R&D personnel (human resources)	Access to capital and substantial financial backing
Patents & other proprietary technology / know-how	Technological point of departure & corresponding industrial know-how
Sufficient size to maintain academic relations	Top management involvement in Project Councils (Executive Committee)
Business development set-up (NKT Innovation)	
Administrative routines & legal expertise (NKT Company Package)	

Source: Own construction.

One of the most important categories of resources is obviously the R&D personnel, due to their research skills, and the research results that they bring about. This category of resources could easily be divided to give a clearer picture of the resource-base, e.g. functionally at a more disaggregated level to identify more specifically the critical elements and competencies in NRC's research portfolio. Still, this is not necessary for this evaluation. More important is to look into the way these resources are activated and bundled in NRC's capabilities.

Capabilities are seen as teams of resources and differ in their level of organizational aggregation. Grant (1996) distinguishes between the following capabilities, increasing in level of organizational aggregation in the order mentioned: single-task capabilities, specialized capabilities, activity related capabilities, broad functional capabilities, and cross functional capabilities[74]. According to these categorizations, a hierarchy of capabilities can be identified with the resource base as foundation. This kind of analysis can be carried out very thoroughly and reveal important relations between resources, lower organizational level capabilities and organizational capabilities. For the evaluation of the suitability of the capabilities view, it suffices to hint at some of the primary resources (as already done) and discuss how these may enter into an organizational capability.

An example of a broad organizational capability distinctive to NRC could be labeled research-based corporate venturing. This could be perceived as the capacity to develop research results and take them through a number of phases until the establishment of an independent company. Keil (2000) also perceives external corporate venturing as *"a higher order capability residing at the organizational level"*[75]. He identifies two key elements, namely the ability to facilitate identification and obtainment of business opportunities from the environment, and the ability to utilize existing capabilities to leverage and exploit these business opportunities. Though Keil focuses on corporate venturing with external partners and inputs, NRC's corporate venturing capability, which relies on both internal and external inputs and partners, must also be perceived as an organizational capability, only slightly more complex.

Figure 3.1 NRC's Research-based Corporate Venturing Capability

Identify Research Areas of Relevance and Potential	
Achieve Research Results In-house	Spot Research Results in Environment
Develop Business Plan	
Evaluate Business Plans and Allocate Funding	
Initiate Business Plan (facilities and personnel recruitment)	
Active Ownership of New Company	Ongoing Support of Operations (administrative, legal and research)

Source: Own construction

This capability incorporates all the identified resources. It is generic in nature in the sense that it can be applied to both internal and external research results within the various research areas that NRC has identified and specialized in.

It has already been argued that when the primary resource is knowledge - in this case R&D - and the primary capability is the utilization of this knowledge, the determination of competitiveness through a capabilities analysis is very appropriate. In the evaluation of a capability, Grant (1996) applies the profit-earning potential of the capability as the overall success criteria. This in turn depends on the extent, the sustainability and the appropriability of the competitive advantage that the capability establishes. Though the success criteria sounds very financial and tangible, the analysis boils down to a discussion, where the weight of the capability's competitiveness is cautiously evaluated along the outlined parameters. As such the analysis is very similar to the analysis of a capability as a core competency, which is the acid test of a capability's competitiveness, so to speak, in the sense that it sets criteria for desirable capabilities.

As has been touched upon earlier, a capability is a core competency, if it is

1/ competitively unique and difficult to imitate *vis-à-vis* the competitors,

2/ widely applicable in terms of markets and products, and

3/ capable of making a *'disproportionate contribution to customer-perceived value'*[76]

NRC is hardly the only company capable of conducting research and developing the results into independent companies in the wider understanding of research-based corporate venturing. Nevertheless, when looking at NRC's specific combination of research areas in combination with its corporate venturing approach, the business model appears rather unique. The competitive uniqueness is not as important per se though, as the issue of imitation is. Here it is important to bear in mind that there is a historicity to the research areas, and in particular the ones, which have translated into commercial successes. For example, GIGA that was sold in spring 2000 at an impressively high price, was established in 1988 and got technologically ahead of its competition by utilizing research results discovered earlier working on wafer production principles, which were actually given up by competitors and generally considered outdated only a few years earlier. Therefore, it can be argued that there is a strong element of path-dependency in research resources; as well as an element of chance, of course. Furthermore, the fact that the capability is organizational and knowledge-based makes it very heterogeneous, and thus hard to imitate, since it is somewhat embedded in organization. Though one of the significant resources, the research personnel may leave, the appropriation may be somewhat secured through patents and the replaceability of employees to a certain degree.

In terms of wide applicability, the broad research portfolio of NRC is paralleled by competencies within a number of technologies, and thus a number product markets. Amram & Kulatilaka have specifically pointed to the fact that *'basic research may in materials may be applied in products used in several industries'*[77] as an example of an investment platform based on capabilities with numerous growth options inherent. This is obviously relevant to NRC. The ability to accommodate external research results within the business model also adds to its range of potential applications. The capability to reshuffle the resources, in particular across research areas, to develop new capabilities with different foci by combining existing resources and acquiring new resources in the shape of research personnel is another example of wide applicability. A prime example is NRC's first venture into medico-technology; i.e. the development of biochips, where parts of the required competencies are available in the organization and others have to be acquired or developed. Some of the technology even comes in the shape of proprietary know-how from earlier research.

With regard to the *'disproportionate contribution to customer-perceived value'*, NRC - and the NKT research prior to NRC's establishment - has demonstrated the ability to create value through divestments worth DKK 11-13 billions, based on an annual cost budget of some DKK 50 millions[78].

Summing up, the preceding presentation of NRC, as seen from the capabilities view, indicates that it holds a strong competitive position, which is based on technological quality capabilities and valuable divestments. Whether the capability briefly investigated is indeed a core competency, is besides the point of this presentation, which was carried out for illustrative purposes. To determine this, more efforts would have to be put into a more thorough analysis. Nevertheless, it is apparent that the application of the capabilities perspective could lead to an understanding of NRC's competitive advantage. Now, the question is to what extent the strategic real options perspective may complement it or even extend it, in the case of NRC.

3.5 Strategic Real Options in NRC

NRC's resource base and research-based corporate venturing capability can quite aptly be seen as an investment platform, which holds and generates growth options. As such the wide applicability and the generic nature of the capability can elegantly be described through strategic real option lenses.

The potential in applying the existing research competencies in new ways and the modularity of the research areas in terms of recombining them - e.g. in the earlier presented biochip example - holds latent capabilities, which may surface to meet opportunities. The applicability of the corporate venturing capability to external results is pregnant with growth options to the extent NRC is capable of handling it. In other words, by being designed as applicable to external research results and consciously targeting these, the option value of the capability has radically increased.

The approach taken e.g. to superconductor technology also holds the contours of real options. Here the small investments can be seen as a pay-to-play or coupon investment approach to research areas with high potential. It effectively holds an abandonment option on the relatively low costs incurred, or maybe better, a call option on growth to paraphrase Kester (1984)[79]. Furthermore, it exhibits the characteristics that Faulkner (1996) outlined as very suitable for the real option framework, which were that the pending investment is high relative to the initial investment, a substantial uncertainty will gradually be resolved, and the duration is long[80]. Basically, the real option approach provides a strategic rationale for an incremental investment policy, where investments are not evaluated on their own, but perceived as options on options to invest if it proves advantageous as the future unfolds.

NRC's overall choices of research targets and in the case of medico-technology also research areas are made, based on expectations of markets where the potential is immense[81]. If it from this statement can be inferred that time horizon required to achieve the targeted research results is longer, and the possible spread of outcomes broader too, this makes sense from an real option approach too. The latter in the meaning that a broad spread implies high uncertainty in the shape of high volatility; i.e. potential for very beneficial developments or the opposite.

3.6 Concluding Remarks on the Applicability of the Strategic Perspective on Real Options

The outline of a potential application of the strategic perspective on real options to the realities of NRC has illustrated two things with regard to strategic analysis.

First of all, the strategic perspective on real options appears to display the potential outlined in the preceding theoretical chapter of extending the capabilities view. In this extension, the wide applicability - i.e. the leveraging of competencies - can be seen as an investment platform containing growth options, among other things due to the ability to recombine research competencies and the generic elements in the corporate venturing capability, as they were defined. Though, explanatory elegant, this insight is actually only complementary in nature. The analysis is still static as such.

However, the strategic perspective on real options may be the foundation for a directional analysis with recommendation as to the approach to R&D investments and the nature of these investments.

Concerning the approach to R&D investments, the benefits of an incremental investment policy can be explained. This was exemplified by NRC's coupon investments in the case of superconductor technology. Another example of this is NRC's approach to the initiation of optical chips production in IONAS. Here NRC invested approximately DKK 100 million by August 2000. After having observed the developments, it has recently been decided to invest further DKK 100 millions, which will increase the capacity four times. This approach is contradicted by theoretical concepts such as first-mover advantages and competitive preemption in the market - and probably also optimal production capacity investments - but makes sense when looking at sequential investments under uncertainty. Whether one looks at it from one side or the other, this can either be considered an option to abandon a small investment with a huge potential, or a small investment facilitating an option for growth.

With regard to the nature of these investments, the dynamic and forward-looking use of the strategic perspective on real options suggests that investments are undertaken with a view to high volatility and long duration profiles. These will respectively create more fluctuation in the underlying value of the investment project with high upside potential, and potentially a larger number of options during the lifetime of the investment, the longer the duration is. Looking at NRC's choice of research areas and research targets, there were indications that this could be both implicitly the case and a beneficial perspective to develop further, though this requires further investigation to conclude upon.

In conclusion, the strategic perspective on real options is applicable to a strategic analysis of NRC, and holds the potential of adding important insight to a strategic analysis, while being compatible with one of the preeminent strategic perspectives, the capabilities view. As such, this can be seen as step towards closing the gap between strategic and financial theory, since quantitative methods are beforehand. With this chapter's brief conceptualization of the real option framework in a strategic perspective, the remains of the paper will investigate to what extent the financial perspective can be coupled and brought together with the strategic perspective in this attempt.

4. Real Option Valuation

This chapter contains a theoretical introduction to the real option approach to valuation. First, real option valuation is positioned relative to the field of valuation. It is explained that real option valuation incorporates the Net Present Value criteria (abbr. NPV), which is also characteristic for a number of other valuation methods. For the purpose of comparison, two of these NPV methods are briefly outlined and criticized in the light of real option valuation's proposed potential for improvements.

Technically, real option valuation is about choosing or developing a mathematical solution that corresponds to the real option at hand, and thereafter estimating the numerical inputs to the variables of the mathematical solution. When this is done the valuation is a straightforward calculation. In order to choose or develop a mathematical solution, the investment project in question must be analyzed with regard to the contingent decision, the uncertainty, and the expiration mode. These aspects make up the configuration and mathematical modeling of the real option, which are required for choosing or developing the mathematical solution. This chapter lays down the theoretical basics of the configuration and mathematical modeling of the real option, before the business case is presented in the next chapter. At the end of next chapter, the mathematical solution can be chosen or developed, according to the presented realities of the business case.

The introduction to real option valuation takes its point of departure in the valuation of financial options, by presenting the fundamentals, the notation, and the Black & Scholes option pricing formula, along with a number of insights. The analogy is spelled out, and a typology of real options is introduced. It is shown that there are quite many ways to configure an option - i.e. to interpret investment projects as real options - in terms of different kinds of contingent decisions. The integration of uncertainty is central to the real option approach to valuation, and the volatility is the most innovative variable compared with conventional valuation techniques. Some statistical considerations on the distributions and processes that depict the uncertainty are made. Additionally, the expiration mode is discussed in the light of different characteristics of project duration.

Finally, a comparison between the NPV methods from the beginning of the chapter and real option valuation is made, in the light of this chapter's theoretical presentation of real option valuation.

4.1 Capital Budgeting

The real option approach to valuation falls within the area of financial theory called capital budgeting. Capital budgeting is defined as '*allocation of resources among investment projects on a long-term basis*'[82]. Valuation is a central aspect of capital budgeting, since the optimal allocation must, of course, follow the value creation, which then has to be measured. Valuation is the term for the activity of appraising the monetary value of a given investment. In the corporate context, valuation can be carried out both for a company as a whole, as well as for investment projects within firms.

The theoretical perspective applied to valuation in this paper is that an investment's value is determined by its capacity to generate future income in the shape of cash flows[83]. This implies the use of the NPV approach. The NPV is calculated by discounting the cash flows to a present value with due corrections for the time-value of money and the risk-profile of the investment. Though, this approach must overcome the practical hurdle of forecasting the future and projecting future income, it is based on the most valid and sound assumptions, and constitutes the most theoretically consistent approach. The applicability of this approach to any kind of investment that generates income is another benefit of the approach, which is widely accepted and used among practitioners, both for valuations at the company level and at the project level[84]. The following presentation and critique of two NPV methods will be carried out with a view to the promises of real option valuation. It is assumed that the reader is familiar with these methods. If not, they are presented in more detail in appendix 2.

4.1.1 Discounted Cash Flow

The dominant method to determine NPV is the DCF method. Following this method, the investment projects are appraised in comparison with alternative investment opportunities on the financial markets; i.e. as if they were stocks or bonds. For this purpose, the following formula is applied. The formula takes the sum of all future cash flows discounted at an appropriate discount rate, and subtracts the initial investment outlay[85]:

$$NPV = -I_0 + \sum_{t=1}^{T} \frac{C_t}{(1+r_t)^t}$$

I_0 = investment outlay
C_t = cash flow at time, t
r_t = discount rate at time, t

The investment outlay is considered known, whereas the formula relies on estimates for the cash flows and the discount rate. The cash flows are simple linear forecasts[86]. The discount rate might change *over time*, though at any given point in time there will be only one value of the discount rate.

The DCF is the most simple and straightforward application of the NPV approach. In its simplicity, it is intuitive, and easy to operationalize and use. However, in the practical application a number of insufficiencies are encountered.

The linear cash flow forecasts presuppose a static and predictable future development of the investment project. If two or more different *scenarios* may take place, or the cash flows may be somewhat dispersed within a range of potential outcomes, this is not incorporated in the simple cash flow forecasts. A more sophisticated DCF model may take these into consideration by attributing probabilities to different scenarios, and then do the calculation on weighted averages. This is the Decision Tree Analysis that will be discussed in the next section.

Furthermore, the static forecasts on cash flows do not take into consideration the *flexibility* management has to alter course as the future unfolds. If for example, the development at an early stage has been so advantageous that an *expansion* of the investment project is considered feasible, or opposite has been so futile that *abandonment* of the project would help avoiding unnecessary costs, this flexibility under *active management* holds a value that the DCF method do not capture. Particularly if contingent decisions - crossroads - can be anticipated, or if expectable contingencies can be foreseen, this flexibility would not be incorporated in the simple DCF valuation. Furthermore, the DCF method envisages a stop-or-go decision at the time of analysis, although the investment project may be deferred until some uncertainties have been resolved. If deferral is an opportunity, this timing opportunity is valuable.

The discount rate in the DCF method relies on the *identification of a similar investment* and the corresponding beta. Beta incorporates the market risk of the project *vis-à-vis* the market portfolio. The identification of a suitable comparable investment is obviously fraught with imperfection. Also the risk attributable to the investment project might change over time, both due to future developments, as well as active management. This would affect the discount rate that would have to be changed accordingly. The DCF is capable of taking this into consideration to a certain extent, but limited by its dependence on one discount rate value per period of time. If the outlined use of *scenarios* is undertaken, different discount rates would have to be applied in the same period of time *in parallel*. Thus, the linear predictions of the development is not capable of anticipating a complex and dynamic risk profile. Furthermore, the perception of uncertainty is simplified to see it as a *risk*, which decreases value, when discounting the cash flows. The event, where uncertainty leads to beneficial developments, is not considered in this method.

4.1.2 Decision Tree Analysis

Decision Tree Analysis (abbr. DTA) is an advanced DCF method. The additional feature compared with the simple DCF method is the use of scenarios and decision points. Thus to calculate the NPV, the cash flows behind the identified scenarios have to be discounted applying the respective discount rates. The discount rates differ according to the risk-profile of the scenarios. Finally, the cash flows of the different scenarios are accumulated as a weighted average according to the probabilities.

The DTA method as an advanced DCF method overcomes a number of the insufficiencies that were pointed out in relation with the DCF method. The use of *scenarios* and corresponding *parallel discount rates* is a significant improvement. By attributing probabilities to the decision points and thus to the various scenarios, the valuation can end up in one figure, based on a weighted average. The *flexibility* that can be incorporated into the decision tree at the outlined decision points is also a step forward compared with the simple DCF. This way, early abandonment or expansion can be incorporated into the valuation. Finally, the mapping of a decision tree encourages *active management* by laying down critical decision points in a way that the simple DCF does not.

Yet, the DTA method has its shortcomings and insufficiencies too. The immediate nature of the valuation with regard to the stop-or-go decision is equally present in this framework. That is, the timing value of the deferral opportunity is simply not caught. Although, the use of scenarios and parallel discount rates is an improvement compared to the DCF, the identification of several discount rates implies a more complicated search for comparable investment profiles. The same goes for the probabilities that need to be attributed. In summary, the forecasts on the distribution of likely outcomes and *scenarios* gets very troublesome, even with only a few decision points, due to the number of detailed estimates that is required. This feature also complicates the application of the DTA method to the valuation at *company level*, since a such object of analysis is extremely difficult to capture in decision points and scenarios. As such, the DTA method is more appropriate for investment projects, where the sketching out of scenarios is less complex. As in the DCF method, the uncertainty is likewise only seen as a value-decreasing *risk*.

The two NPV methods presented will in the following be referred to as conventional valuation techniques, especially because of the DCF method's widespread use, both in its simple form, as well as in more advanced forms which resemble the DTA method. The evaluation of the distinctive characteristics of real option valuation on a theoretical base will be done at the end of the chapter, after presenting the real option approach to valuation in the following. The overall conclusion on the real option approach to valuation and its practical applicability *vis-à-vis* the conventional valuation techniques will be undertaken at the end of the paper, after it has been applied to the business case in the next chapters.

4.1.3 Real Options and the NPV Approach

The real options approach to valuation is also an NPV method[87], though it utilizes quite different factors to discount and risk-adjust the future cash flows, and to capture the spread of potential outcomes. This has implications for the way the dispersion of potential cash flows is modeled, the way the flexibility of active management is incorporated, and the perception of uncertainty with regard to value implications. The value estimate of real option valuation is often referred to as Expanded Net Present Value. By this is meant that the Expanded Net Present Value conceptually is the sum of two components; the static NPV and the option premium. The former is in principle equivalent to the simple DCF, whereas the latter is the extra value from the flexibility to adapt to future developments in the shape of reaping the benefits from supportive developments and limiting the undesired impact of negative developments. Though conceptually presented as a simple addition of two components, this is not the way the actual calculation is done, as will be shown later.

4.2 Financial Option Valuation

The concept of a real option originates from an option as a financial derivative. The characteristic of a financial option is that for a certain price, a right is bought to buy or sell an underlying asset at a prespecified price at a specified future point in time, with no obligation to do so. If the option holds the opportunity to sell, it is called a *put option*, and if the option is to acquire, it is called a *call option*. In the case, where the option can only be exercised at a fixed point in time, the option is said to be *European*. Options that can be exercised at anytime up until the exercise date are said to be *American*. These are open options in the sense that they can be exercised anytime from purchase to the exercise date. The underlying asset is most often an exchange-traded asset, such as stocks or commodities - e.g. oil, gold, coffee, etc. The prespecified price at a future point in time is called the exercise price.

The critical feature of an option is that no obligation is attached to exercise the option - i.e. to buy or sell – it is only a right / an option. This way the downside risk is limited to the initial investment, whereas the upside potential is unlimited. Therefore, options are popular instruments for hedging unwanted risk exposure and for highly geared speculation.

Black & Scholes (1973) proves that if the following assumptions hold, the below formula can be applied to option valuation:
- *'There are no transactions costs and no taxes.*
- *The risk-free interest rate is constant.*
- *The market operates continuously.*
- *The stock prices are continuous, i.e. there are no jumps in the stock prices ...*
- *The stock pays no cash dividends.*
- *The option is European (exercisable only at expiration).*
- *Stocks can be sold short without penalty and short sellers receive the full proceeds from the transaction.'*[88]

$$C_0 = S_0 N(d_1) - E_x e^{-r_f t} N(d_2)$$

where:
- C_0 = the current call price (value of option),
- S_0 = the current stock price,
- E_x = the exercise price,
- e = base of natural logarithms – approximately 2.7128,
- r_f = the risk-free interest rate (annually),
- t = the time to maturation (as fraction of a year), and
- $N(d_1)$; $N(d_2)$ = the values of the cumulative normal distribution at points d_1 and d_2 respectively where:

$$d_1 = \frac{\ln(S_0/E_x) + (r_f + \tfrac{1}{2}\sigma^2)t}{\sigma \sqrt{t}}$$

$$d_2 = \frac{\ln(S_0/E_x) + (r_f - \frac{1}{2}\sigma^2)t}{\sigma \sqrt{t}} = d_1 - \sigma \sqrt{t}$$

- σ = the standard deviation of the continuously compounded annual rate of return, representing the volatility of the stock price.

From the formula, it can be seen that the terms S_0 and E_x constitute the value components, respectively incorporating the value of the investment project and the required investment. However, S_0 is in present value and is adjusted for the time-value of money before it enters the formula, whereas E_x is a nominal future value. Therefore E_x is discounted by the term e^{-rt}, which is a discounting in continuous time. For the sake of comparison, this can be thought of as similar to the term $(1+r_t)^{-t}$ from the DCF formula of section 4.1.1, which in contrast is in discrete time. The two terms $N(d_1)$ and $N(d_2)$ respectively model the upside and the downside risk of the option by integrating the volatility and the time factor[89] into the formula.

Though the option priced is a European call option, the formula can be extended to American type options and put options too. The range of assumptions may seem somewhat restricting to the formula's usability. Some of the assumptions, however, primarily have been made for the sake of deriving the formula. The main principle behind the derivation of the formula is to create '*a portfolio of traded securities which has the same payoff as the option, and which mimics its fluctuations in value over time*'[90]. Hence, the assumptions related to the absence of transaction costs and taxes, the continuous stock prices and operating markets, and the short-selling of stocks can be considered idealized with little impact on the relations presented in the formula and its validity. The assumptions related to the constant risk-free interest rate, the absence of dividend pay-outs, and the European expiration mode are conceptually restricting, but solutions have been developed that transcend these limits.

Based on this, appraising the value of a financial option is rather straightforward, since the inputs for four out of five variables are readily available, when the shape of the option has been laid down. The only variable that needs to be estimated is the volatility. Conceptually, this estimate should be of the expected future volatility. In practice, historical data are frequently used[91].

In the following table, the effect on the value of the option (C_0) of an increase in the other factors of the formula is depicted[92]:

Table 4.1 Effects of Increases in Variables for the Option Value

An increase in … :	S_0	E_x	σ^2	t	r_f
… has this effect on C_0:	↑	↓	↑	↑	↑

Source: Own construction.

It is worth noticing that the maturity (t) is only present in the formula multiplied with the interest rate (r_f) and the volatility (σ^2). Therefore, equal percentage increases in maturity, interest rate, and volatility (σ^2) as a variance have the same effect on the value of the option (C_0)[93]. The point that the option value increases with increases in uncertainty in the shape of volatility and with increases in the time to maturation may appear counterintuitive, from the point of view that exposure to uncertainty is rather avoided, and if necessary, then for as short a period of time, as possible; that is seemingly plain risk aversion. Nevertheless, this is one of the central lessons from option pricing theory. It is caused by the limited downside, but the potentially unlimited upside.

Another lesson from option theory is that an option should not be exercised, before its ultimate expiration date. This is because the option holds the potential of a further increased upside, if the price of the underlying asset develops even more favorably. Put another way, the option on the remaining time to maturation can be sold on as a call option, thereby having a higher value than the sheer pre-mature exercise value. In other words, the option is more worth unexercised - a.k.a. 'alive', than exercised - a.k.a. 'dead'. This only goes for options, where the underlying asset does not pay cash dividends. When there are no dividend payouts, an American option is worth the same as a European option[94]. Oppositely, if there are dividend payouts, the option may profitably be exercised prior to the dividend pay out date. Since the underlying asset - in this example a stock - is acquired upon exercise, the owner of the stock receives the dividend pay outs. If these are higher than the remaining option value, premature exercise will consequently be optimal. As a consequence, American options are more valuable, than otherwise similar European options, when there are dividends.

The earlier mentioned approach to option valuation put forward by Cox, Ross & Rubinstein (1979) using a binomial approach, did also gain ground in real option valuation. The advantage of the binomial approach is its incorporation of discrete observations, as opposed to the normal distribution's continuous observations, i.e. stepwise and fixed time intervals. Thereby, the binomial approach is easier to grasp intuitively, since it is basically modeled as a decision tree with sequential steps and decision notes outlined. Furthermore, the modeling of the real options can be tailored to more complex options; i.e. multiple or compounded options, whereas the Black & Scholes formula has its limitations in terms of incorporating and evaluating more complex real options.

The binomial approach is more demanding in terms of sketching out the alternatives. For the more complex real options, this approach involves longer equations that have to be laid out and calculated backwards, and is as such more complex mathematically. This approach provides so-called numerical solutions in cases where analytic closed-form solutions like the Black & Scholes formula are not at hand. Analytic closed-form solutions can also be found for the simpler real options using the binomial approach. The Black & Scholes formula can for example be derived from the binomial approach, when this is approximated to the normal distribution by decreasing the discrete intervals[95].

With the above terminology in mind, the following developments can be traced in the research on the quantitative applications of real option valuation. Initially, the solutions developed to the cases at hand were analytic closed-form solutions related to simple and isolated options. Later, complicated analytic closed-form solutions to more complex options (multiple and compounded options) were developed, and it was learned that '*the incremental value of an additional option, in the presence of other options, is generally less than its value in isolation and declines as more options are present ... option interactions can be small or large and negative as well as positive*'[96]. The last stage in the search for exactitude has been to appraise so complex real options that no analytic solutions could be developed, and numerical solutions had to be developed[97].

The advances made within the quantitative analysis of real options have been quite substantial and enabled sophisticated modeling and high mathematical precision of very complex multiple and compounded real options. Through these advances, the academic approach to valuation has become more comprehensive, demanding and complex. Early real option valuation focused somewhat narrowly at simple single options, which made it intuitively and conceptually easier to understand and the corresponding analyses easier to carry out. In contrast, the more complicated quantitative analyses presented in the literature today almost require a specialized mathematical background. Compared with the DCF approach, which is widely used among corporate practitioners, the requirements for understanding the analysis of simple single options may not be that much more complex though. Today's general familiarity with beta, and the CAPM analysis, which is most often used to determine the beta, has come through decades of use. Likewise familiarity with the real option valuation, and in particular the concept of volatility, which is conceptually the most difficult to understand, might evolve. Actually, the two concepts, beta and volatility, do not differ much in sophistication, complexity and difficulty, seen both intuitively and theoretically[98].

4.3 The Analogy; Real Options

The analogy between real options and financial options rests on the use of the same formulas and mathematical principles for option pricing. The first part of the term, real, points to the fact that the object of the analysis is not a constructed, financial instrument, but a concrete, tangible investment project in a corporate setting.

The definition of the real option is slightly changed from the financial option. It says that a real option is present when '*(t)he owner of the discretionary investment opportunity has the right – but not the obligation – to acquire the (gross) present value of expected cash flows by making an investment outlay on or before the anticipated day when the investment opportunity will cease to exist.*'[99]

In the analogy, the contractual and predefined agreement of the financial option between two participants to the transaction translates into an unrestricted discretion that the owner of the real option has on the underlying investment project[100]. As a one-participant notion used for the sake of valuation, the owner of the real option does not have to stick to the course of action laid down in the real option. In that sense real option valuation is only an instrument for valuation at a given point in time. Though it may help explicate the important strategic infliction points and prepare for various contingencies, and thus may support strategic planning, it is important to realize that valuation of corporate investment projects does not imply the fixation of one course of action from the valuation date, the way contractual financial options do.

Though it could be speculated that real options for one reason or another may in fact be traded, the potential in terms of establishing contractual arrangements for corporate investment projects is limited by the lack of an objectively observable price to set up the contractual agreement around. Therefore, the above definition's focus on real options as discretionary, one-participant investment projects makes sense.

The definition of real options focuses on call options by the words *'to acquire'*. In fact, real options on e.g. salvage value have been analyzed as put options. Still, the main potential of real options lie in call options, and their above outlined fit with discretionary, one-participant investment projects.

As have already been touched upon, more elaborate and encompassing mathematical techniques for option pricing than the Black & Scholes formula have been developed. By using a binomial distribution, more complex options can be appraised by developing what is known as numeric solutions. Anyway, the variables that enter into these solutions are still the same, so for this chapter's theoretical discussion of real option valuation, Black & Scholes' option pricing formula will be used. When the formula is applied to the real option application in order to evaluate an investment project, the formula remains the same, but the content of the variables changes, as presented in table below.

Table 4.2 The Analogy between Financial and Real Options; Content of Variables and Notation

	Financial option (derivative)	Real option
C_0	Purchase price	Value of investment project
E_x	Exercise price	Required level of investment at the time of decision
S_0	Current stock price	Present value of expected cash flows derived from the project
σ^2	Volatility of the stock price	Volatility in the driver of project value
t	Time to maturation	Project duration
r_f	Risk-free interest rate	Risk-free interest rate

Source: Own construction.

In the application of the formula to appraise the value of an investment, the required level of investment (E_x), the present value of expected cash flows (S_0), and the risk-free interest rate (r_f) are familiar factors to take into consideration. The additional insights from the valuation in terms of variables lie in the volatility and the project duration. Conveniently, the insights from the presentation of the Black & Scholes formula with regard to the impact on the option value by an increase in one of the variables in the formula, as illustrated in table 4.1, also applies to real option valuation. The impact will be exemplified in the following.

The fact that the higher S_0 is and the lower E_x is, the more valuable the investment project will be, must be considered common business sense. This is basically the same as realizing that the higher the spread between revenues and costs is, the more feasible the investment project is. So no new insights from these variables.

Increases in the risk-free interest rate surprisingly increases the option value. This variable enters into the formula to take into account the time-value of money, so should it not be expected that an increase would decrease the option value. The crux of the matter is that this insight does only relate to the formula, where S_0 has already been discounted, before entering the formula, whereas the exercise price, E_x is discounted in the formula, as the only variable. Since E_x is a cost, an increase in the risk-free interest rate, with which E_x is discounted, decreases the costs, and hence increases the option value. An evaluation of the overall impact of an increase in the risk-free interest rate, before S_0 is discounted[101], is more ambiguous, and depends on the proportions of S_0 and E_x. Though it is important to know the impact of and the sensitivity to changes in the risk-free interest rate, there is little to be done about it in terms of seeking out real options with interesting features, since it must be considered given.

The variables of volatility, σ^2 representing uncertainty as a variance, and project duration, t, have the most interesting impact on the option value. Their value-impact is the mathematical corner stone of real option valuation. This was already presented conceptually in section 2.4 in order to establish a basic understanding hereof, before the strategic perspective on real options was rolled out in the analysis. For the sake of presenting the analogy in its entirety in this introduction to the financial perspective on real options, the next two pages repeat this introduction. The benefit of real option valuation is that it incorporates the value of the option for management to alter course, when uncertainty is gradually resolved in the course of time, and a contingent investment decision can be identified. The contingent decision may come in many shapes, as will be explained in next section's presentation of a real option typology. The real option typology introduces the different kinds of flexibility that can be incorporated in real option valuation.

The uncertainty is perceived as the price fluctuations of the underlying asset, expressed as the variance. The notion is that uncertainty is distributed with changing probabilities for positive and negative developments relative to a mean value. This means that uncertainty is not just perceived as possible losses (risk per se), but equally so as potential gains. Consequently, the higher the uncertainty is, the broader the spectrum of possible outcomes will be. Since the investment project is seen as an option in the sense that management may continue the project by investing, but are not obliged to do so, the downside can be limited to the investments prior to the contingent decision, if developments have been unfavorable to the project. On the other hand, the upside can be reaped, if developments have been supportive. That is, the higher the uncertainty and the longer the project duration, the better the chance is that the investment will be worthwhile at a given point-in-time in the future. The cone-shaped figure below illustrates the point.

Figure 4.1 The Cone of Uncertainty

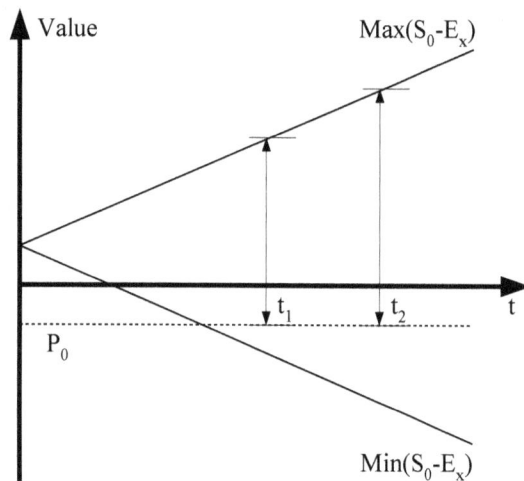

Source: Own construction, inspired by Amram & Kulatilaka (1999) pp. 15-17.

P_0 is the investments undertaken prior to the contingent decision, and thus represents the highest possible loss, if the option is not exercised. As it can be observed, the longer the project duration, and consequently the longer the investment project is exposed to the uncertainty, the wider the range of possible outcomes will be. Graphically, the higher the uncertainty in terms of volatility is, the wider the cone will be. As illustrated, the downside is maximally P_0, whereas the upside changes notably from t_1 to t_2. The difference between Max (S_0-E_x) and P_0 is the range of outcomes.

The uncertainty in the reality facing the investment project may come in many shapes. Yet, it is important that high uncertainty is not perceived as equal to high risk, when risk is perceived as a high probability of failure. For the uncertainty to be value-creating as proposed by real option valuation, the probabilities must be distributed with chances for both positive developments, and risks of negative developments. Technological or market uncertainties have to exhibit these properties, in order to be valuable. Therefore, when spotting areas with high uncertainty, e.g. industries that have shown volatile developments, which are cyclical, are more interesting for real option valuation, than industries that are stable at a high or low level, or historically showing only developments in one direction; i.e. positive or negative developments. This is, of course, not to say that industries showing only positive developments are not interesting. For most cases, it suffices to evaluate whether the spread of potential outcomes is wide, and the feasibility expected to change over a long period of time.

The integration of active management in investment projects with spectacular risk profiles makes the framework particularly useful for long-term projects under high uncertainty involving sizable investments. Examples of such projects are natural resource extraction, such as mining and oil drilling, real-estate development, and R&D projects. The option might come in many shapes that share the same basic characteristics. If for example, the investment outlays and the progress of the project are staged, a sequence of decision points can be identified, each of which has an improved foundation for deciding whether to proceed with or abandon the project, or whether to contract or expand the scale or the range of the project.

However for valuation of a company as a whole, the real option approach to valuation may not be that suitable. In that case, the configuration of the option becomes too complex, since the underlying asset then becomes the company itself. This has the consequence that a relevant contingent decision is difficult to identify, and an appropriate volatility, time horizon, and exercise price likewise. Seen from the owners' point of view, it makes little sense to say that, if the company increases in value, they can buy it a fixed exercise price, due to an initial investment. They already own the company and have as such invested the required investment to own the company. Neither does it make sense from the owners' perspective to talk about a limited downside, since this is equal to bankruptcy, which must be considered rather costly in its total destruction of the company value. For the owners of a going concern, the 'exercise' (i.e. continuation) of the company as a whole is simply not optional, in a real option sense.

4.3.1 Types of Real Options

Like the presentation of the mathematical principles behind the value-impact of uncertainty / volatility and project duration, the various types of real options have been briefly introduced before, namely in section 2.5. It is presented once gain but more detailed here for the sake of presenting the analogy in its entirety. As established, active management, perceived as the action of altering course as the future unfolds, can be incorporated into real option valuation by identifying the contingent decisions in the investment project in question. Thereby, the extra value of the option(s) is captured, compared with the passive management anticipated by the

DCF approach's static projections. The contingent decisions that can be analyzed as options come in a number of different shapes. Basically, they can be divided into three categories. These are *flexibility options* that are present in investments that are rolled out in stages in which directional changes can be made by management, *timing options* that take into consideration optimal time of initiation and non-operation, and *growth options* that create subsequent investment opportunities.

The flexibility options can be *options to expand or to contract* the scope of the project according to future developments. If for example consumer demand for a given innovative product exceeds expectations, then an option to increase production capacity has value. And vice versa, if the demand is less than expected, an option to contract is valuable too.

Another set of flexibility options is the options to terminate an investment project, if the development has been worse than expected. An *option to abandon* a project, before investing heavily in a final and expensive phase might be valuable, where initial investments are in preparation or preliminary efforts, such as market research on consumer perception of product or prototyping. E.g. in the case of pharmaceutical drug development, the final and very expensive clinical testing (phase III testing)[102] may be avoided if the market conditions have developed unfavorably. From the point of initiation of the investment project, this has a value. A similar option is the *option to default on staged investments*. This is basically the abandonment option in investment projects with multiple stages where stop-or-go decisions can be made based on the development.

A final flexibility option is the *option to switch* use of an asset, either on the input or the output side. If for example a given production set-up can run two different products, the option to switch according to developments in the markets for the two products - the output side - is valuable. The same goes for possible changes on the input side, if for example a given production set-up can use two different kinds of energy sources, e.g. coal and oil. Then the option to switch according to relative price changes has a value.

Two kinds of timing options can be identified; *options to defer* and *options to temporarily suspend operations*. If no pressure is on the investment project in terms of time, i.e. the project is not in a window of opportunity, the option to await the development of the market or the resolution of other kinds of uncertainty might hold value. This value is present in almost any kind of investment project that is confronted with conditions of great uncertainty and volatility, but with no pressure for a quick, preemptive investment. The option to temporarily suspend operations is particularly critical for investment projects or businesses with heavy sunk costs or substantial price changes that cannot be transferred to the end-customers. If the market thus turns against these kinds of projects or businesses, an option to shut down and restart operations at a later, more beneficial point of time, is valuable. A classical example is mining.

The final category is the growth options. These are present, when sizable investments are undertaken with no direct or obvious laid down target, but numerous possible outcomes. This kind of platform investment creates growth options. A typical example could be the initiation of research in a field that is expected to hold high future potential, with no direct application in mind. The more specific the growth opportunity inherent in the real option is, the more similar the growth option is to an option to abandon. Thus when predictions can be laid down rather accurately, the growth option becomes a simple call option on the underlying asset. Like a financial call option that is not exercised, if its exercise price is higher than the current stock price - a.k.a. an out-of-the-money option (abbr. OTM) - the investment project might be discontinued, just as it will be exercised, if it the exercise price is higher - a.k.a. an in-the-money option (abbr. ITM). This corresponds to the investment project turning into a growth opportunity that can be invested in; i.e. a growth option. In other words, the growth option and the option to abandon can be seen as two sides of the same classic call option with a limited downside and an potentially unlimited upside, when one (or few) identifiable and projectable growth option(s) is present. For completeness, it should be mentioned that an option where the exercise price is equal to the current stock price is known as being at-the-money, which is abbreviated ATM. These abbreviations will be used repeatedly throughout the estimation of numerical inputs in chapter 6.

Some of the presented options have characteristics that correspond to the ways investment projects naturally develops - e.g. options to abandon and to expand, and growth options, whereas others seem to hold characteristics that need to be prepared for or build into the investment projects - e.g. options to switch or temporarily suspend operations. This way the real option approach is not only a method for valuation with templates that approximate the reality, but does also suggest aspects to be taken into consideration, as value creating, when designing investment projects and laying down their strategies.

A prerequisite for applying the real option approach to valuation is that one can be rather specific and explicit about future scenarios. Some types of options are more easily applicable, than others. For example the option to defer is quite early in the lifetime of an investment project, and thus do not rely on predictions long into the future. Likewise, the option to abandon does not require complex future forecasts per se, since this is simply the no-go alternative. Opposite to these two examples, the growth options are more difficult to analyze, since this kind of broadly oriented investments may not be undertaken with an application in mind, or the potential applications may be so numerous that identification of the various scenarios gets troublesome. The option to switch is equally one of the more complicated option types to apply, since it requires consideration of more variables, and their interactions to be forecasted in parallel; e.g. future price developments on alternative inputs or outputs.

One investment project may hold more types of options in its forecasted development. For example, an investment project could have an open abandonment option, an option to expand,

and an option to defer the initial investment, possibly at different points in time. Actually, it is possible to interpret almost all investments as holding many options, if one chooses to do so.

It is perfectly possible to calculate these multiple option investment projects using more complex numerical solutions and different models for uncertainty. If this is done, it is important to keep in mind that the value of more options combined, which is called a compound option, only is a simple addition of the individual values of the respective options, when there is no interaction between the options. This is rarely the case. Often there are interdependencies, when the exercise of one option kills another option, or otherwise influences other identified options. This means that the incremental value added of an extra option usually is decreasing[103]. This is known as the 'diminishing option-value effect'[104]. Consequently, the most important thing is to identify and focus on the crucial option(s), despite of the many options that may be identified. Working with complicated, compound options can easily induce more complexity and model problems, than is added of explanatory power and value precision[105]. This issue will be further looked into in the configuration to the business case as a real option in next chapter.

4.3.2 Evaluation of the Analogy

Conceptually, the transfer of the option pricing formulas and the mathematical principles has been well put down by the various theoretical contributors, as described above. Still, the question is whether it is reasonable to adopt a formula applied for pricing of derivatives under certain assumptions to the quite different area of capital budgeting. Theoretically, the crux of the matter is whether the application of the formula, developed for traded, financial assets, makes sense for non-traded assets[106]. But as we saw in the beginning of this chapter, this is also the case for other valuation methods. For example, the theoretical foundation of the DCF approach is the valuation of stocks and bonds, that is, also here a theory for valuation of financial instruments is transferred to the 'real' investments of capital budgeting. Furthermore, the use of betas relies on the same assumptions of market efficiency - i.e. identification of similar investments and comparable companies - from the investors' point of view. As we shall see later, a similar approach can be applied for real options, when volatility estimates have to be found and applied. In other words, the assumption of market completeness is a prerequisite, if a valuation technique is to be independent from various, individual utility preferences, and hence for the valuation approach to have universal validity in this regard. Basically, the use of valuation methods to appraise corporate investments has to be in accordance with the financial market valuation of traded assets; i.e. the objective is to appraise the corporate investments as if they were to be traded[107]. Hence, the conclusion is that not only is it defensible to use models based on strong market assumptions in capital budgeting, but it is actually very important that the valuation models are in accordance with the financial markets, which they, based on the assumptions, become both in the case of real option valuation and DCF.

Though the analogy between the financial options and the real options can be legitimized, there are still a few differences to be aware of. These differences point to the importance of using real options as a stylized and conceptual approach, more than as a method to achieve the exactitude of the formula, when applied to financial options. The differences are all related to the financial option's well-defined contractual character compared with the real option's embodiment of complex and strategic corporate interactions and decisions. The setting of the financial option with its clear-cut exclusivity of ownership and right to exercise, clearly defined conditions in terms of exercise price and identifiable underlying asset which is easily priced, independence of outside factors, and its tradability is very much in contrast with the real option in the corporate context. Here the threat of competitive interactions might kill an option or force an option to be exercised prematurely, while the basic conditions in terms of exercise price and underlying assets are less clear, particularly due to the non-traded nature of the option and its focus. Furthermore, the options are rarely clear-cut and isolated options, but rather dependent on complex corporate interactions.

The evaluation implies the necessity of carefully interpreting the results of the real option valuation, due to the more dynamic reality of the investment projects behind the real options. Compared with the valuation of financial options, there are potentially many more factors that might influence the value along the course of the project. Most are factors that cannot be expected to remain fixed, and will change subsequently with implications for the value of the investment project. Nevertheless, the estimated value stands at the time of the valuation.

4.4 Real Options and Mathematical Solutions

The first step in applying the real option approach to valuation is to establish the mathematical solution, whether it needs to be developed or exists. The mathematical solution is based on the configuration and the mathematical modeling of the real option. It must take into account aspects, such as the contingent decision(s), the uncertainty, and the expiration mode. When these aspects have been analyzed, it is clear whether the real option in question can be satisfactorily appraised with existing analytic solutions, such as the Black & Scholes formula, or specific, customized numeric solutions must be developed. The complexities of tailoring mathematical solutions can be quite profound. The choice of Black & Scholes' formula was made for easier explanation of general option pricing aspects. In the following theoretical presentation of the configuration and mathematical modeling it will be maintained.

4.5 Real Options and Contingent Decisions

For the interpretation of the reality of the investment project as a real option, a number of real option types exist. A broad typology was presented earlier in this chapter. The identification of the contingent decision(s) cannot be theorized more, but must be done in the light of the empirical focus.

4.6 Real Options and Uncertainty

In section 4.2, Black & Scholes' option pricing formula was presented. From the content of the formula, it can be seen that this calculation of the option value incorporates a normal distribution function. A fundamental assumption behind the application of many option pricing techniques is that the dynamics of the underlying assets must be explainable and demonstrable through a stochastic process. In the case of Black & Scholes' formula, this is the normal distribution.

Stochastic processes describe changes in the value of a variable that is uncertain over time. Stochastic processes this way depcict uncertainty, but not to the extent of complete randomness. Therefore, stochastic processes often depict the uncertainty as quite unpredictable in the short term, but expected to follow a trend in the long term[108]. The volatility in the driver of project value, σ is the key numerical input with regard to the stochastic variable. The uncertainty can be modeled in a number of ways.

The geometric Brownian motion is probably the most common stochastic process for option pricing[109]. It is the one used in the Black & Scholes formula. This stochastic process is often preferred for option pricing, because it resembles the characteristics of financial traded assets well, in the sense that it cannot become negative, i.e. the price of the underlying asset cannot be less than zero, and the dividends and the variance of the asset are not influenced by the absolute value of the asset. The geometric Brownian motion will be used in this paper.

Of other processes that can be applied to option pricing, the mean-reverting process and the Poisson process should be mentioned. The mean-reverting process has a long-term equilibrium trend that in some cases captures the behavior of underlying asset in question well. For example, oil and copper prices have been shown to display these characteristics[110]. Therefore, a real option on an oil drilling investment project could benefit from using this stochastic process. The mean-reverting process is primarily used in special cases that call for it. The Poisson process is a so-called jump process. This can be applied for variables that do not just follow continuous, stable long-term trends, but also might show sudden disruptive movements. For the underlying assets of financial options, a such occurrence could be a sudden bankruptcy of the company behind the stock. Integration of the Poisson process is technically rather complicated in terms of estimation and formula mathematics, and since it is consequently not anticipated to add significant explanatory power, it is not used in this paper. Generally, the choice of stochastic process should follow the characteristics of the underlying variable. But only where circumstances are particularly obvious for choosing a different process than the geometric Brownian, should this be done[111]. There are numerous other stochastic processes, which will not be further explored. Suffice to say that a big part of the ongoing research in option pricing is focused on this area, in attempts to model the uncertainty more precisely.

Stochastic processes either unfold in so-called discrete or continuous time. Discrete time is when the changes in the stochastic process only happen at certain designated points in time, whereas it may be happen continuously in continuous time. The normal distribution is per definition in continuous time, whereas Poisson and binomial distribution are in discrete time. As explained the Poisson process, and hence the Poisson distribution is not used in this paper. The binomial process can be used for real option valuation, and is particularly useful for more complex options that require, customized, specific numeric solutions. When the intervals between the designated points in time diminishes - i.e. get close to zero - in the binomial distribution, it becomes a close approximation to the normal distribution, and the two approaches give similar results.

Which of the two distributions the real option of the business case calls for will be determined after the choice of empirical focus and the presentation of the business case, in the next chapter.

4.7 Real Options and Expiration Modes

The project duration (t) is often explicitly forecasted in investment projects. As in the case of the financial option, this is basically the time until the opportunity disappears[112]. The project duration is the time from the date of the option pricing - the valuation date - until the point in time, where the option has to be exercised, i.e. a decision has to be made. But in contrast to the financial option, where the time of expiration is contractually set, for a real option three kinds of project duration might occur, each having different implications for the configuration and the mathematical modeling of the mathematical solution[113].

4.7.1 Three Kinds of Project Duration

First of all, the project duration might be influenced by changes in market conditions, such as actions of competitors or changes in consumer preferences. This way, the option may suddenly expire, demanding immediate exercise or else become worthless. This kind of sudden, disruptive market impact appears to be relevant for many industries, and thus many investment projects and real options. It could be captured by a Poisson distribution, as described in the previous section. Still, the frequency and the extent of the impact is very hard to predict and estimate. In the cases, where external developments may suddenly have an impact, the project duration can be considered *unknown*, but *finite*. The same goes for investment projects, where internal developments may lead to early achievement of development targets.

Secondly, the time of the opportunity might for some kinds of investment projects be infinite. This could be the case, when some sort of monopoly is attached to the option. This kind of option is presumably rare. Here, the project duration can be considered *unknown* and *infinite*.

Finally, the situation, where the owner of the option has an exclusive and discretionary right that is not influenced notably from external factors within a certain time frame, leads to a project duration characterized as *known* and *finite*. This is the case, when the investment project is patent protected or a license contract, such as a state concession. Also very unique investment projects may be entirely under the discretion of the owner, leading to a predictable project duration with no risk of external impact, enabling a known and finite project duration.

The latter kind of project duration is the preferable as regards the calculation of the option value, since the predictions are more exact and thus easier to estimate precisely. Nevertheless, it is important to have the two other kinds in mind, when applying real option valuation to an investment project.

4.7.2 Project Duration and Exercise Mode

Another time aspect related to project duration is whether the option is likely to be exercised prematurely, and whether this is possible. This discussion has been touched upon earlier; i.e. whether the option is European or American.

According to the above, if the project duration is expected to be either unknown and infinite, or unknown and finite - the first two kinds of project duration in the above - the option is in effect likely to be American. That is, the option is open for continuous exercise, since it is not possible to establish a fixed project duration, given the fact that the project duration is unknown. In general, corporate real options are seldom under contractual restraints or the like that limit the opportunity to exercise. Therefore, it would appear obvious primarily to perceive real options as American options.

On the other hand, for some investment projects with project durations that are known and finite, it may be appropriate to consider the options European, because it can be anticipated that a certain time frame is necessary to develop the foundation for the exercise of the options. That is, before the end of the project duration no option can be exercised, because the underlying investment is not ready and too incomplete for exercise; e.g. R&D investment projects.

Table 4.3 Aspects of Project Duration and Effect on Exercise Mode

	Unknown	**Known**
Finite	Sudden unforeseeable impacts. E.g. competitive actions & changes in demand. (American)	Proprietary, exclusive, and discretionary within a certain time frame. E.g. patents and licenses (may be European).
Infinite	Completely shielded. E.g. Monopoly (American)	n/a

Source: Own construction.

In conclusion, the project duration is often rather uncertain, or maybe better not very exact, and completely discretionary to management, which suggests that real options primarily are American in nature. Yet, the difficulties of incorporating external influences when the project duration is *unknown and finite*, along with the discretionary and preliminary nature of many real options when the project duration is *known and finite*, because it is used to establish a foundation for the exercise of the option, suggest that it may be conceptually reasonable to apply the European view of project duration and exercise mode to many real options. Technically, it is easier to calculate and model a European option.

4.8 Concluding Remarks on Real Options and Capital Budgeting

Real option valuation clearly has some distinctive characteristics compared with the two presented NPV methods. The comparison in the table below sums up the differences.

Table 4.4 Comparison of NPV Methods and Real Option Valuation

	Discounted Cash Flow	**Decision Tree Analysis**	**Real Options**
Suitable object of analysis	Company and investment projects.	Investment projects. Problematic to outline scenarios for a company.	Investment projects. Problematic to interpret a going concern in terms of contingent decisions
Time-value of money	Yes	Yes	Yes
Dispersion of future cash flows	Linear	Parallel	Probability distribution
Modeling of uncertainty	None	Scenarios	Stochastic
Perception of uncertainty	Risk	Risk	Risk & opportunity
Impact of uncertainty	Decreases value	Decreases value	Increases value comparatively, due to opportunity
Variables behind uncertainty	One beta	Possibly several betas	Volatility and beta
Operationalization of variables	Straightforward	Complicated in terms of scenarios and betas	Complicated in terms of volatility, less complicated scenarios,
Complexity of calculation	Easy	Relatively easy	More difficult, can be mathematically demanding
Intuitiveness of method	Simple	Easy overview	Complicated

Source: Own construction.

With regard to incorporating dispersed cash flows and uncertainty, the use of stochastic processes makes for a more subtly outlined spread of potential outcomes. The simple DCF is incapable of incorporating alternative outcomes, while the DTA method may do so, but only through very elaborate and extensive forecasts, if the same nuances are to be captured.

Real option valuation is dependent on the identification of at least one contingent decision, if the value of flexibility is to be integrated in the valuation. When this can be done, the real option approach to valuation captures the value of awaiting the resolution of uncertainty in a way that the two other approaches do not. On the other hand, the dependence on the identification of a contingent decision limits the applicability of real option valuation, since this makes it rather unsuitable for valuation of companies.

In conclusion, the three methods each have their most suitable context to be applied in.

The DCF method is the primary one for company valuation. It may be sophisticated with a simple DTA addition, but the number of scenarios that can be taken into account is quite limited, due to the complexity of forecasting scenarios at this level. In other words, more sequential lines of decision points are presumably hard to predict for a company as a whole. The real option approach's inadequacy in this regard is similar in its dependence on the identification of a contingent decision. Furthermore, the DCF method may be the most appropriate for short-term investment projects, where the uncertainty is minimal to the extent that it is hard to model it meaningfully.

The DTA method is the most appropriate for investment projects, where no contingent decisions can be identified, but where the alternative paths are natural consequences of initiating the project in the first place, and the outcomes of these paths can be estimated. Furthermore, the DTA method may be the most adequate in the cases, where the estimated outcomes simply are better approximated by a number of laid down scenarios, than by a volatility and a stochastic distribution, or when a volatility is unidentifiable.

The real option approach has the potential of capturing flexibility value that the two other approaches cannot. Beyond, the prerequisites of the two other approaches this requires that a contingent decision can be identified and that the uncertainty can be depicted as a volatility. Since uncertainty is such an essential part of this valuation approach, the application makes the most sense, when the uncertainty is substantial and the time horizon is long. This is because the progress of the investment project in these cases is more likely to be made up of different stages with a wide distribution of potential outcomes. Consequently, the investment profile is more likely to be staged also, with a number of subsequent investments or investments that can meaningfully be split up, which implies a potential for contingent decisions. After this theoretical presentation and comparison with conventional valuation techniques, the rest of the paper will look into the practical application of real option valuation. This way, it can be tested whether the promises outlined translate into meaningful results.

4.9 Concluding Remarks on the Theoretical Presentation of Real Option Valuation

This chapter's presentation of the theoretical aspects behind the configuration and the mathematical modeling, has made way for the first step in real option valuation; the determination of the mathematical solution. The identification of the contingent decision(s), modeling the uncertainty, and determining the expiration mode are challenging tasks of great importance to real option valuation. These aspects will be laid down in the following chapter, after the empirical focus of the case company has been chosen.

With these aspects analyzed, the mathematical solution can be determined. Only after that is done can the numerical inputs to the variables be estimated. This is done in chapter 6.

5. Empirical Focus and Configuration

In this chapter, the unit of analysis in the shape of the business case will be chosen, presented and the real option configured. First, a suitable empirical focus is chosen. This is done in the light of the realization from the theoretical discussion that a company focus may not be expedient for real option valuation. Therefore, the chapter begins with the identification of the most suitable focus within NRC and its research activities with regard to potential applicability. In so doing, a number of aspects of the preceding analysis is anticipated. After having decided on an empirical focus, the business case behind it is presented. Finally, the business case is modeled along the conceptual parameters of a real option in the configuration. The configuration looks into the contingent decision and the contours of the real option, the sources of uncertainty, and the expiration mode. These aspects are all modeled into a mathematical solution at the end of the chapter.

5.1 Empirical Focus of the Analysis

The process of interpreting the reality of the business situation as a real option, and modeling the mathematics of real option valuation to match the business case is called the configuration. Though the real option approach to valuation can be adapted to many situations, it is obviously more relevant for some applications, than for others. As most investment projects, in fact, can be influenced by the responsible decision makers throughout the lifetime of the project, most business cases *can* be modeled as real options. Therefore, for the analysis to be useful, care must be taken, *not* to force the reality of an investment project into the framework. Instead, the focus should be on business cases, where natural and identifiable strategic decision points already have been identified, or implicitly are present and important in the venture. An equally important prerequisite is the availability of data, based on which the numerical inputs can be estimated. These data may stem from both NRC, as well as other external sources. Therefore, the perceived empirical applicability of the empirical focus is evaluated *prior* to the analysis.

Figure 5.1 Choice of Suitable Empirical Focus

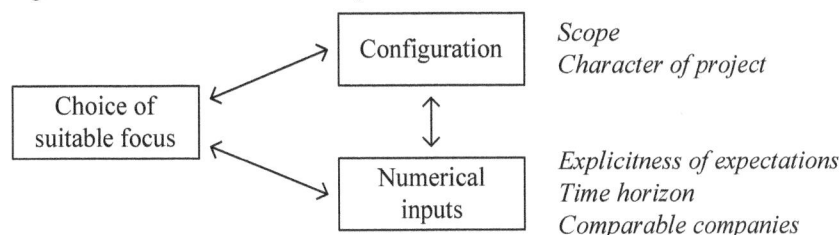

Source: Own construction.

As illustrated in the figure, the configuration and the estimation of numerical inputs are mutually dependent. Hence, both have to be taken into consideration in the choice of a suitable focus. Still, the configuration is the most obvious to undertake first, because it effectively delimits a wide field of potential applications. Thus, the *scope* is decided first since it establishes the unit of analysis which can be captured by the theoretical framework. By *character of project* is basically meant whether the empirical focus exhibits option-like characteristics; i.e. can the contours of an option be identified in the shape of a contingent decision. The *explicitness of expectations* refers to the estimation of the preset value of the expected cash flows and the investments required at the time of decision, while the *time horizon* is important as to the credibility of the forecasts, the timing of the contingent decision, and the nature of the project duration and expiration mode. The availability of *comparable companies* is related to the estimation of volatility in particular.

Three contributions on real options and R&D are relevant for the choice of empirical focus. Mitchell & Hamilton (1988) were the first ones to look into the appropriateness of appraising and interpreting R&D as real options in detail. The authors identify three different stages that the research can be in on its way from idea to market, and argue that the financial approach to the resource allocation should vary with these stages. The three stages differ in terms of the uncertainty of the R&D and the resources committed, as illustrated in the figure below. The three consecutive stages are knowledge building, strategic positioning, and business investment. The knowledge building is characterized as exploratory in nature and too general to be approached with valuation techniques. Rather the resources should be allocated as fixed costs of doing business. Oppositely, in the stage labeled business investment, the R&D is directed at a specific targeted product, close to market introduction. This investment should according to the authors be appraised using conventional valuation tools, such as ROI, which is an NPV method similar to DCF. In between, Mitchell & Hamilton identify a kind of R&D that falls in between the two funding criteria of the two other stages. Due to its strategic significance and closeness to market, it can neither be treated as pure knowledge building, nor can it satisfactorily be evaluated using ROI or DCF. This R&D is called focused research / exploratory development, and found in the stage labeled strategic positioning. According to the authors, this kind of R&D should be appraised using real option valuation.

Figure 5.2 Progression of Strategic R&D Programs

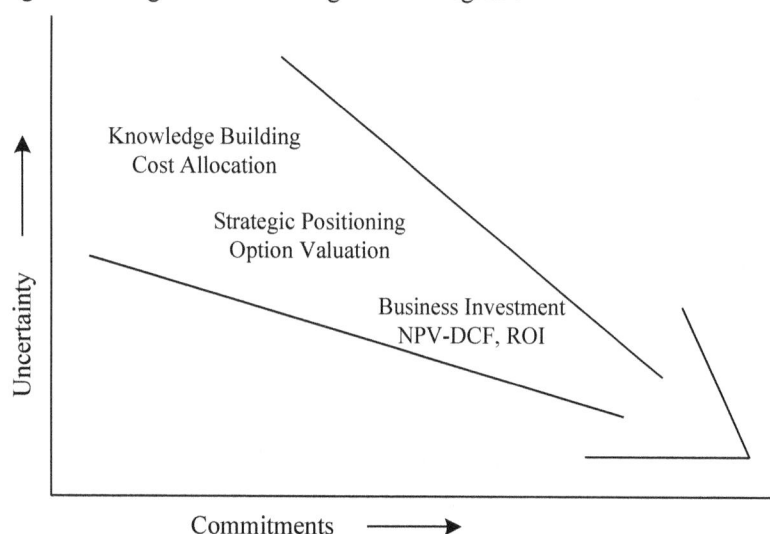

Source: Mitchell & Hamilton (1988) p. 16 with financial approach in each stage added, as outlined in original paper.

The above figure is also used by Matthews (1997)[114], who assigns time frames to the three stages of R&D. Though, the placement of R&D projects in the figure is obviously related to the time before market introduction, the corresponding time frames may of course vary with the specifics of any given R&D project, which may deviate from the simplified estimates of time horizon. Nevertheless, the estimates presented are illustrative. Matthews (1997) identifies the time frame for knowledge building as 6-10 years, strategic positioning 4-5 years, and business investments 1-3 years. In short, the recommendation is that real option valuation is most appropriate for R&D investments, whose time horizon is 4-5 years.

Faulkner (1996) recommends cases, where the pending investment is high relative to the initial investment[115], a substantial uncertainty will gradually be resolved, and the duration is long. In his argument, these are the cases where the DCF method is the least appropriate for R&D investments compared with real option analysis. The following choice of empirical focus will keep these recommendations in mind.

The first step will be to identify the *scope* of the empirical focus, which is equal to the unit of analysis. With regard to valuation and NRC, the below figure divides NRC into different levels of aggregation, and thus potential empirical foci. A more thorough presentation of the different levels and the four business maps mentioned in the following can be found appendix 3.

Figure 5.3 Different Levels of Aggregation for NRC

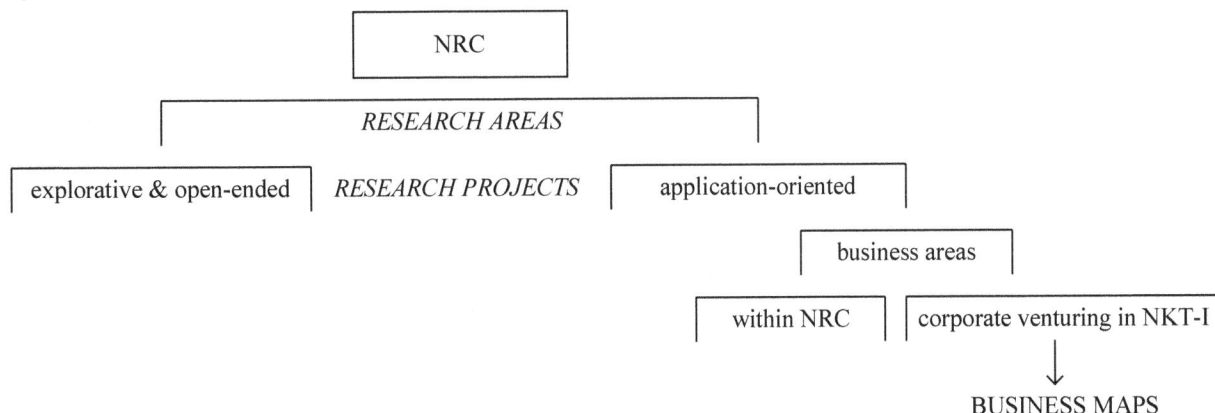

Source: Own construction.

So beginning with the larger valuation unit, it makes little sense to appraise NRC as a *whole company* using the real option approach. This was already argued theoretically in section 4.3. It is true that the parent company may see NRC as a growth option, 'producing' business concepts[116] for it to consider initiating within its corporate venturing set-up, but still this is at a very abstract level. The biggest problems are to configure an option in the going concern, to determine a time horizon and estimate a volatility. Therefore, the company as a whole is too aggregated to be the empirical focus.

The *research areas* of NRC are superconductor technology, cleaning and environmental technology, optical fibre technology, and polymer and surface technology[117]. Although, the research areas are more consistent than NRC as a whole, they are too broad to concretize the configuration. For example, the activities of the different research projects within each research area may be hard to aggregate meaningfully, and thus complicate the estimation of many of the numerical inputs. Some of the activities within each research area may also be time-wise open-ended and only vaguely application-oriented research for which few of the variables can be estimated, and for which the configuration of the real option is impossible, among other things, due to the lack of a decisive time horizon for research that is explorative in nature.

The subgroupings under each research area that are labeled *research projects* can be either teams of researchers working on parts of the technologies without a completely fixed application focus - the explorative and open-ended research projects in figure 5.3, or teams with designated and application-oriented research targets. Obviously, only the latter kind with the most concrete and application-oriented foci is turned into *business areas*. Some of the research results have been developed into business areas, without being established as independent companies. These lines of business are taken care of within NRC, and not integrated in the corporate venturing set-up.

Other research projects that are currently business areas have been pinpointed in NKT Innovation's screening of NRC research with commercial potential. If the research projects chosen in the initial screening are approved for further consideration by the Project Council, business maps are made subsequently. If these business maps are then approved by the Project Council and allocated funds, they become independent companies. The research projects that become business maps are the most obvious to apply real option valuation to. These research projects have been evaluated to contain enough commercial potential to build a business concept around. The fact that NKT Innovation makes a business map that explicitly outlines the context of the business concept, and projects the targeted development, makes it easier to estimate many of the numerical inputs in the real option valuation, among those the time horizon. Quite often, the research projects are made into business maps and separate businesses at a time, when some application-oriented and targeted research is still needed to perfect the technology and / or to establish proof of concept.

Four business maps were available to the analysis. Remarkably three of them exhibited option-like features. Of these three, Crystal Fibres was discarded, because the alternative paths in the contingent decisions were the most vaguely concretized and most uncertain, and the identification of comparable companies made difficult by the fact that this kind of research either takes place as minor activities in large companies, or in academia. The business map on SQUID technology was partly dismissed on the same grounds with regard to the identification of comparable companies. Furthermore, the time horizon was extremely long; namely 15 years, which was perceived to discredit the forecasts. The choice fell on Scandinavian Micro Biodevices, which is rather explicit about future strategic actions and estimates, though the market estimates are vague to say the least. The business context is very option-like, with a decision point with clear cross-roads identified three years ahead. The business concept has many comparable companies, due to the early stage the industry is in with many start-ups. The business case of Scandinavian Micro Biodevices will be carried forward in the analysis and presented in the following.

In terms of the theoretical recommendations that were presented before the choice was made, the three business maps fit more or less with Faulkner's (1996) three criteria; i.e. high pending investment, substantial uncertainty, and long duration. With regard to Mitchell & Hamilton (1988) and Matthews (1997), it is interesting that SMB is the one that comes closest to the 4-5 year time horizon. In comparison, Crystal Fibre and SQUID's forecasts have much longer time horizons, which actually make the forecasts problematic and the contingent decisions harder to outline.

5.2 Presentation of Scandinavian Micro Biodevices[118]

Scandinavian Micro Biodevices (abbr. SMB) is a venture into the medico technological market which is a new business area for NRC. Medico-technology has been identified as a new focus area with a high long-term potential and a strategic importance to NRC.

Within medico technology, NRC has identified biochips, equal to the 'micro biodevices' in the company name, as a promising product technology underway. This is a product technology where NRC with its current competencies and patents has the potential of adding significant value by combining existing and new research competencies. The product technology behind biochips is rather complex and draws on a number of scientific disciplines, as will be explained later.

SMB's aim is to manufacture the biochips based on its customers' design; a so-called foundry production. Therefore, the customers will have to be companies with biotechnology competencies related to the design and development of biochips. From its other research activities, NRC has capabilities in parts of the technology value chain required to manufacture biochips. For example, NRC has relevant know-how within materials and surface technology, which is a prerequisite for the production of biochips. NRC also has experiences with micro level research from its development within optical fibre technology; especially from integrated optics and the optical components of e.g. IONAS and GIGA[119]. However, some of the competencies required are not present in NRC, but have to be acquired or developed in SMB. Among these are primarily the necessary biotechnological know-how and the ability to go to industrial scale with the technology. The recently initiated optical microchip production in IONAS may in time become a source of know-how for the latter challenge.

5.2.1 Field of Research

The development of biochips has been enabled by the integration of research from many scientific disciplines. The field is truly multidisciplinary drawing on insights and principles from chemistry, physics, biology, electrical engineering, and mechanical engineering for areas such as fluid dynamics, micro electronics, organic and biomolecular chemistry, genomics[120] & genetics[121], opto-electronics, surface and materials technology - a very eclectic field of research indeed[122]. For the most sophisticated biochips, it all combines to a technology labeled microfluidics[123].

This field of research began in the mid- to late 1980's in Silicon Valley, America. The combination of intense government funded research efforts, the existence of venture capitalists, a culture of high-tech entrepreneurship, and the complementary insights from the development and manufacturing of microchips in the semiconductor industry provided an excellent breeding ground for biotechnology start-ups with this focus. Since then government funded initiatives, notably for biological warfare purposes and the Human Genome Project, have fueled the development further. The start-ups have also enjoyed significant capital infusions from major pharmaceutical companies. In the mid- to late 1990's, when the field of biochips began to take off in America with a number of the largest companies going public and the number of new start-ups increasing, European research in this field began to reach a substantial level, primarily through public regional industrial development funding. Though European academic research has largely caught up with the American level, the existing companies in America have a significant lead, and easily outsize their European counterparts[124].

5.2.2 Product Technology

Biochips (micro[125] biodevices) *'is a category of devices which can be characterized as:*

- *devices with functional structures in μ m dimensions (1μ m = 1/1000 mm) – typically 50-100 μ m, (micron)*
- *devices applied for purposes like analysis and screening, and*
- *devices used together with samples of liquid solutions.'*[126]

According to another definition, biochips are: *'miniaturized and selective measuring and screening systems aimed at biological cells and molecules'*[127].

Biochips can be divided into two categories; microarrays and microflow systems[128]. Microarrays are the simpler of the two kinds. Microarrays only test the sample for a predefined target, whereas microflow systems perform a number of steps in an analysis. Microarrays are sometimes referred to as first generation biochips and microflow systems as second generation biochips[129], since microflow systems incorporate the functionality of the microarrays in their extended functionality. The extra steps that microflow systems do are preparatory steps, such as separation of molecules or identification and isolation target probes[130].

The distinction between the two kinds of biochips is not important in the following presentation of the applications and the technological improvements and value creation of the biochip concept, and will consequently not be upheld. However, the distinction becomes important later when the choice of comparable companies is explained. It is important to stress that today only the microarrays have been launched commercially as products. The microflow systems are still being developed. Sophistication of the microarray technology is still a critical issue for the industry, as is the price-performance relationship.

The Human Genome Project[131]

The primary driver of the biochip industry is the recently concluded efforts to sequence the human genome. This extensive task has been undertaken as a public-financed project, which is known as the Human Genome Project. It was carried out in international cooperation, but was initiated in the late 1980's by the American government, who has been the dominant source of funds for the project. The aim of the project has been to establish one complete map of a human genome[132] that genetic variations can be tested against[133], which can also be used to identify physical points in the genome. Both prospects are very relevant for genetic research. When President Bill Clinton on June 26, 2000 announced at a White House press conference the completion of the mapping, it was in effect the completion of a working draft containing some 90% of the total DNA. Therefore, only about half of the genes had actually been sequenced. The identification, mapping and sequencing of the genes is maybe the most important result from the Human Genome Project, so critical steps are still ahead following the completion in February 2001[134].

Fundamentals of Genetics

A genome contains '*the master blueprint for all cellular structures and activities for the lifetime of the cell or organism*'[135], which also means that all living organism have a genome. The human genome is the most complex of the genomes. It can be found in '*every nucleus of a person's many trillions of cells*'[136]. The human genome consists of some 3 billion base pairs (abbr. 'bp') that are placed on long strands in a double-helix pattern. The strands can be pictured as two long strands of 3 billion entities that are matched and connected in pairs, but cut into strands of varying length in the nucleus of the cell. The strands of DNA in the genome can be divided into 23 chromosomes and approximately 30.000 genes.

The way that the DNA sequences are translated[137] into genetic instructions, and these instructions are executed, goes through the genes. The composition of each gene in terms of base pairs holds the key, or rather the code, to the construction of a protein This is also known as protein synthesis or gene expression. The protein is the central structural component of cells and tissues, as well as of enzymes for essential biochemical reactions. The 3 billion base pairs (3×10^9) in the human genome may vary between any two individuals in about 3 million bp's (3×10^6) or 0.1% of the bp's. Thus, our biological differences stem from these variations, which also hold the reasons for our differences in predispositions for certain diseases[138]. The variations in the DNA sequence are known as polymorphisms, since these are the places on the genome that literally can take alternative forms; i.e. they are literally polymorphic. Variation is caused by recombination[139] and mutations[140], and leads to changes in the DNA sequences. By enabling the tracking and marking of these variations, the Human Genome Project greatly helps in the determination of genetic causes for diseases. As such, this is an important first step towards the treatment of a disease.

Biochips are the perfect tools for the process of screening and identification. Due to the sheer amount of genes, and the number of base pairs they consist of, the screening and identification tasks at hand are quite considerable. Biochips help speed up the process and make it cheaper. This shift in focus towards the determination of the gene functions has been called the Post-Human Genome Project, and has as such been initiated already.

Functional Application of Biochips

The reason that the Human Genome Project is the primary driver of the biochip industry is the usability of the project's findings, when combined with the functionality of the biochips for the pharmaceutical industry. First of all, the biochip industry receives significant funding and excellent testing grounds from the pharmaceutical companies that see the potential of this technology for shortening and making more efficient the very long and expensive drug development process[141]. Secondly, the investors are presumably more willing to invest in the biochip industry, when the potential is related to the huge pharmaceutical market. Hence, the primary commercial potential of biochips is in *diagnostics*[142]. The improvements are in the laboratory tests conducted in the screening for protein targets and potential drugs, and the better testing of their usability in laboratory, before the expensive clinical trials.

A number of other molecular medicine applications exist. *Pharmacogenomics*[143] utilizes the biochips to better understand the genetic conditions of the patients, and the variety herein. The benefits from this improved knowledge of the patients' genes and thereby their reaction to drug treatment are much more targeted drug development and drug prescriptions. Also, the two related areas of *genomics*[144] and *bioinformatics*[145] are greatly helped by the biochips. Where genomics is focused on establishing information on the structures of the genome, *bioinformatics* is computational analysis of '*genomic and protein information to identify new targets for drug discovery*'[146], and other computational ways of improving the drug discovery process through the establishment of databases with DNA sequences of genomes, genes, proteins, molecule compounds, chemicals, etc., and analysis hereof[147]. Furthermore, biochips may be utilized in relation with research on human gene therapy[148], i.e. correction of genes to avoid diseases that people are genetically disposed for, and comparative genomics, where genetic experiments with animals may provide new knowledge, due to the substantial genetic similarities between e.g. mice and men.

Most of the other uses may not be as commercially viable as for the molecular medicine applications described above, but gives a good impression of the wide range of applications for biochips, and consequently the wide market potential. In the field of *microbial genomics* research on new energy sources (biofuels), environmental pollution, and biological / chemical warfare may be greatly improved. Within *DNA forensics*[149], great steps have already been taken, which may be further implemented in criminal cases. Biochips may also be used for *risk assessment* related to research on the causes of genetic mutations, such as exposure to radiation, chemicals and toxins. Additionally, biochips may improve genetic research into *agriculture, livestock breeding, and bioprocessing*, which has been practiced for ages, but may now be carried out in a scientific way. Genetic manipulation in the field of agriculture is the most advanced to date, but also very problematic, due to the easy crossover for plants, and thus unintentional and uncontrolled spread to the rest of the ecosystem.

Summing up, it should be emphasized that the outlined revolutionary perspectives opened up by research in genetics is not directly caused by biochips, since the biochips do not offer functionalities that have not been achieved or cannot be achieved with regular laboratory equipment. Rather the biochips propel the direction by supplying very powerful and potentially economical tools for research in molecular genetics and certain kinds of organic analysis at the molecular level[150].

The main advantages of biochips are efficiency and costs. The efficiency improvements that biochips introduce are speed, parallelism, and automation[151], which all come from putting the chemical analysis on a chip. These three primary gains from the miniaturization are obviously intertwined in their effects, and have the following cost advantages:

The higher *speed* leads to higher efficiency, and thus lower costs. This is particular evident in the pharmaceutical industry, where reductions in the time of the drug development process can save huge amounts. It is estimated that every day that the time of patent protection, for an average drug is prolonged, is worth DKK 7 million[152]. The efficiency gains from the *parallelism* offered by biochips, and the proportions of the reductions in sample size, are dramatic as explained earlier. This obviously lowers the use of reagents[153], and thereby the costs, but is also part of the reason for the improvement of speed. Finally, the *automation* basically means reduced hands-on time for laboratory workers that historically have been a significant, though decreasing part of total costs.

5.2.3 Industry and Competitors

In the microflow systems industry, there are around 80 players worldwide, of which approximately 50 are situated in America[154]. They vary in size from the biggest most established firms (Motorola, PE Corp.), where this business is only a small part of the whole portfolio of activities to small start-ups with this singular focus. A few IPOs[155] have taken place within the microflow systems industry in America during the first half of 2000 starting with Caliper Technologies in December 1999 and ACLARA BioSciences in March 2000, which were both established in 1995. They have emerged as industry leaders[156]. Microarrays are more perfected products, than microflow systems. The first commercial introduction happened in 1996, but the products are still being developed and sophisticated. There are at least as many industry participants as in microflow systems. The industry leaders are two well-established publicly listed companies; Affymetrix Inc.[157] which more or less has founded the industry and Incyte Genomics Inc.[158] In Europe, the commercial research and development on biochips is smaller in scale. The biochip companies in Europe have typically grown out of academic environments rather recently, compared with their American counterparts.

The companies in the biochip industry vary in the scope of their activities. They differ in the extent that they spread over the range of activities that are related to the development, production, and use of biochips.

The most narrowly focused companies only supply the biochip products to the customers, i.e. biotechnology and pharmaceutical companies, for these companies to utilize the biochips in their drug development, or wherever they are required. This is a so-called *foundry production* that can be based on both standard designs developed by the company, or designs from the customers. This kind of company will typically produce the more complex biochips, based on designs from the customers.

Other companies with a broader range of activities are so-called *contract research organizations* (abbr. CRO) that have specialized in carrying out parts of the biotechnology and pharmaceutical companies' research. This way, the customer companies outsource the extensive laboratory tests that are conducted for example for the purpose of screening for a drug target. These companies' interest in biochips may stem from a desire to further improve the extensive combinatorial tests that have previously been carried out using the so-called microtiter approach, which is heavily automated experiments conducted using tiny test tubes. These CRO companies may also directly market the biochips to the end-customers - i.e. foundry, but have extended their range of activities compared with foundry companies to also supply 'in-house production' of contracted research tests. But like the pure foundry companies they depend on the customers to supply the content, such as the probes and the samples, and the design of the chip that need to be tested, i.e. to design the experiments and tests undertaken.

The final group of biochip companies makes use of the biochips for research that is self-initiated. Here the target is to sell or license new drugs or drug targets to biotechnology and / or pharmaceutical companies that can finalize the development and market the drug. These drug targets have already been through a number of the initial phases in the drug development process in the biochip companies. This group of biochip companies also contains the ones that use the biochips to collect and / or to analyze genetic information, before it is sold to the biotechnology companies or the pharmaceutical companies. They may also sell the biochips or offer contract research to the customers. These biochip companies are so involved in the drug development and the treatment aspects that they are in effect as much into biotechnology, as medico technology. In the figure below, they are labeled *biotech companies*.

Figure 5.4 Range of Activities for Different Kinds of Biochip Companies

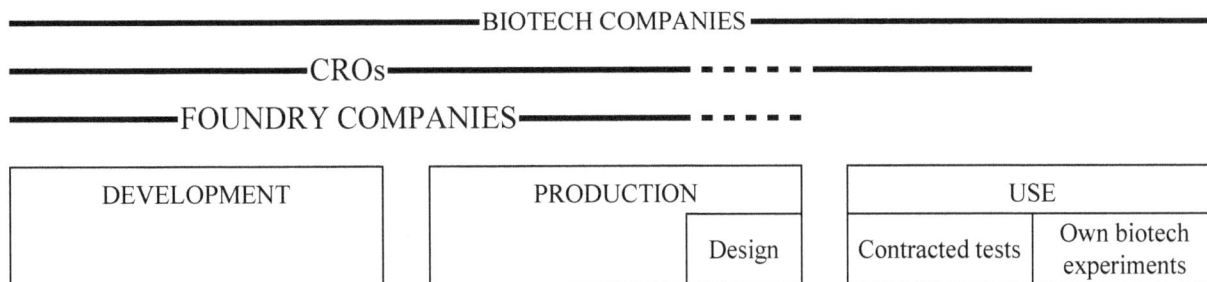

Source: Own construction.

Most of the biochip companies have foundry production. Still, some of the most notable exceptions to this, that is, the companies that do have biotechnology-related activities, are among the most established microarray companies, such as Incyte and Affymetrix. The biochip companies active in microflow systems appear to be less ambitious in terms of range of activities and more like the foundry producers and the CRO companies. Both Caliper Technologies and ACLARA are based on the production of microflow system with emphasis on foundry. The European companies appear to be more narrowly focused on foundry production with regard to the pharmaceutical and biotechnology applications, and this is also the role SMB intends to take.

As has been mentioned, the application of real option valuation often depends on the existence of comparable companies. Naturally, these are most frequently found in the industry in question. For the comparable company to be useful, it must be listed in order for the analysis to identify and make use of its stock exchange data. Hence, the European companies, which are predominantly not listed, cannot be utilized in the analysis, though they are more comparable in terms of phase of development, size, and set-up. Among the listed American companies, NRC has identified the two technology leaders active in microflow systems, ACLARA and Caliper Technologies, as the most comparable. These are the only two companies with focus on microflow systems that are listed. They have been chosen, because of their foundry-focus, which gives them a role as suppliers only and not direct participants in the pharmaceutical and biotechnology industries, as compared with some of the microarray companies and the microflow systems companies with CRO activities. Furthermore, the complexity of the R&D ahead and the short time they have been listed make them the most similar to SMB of any companies listed. Summing up, the main similarities are in core technology and appropriation, both related to the chosen range of activities.

5.2.4 Production Technology

SMB's business concept is targeted at a foundry production of biochips; both microarrays and microflow systems. The main difference to currently marketed biochips is the material that the chips are made of. Here SMB focuses on polymers as a cheaper and more appropriate material in terms of the trade-off between price and quality, than the currently used glass or silicon for microarrays. SMB is not the only company with ambitions in this direction; Caliper, ACLARA, and the Swedish company Åmic are among a few that have explicit research and development goals for this kind of material too. This is not just a raw material issue though, but has implications for the production process and choice of production technology too.

The technological and research challenges can be categorized into the choice of material and the surface consequences hereof, the biotechnological design of the biochip, and the detector system.

The choice of *material* is the point, where SMB's main difference is compared to the biochip industry at large. Silicon and glass are currently the preferred materials for marketed biochips, since the production of these are based on the microfabrication techniques from semiconductor microchips, where a high degree of precision in the manufacturing has been achieved primarily using silicon. SMB's target is to manufacture polymer-based biochips.

Polymers are giant molecules that consist of long chains of smaller molecules. Polymers are easily manipulated, and high levels of thermal, electrical, optical, chemical, and physical stability have been achieved through research and development. The fact that synthetic polymers can be developed with a number of customized properties makes polymers useful for a number of purposes; plastics is probably the most well-known of them, and the applications are manifold. NRC utilizes its competencies in polymer analysis to identify the most appropriate polymer available with regard to the requirements for biochip application. An extensive number of polymers have been developed and are available in the market. It would be too expensive and unfeasible to develop a new kind of polymer for this venture; i.e. SMB.

The choice between polymer, silicon or glass as base materials for biochips has consequences for the production method. Silicon and glass chips are primarily etched, whereas polymer-based chips have to be molded. This difference has important implications for the cost profile. The fact that a mold has to be created for each kind of polymer-based biochip makes the pre-production equipment costs - i.e. the fixed costs - incurred with each batch higher. On the other hand, the general production equipment and the material costs are lower. The overall effect in terms of costs is that polymer-based production is preferable with increasing batch-size, since the unit costs decreases with increased quantities produced. The turning point depends on the savings on materials and general production equipment compared with extra costs of the pre-production equipment in the shape of the mold.

Figure 5.5 Idealized Cost Profiles for Three Kinds of Base Materials

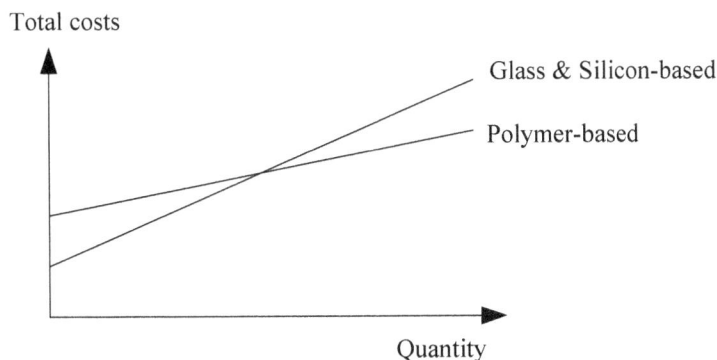

Total costs

Glass & Silicon-based

Polymer-based

Quantity

Source: Own construction.

The *surface* considerations are closely related to the choice of material. The polymer-based biochips do not possess the potential of achieving quite the same quality of microstructures as glass and silicon. These issues of surface roughness and chemical resistance are to be resolved through the research for the most appropriate polymer.

Regarding the *design* of the biochips, NRC and SMB lack some capabilities within biotechnology, or more specifically molecular biology and molecular genetics. Though designs for particular biochips may be specified or provided by customers, the interfaces of course need to be prepared for and managed. This requires biotechnology capabilities. To cope with that need, NRC has decided to a establish biotechnology laboratory at NRC, from which the necessary knowledge will be transferred to SMB[159].

The *detector system* is related to the monitoring of the chemical reactions on the chip. By using special dyes that change color or glow when a reaction has taken place or a chemical substance is present, the results of the experiment can be monitored through optical detection instruments. It is uncertain whether the best solution for NRC and SMB is to use an existing detector system, modify an existing system, or develop one in house, but either way NRC has sufficient competencies in optics and microelectronics from its earlier research in integrated optics and optical components in the field of optical fibre technology to determine this, or potentially develop it in-house.

NRC has some of the capabilities required in the three research areas that meet in the production technology behind this application. With regard to materials and surface technology, NRC has a solid background in *polymer research*. It is here NRC's distinctive capabilities are expected to create most of SMB's value. This competitive edge is particularly related to NRC's laboratory competencies in analyzing the properties of polymers and identifying the most appropriate polymer. Some of the major technological challenges in this research area are the usefulness and quality of the polymer-based biochips, and SMB's capacity to take it to an industrial scale. With regard to the latter, the experiences of the NKT subsidiary, IONAS, which has recently started an optical chip production may be helpful. Furthermore, the attractiveness of the cost profile depends on the degree of customization that the market will demand, which is unclear yet. Obviously, the more differentiated the demand is, the less attractive standard solutions and the presented cost profile will be. For the research area of *optics & electronics* related to the detector system, the research challenges are not so significant, and it is anticipated that NRC's know-how within microelectronics should be sufficient. Finally, *biotechnology* is the research area, where NRC has the least experiences and current competencies to rely on. SMB's value propositions with regard to the biochip industry is on the production technology side and targeted at the development of a polymer-based chip. This material alternative might facilitate costs and price improvements through a molding production process. This way, large-scale biochip production would lead to cheaper biochips.

5.2.5 Market

Among the forecasters of the biochip market potential, there is widespread agreement that the potential is a lot bigger than the current market. A common approach for new products or technologies that have not been commercially introduced, is to use the current market size of the products or functionalities that the product or technology, in casu biochips, are expected to replace (the substitutability) as a an indication of the level that the technology has the potential to reach[160]. One indication for this is the worldwide market for '*various analytical instruments used in chemistry and biotechnology*' that approximately equals USD 16 billion a year[161]. Another indication is the '*market worldwide for in vitro*[162] *diagnostics*', which is generally acknowledged to be the most significant for biochip application, estimated to USD 17 billion and 19 billion in 1997[163].

The level of these indications, and forecasts based on the substitutability effect, may both overestimate and underestimate the market potential. Overestimate since the technology is unlikely to replace all the functionalities of the outlined products and services, and underestimate because the groundbreaking technology may enhance demand by making more experiments feasible, e.g. in diagnostics, or devising new applications, and thus new markets, such as point-of-care or home use, in vivo[164] surveillance of diabetics, food monitoring for fresh products, etc.

A number of estimates on the current size of the biochip market have been published, along with forecasts for the biochip industry. These estimates show some variations that can partly be explained by differences in focus, i.e. microarrays alone or both product technologies, time horizon, i.e. technology breakthrough included or not, and time of appraisal. The estimates are all but one below the estimates presented above, which were based on substitutability. This reason behind this could be that the full substitutability is not anticipated within the time frame of the below figures, except for the one that stretches to 2009.

Table 5.1 Market Forecasts from Various Sources

Source	Most current	Future	CAGR
NIST[165] (1998)	2000: USD 300 mill.	2007: USD 4 bill.	45%
Business Week (1999)	1999: USD 1 bill.	2009: USD 40 bill.	45%
BioInsights (1999) - only microarrays	1999: USD 176 mill.	2005: USD 950 mill.	32%
Frost & Sullivan (1997)	2001: USD 950 mill.		n/a

Source: Presented in table and listed in references at the back of the paper. CAGR is Compounded Annual Growth Rate.

From the presentation, it can be seen that the forecasts show significant growth over the next five to ten years. Two of the compounded growth rates are in the area of 45%, while one for microarrays isolated says 32%. The big difference in the most current estimates on market size is remarkable. This is an indication of the difficulty that is associated with estimating the market, as discussed above. Nevertheless, the forecasts do explicitly or implicitly seem to anticipate that once the technology has been perfected and the price level has dropped, the breakthrough will increase the market immensely. The estimates that NRC expects are shown below. NRC's expectations are much in line with the other predictions in terms of growth rates, presumably relying on a technological breakthrough within the next five years. NRC's forecasts depict an expected 48% yearly increase up until 2007, but is not as optimistic as the most highest forecast in terms of starting point for the projections, as the current market is estimated at a lower level. NRC's forecasts will be used in the following chapter on the numerical inputs.

Figure 5.6 NRC's Market Forecast for Biochips Worldwide 1998-2007

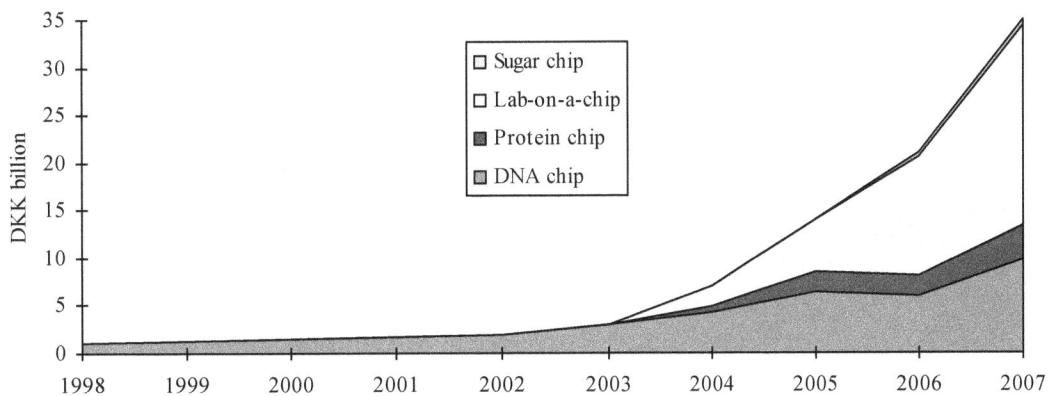

Source: NRC's Business Map on SMB.

5.2.6 Strategy

NRC has identified SMB's first challenges to be the establishment of technological proof of concept and the determination of competitiveness. The first step is for SMB to generate the necessary know-how and small-scale production capacity. Thereafter a strategic decision has to be made on whether to continue with the establishment of full-scale production. This in turn depends on the development of cost-efficient production technology and sufficient demand.

In NRC's operational strategy for SMB, a three-year time horizon has been applied, and the microarrays and the microflow systems are seen as parallel developments. '*A number of possible strategies have been identified. The strategic options are to focus solely on microarrays, or to focus solely on microflow systems, or both at the same time.*'[166]

The development of manufacturing capabilities for microflow systems is more complicated and time consuming, than for microarrays. Still, the capabilities that have to be developed and the technology that needs to be perfected for microarrays are prerequisites for mastering the production technology for microflow systems too. The perspectives for the two applications are illustrated through the following two quotes.

> '*Within microarrays, a mass market (commercial breakthrough) will come into being in 2-4 years. There is some competition, though less than for microflow systems, and a relative low risk for NRC. An evaluation of the feasibility is possible in 1½ years.*'[167]

> '*Within microflow systems, a mass market (commercial breakthrough) will appear in 4-6 years. The competition is intense, and the risk is high for NRC. An evaluation of the feasibility is possible in 3 years.*'[168]

The parallel developments can be illustrated as in the figure below.

Figure 5.7 Parallel Developments and Strategic Option in SMB's Operational Strategy

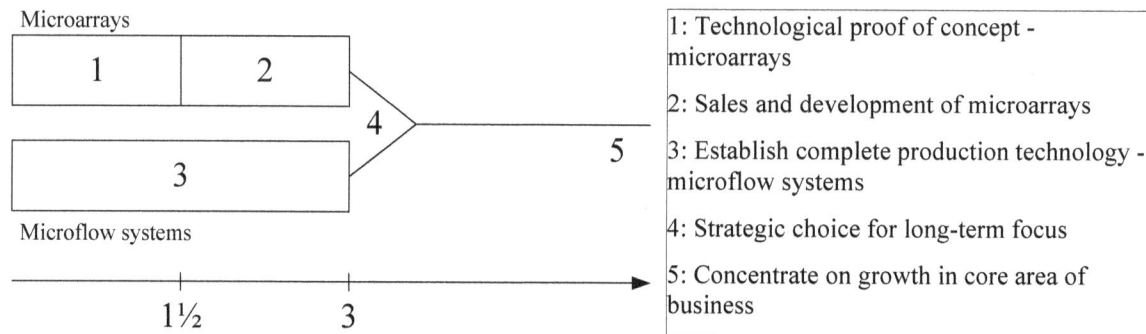

Source: NRC's Business Map on SMB.

Regarding phase 4, NRC has identified four alternative courses of actions that have to decided upon after three years. These are:
- '*close down all activities*
- *concentrate on surface technology (microarrays) and close down microflow system activities*
- *concentrate on microflow systems and invest in further development of the technology value chain* (production technology)
- *focus on both product groups and potentially split them into two companies with each their focus areas.*'[169]

Along with the operational strategy, a rather detailed financial roll-out plan has been formulated too. The essence of the corresponding budget is shown in the table below. It shows that personnel costs is by far the most significant part of the costs. Not surprisingly, the sales generated the first three years does not balance the cash-burn.

Table 5.2 Budget for SMB 2000-2003 in DKK 1000's

	2000	2001	2002	Accumulated
Salary	1840	6000	8000	
Total costs	7110	9200	10,500	26,810
Sales	100	1125	4000	5225
Cash burn	7010	8075	6500	21,585

Source: NRC's Business Map on SMB.

5.2.7 Future Issues for the Biochip Industry and SMB

Beyond the three-year time horizon of the business map, the obvious preferred outcome as seen from the point of view of NRC and SMB is that the research and development on biochips leads to the establishment of a competitive foundry production in a high-growth industry. If the industry takes off and the production technology facilitates a sufficiently low price level for a broad range of applications, the potential seems overwhelming. The impact on society, if this should happen, has been compared to the revolution that the microprocessors and personal computers have caused within the last 20 years. The parallel between the historical development of the microprocessor and the potential of the biochip is, among other things, that the microprocessor industry; a.k.a. the semiconductor industry, through continuous improvements and cost reductions have made microprocessors something that could be afforded in increasingly powerful computers for everybody, and not just for huge, mainframe computers. The same way, biochips' ultimate challenge is to '*make it personal*'[170]. Like the microprocessor took the computer from mainframe computers to personal computers, one of the promising perspectives in biochips is to take these new genetic tools from the laboratory to the personalized, genetics-based, point-of-care health care such as outlined in the presentation of the pharmacogenomics applications.

Standards

For the biochip development to imitate the evolution of the microprocessor industry however, there has been pointed to the necessity of a standard in the biochip industry. A shared technology base or / and a clear improvement criterion for the development, it has been stated, would stimulate the development towards a standard, which is a prerequisite for a groundbreaking and widespread breakthrough, as massive as in the microprocessor / semiconductor industry[171]. Through agreed upon technology and fixed improvement targets, industry participants and industry suppliers would be capable of directing their development efforts into the kind of concentrated progress witnessed in the microprocessor industry, which is required to reach the necessary performance improvements and cost reductions for a similar industry take-off. A standard could provide the industry at large with the '*figure of merit*'[172] that have worked as a focus for the microprocessors in terms of performance[173], while maintaining a stable price. The clear focus here has had the effect that a large share of the improvements over the last 35 years have come from the industry suppliers[174].

The fact that biochips need to become even cheaper, than microprocessors to reach the whole market and range of applications only point further to the necessity of a standard. A standard could enhance the scale advantages and speed up the development towards cheaper and better biochips. The reason that it appears possible to expect lower prices than microprocessors is that the market potential in units gives far more room for amortization of R&D costs, if one or a few kinds of biochips emerges as the industry solution. Still, regardless of the benefits of a standard for the evolution of the biochips, it has been put forward that standardization is difficult, due to the complexity of the biochip technology, and the diversity of the applications. Several barriers to standardization, such as inconsistencies across participants with regard to substrate materials, fabrication processes, packaging technologies[175], characterization techniques and design methodologies, have led some to conclude that this is only possible at a higher system level[176]. This would imply less similarities across the industry, and few shared improvements targets. Affymetrix, the company with the by far biggest biochip sales today, has committed itself to an open systems architecture approach[177], which eventually might evolve into a defacto standard solving some of the above issues (e.g. the packaging technique as described in footnote). Nevertheless, the affiliation to highly regulated industries, the differentiated nature of demand, and the different product characteristics do provide obstacles with regard to the biochip industry imitating the growth model of the semiconductor industry[178]. Although, it appears unlikely that the scenario of the semiconductor industry will repeat itself for biochips, it should not be expected that the lack of an industry-wide standard and a shared figure of merit precludes industry take-off at large. Instead, it may prevent the explosive growth witnessed in the semiconductor industry. It must be emphasized that the earlier presented market forecasts do not presume the same groundbreaking standard effects, as experienced in the semiconductor industry.

Patents and Appropriation

Another issue for the take-off of the biochip industry is the massive R&D investments that are required to develop the technology. For these investments to occur, the research results must be appropriable, and in particular competitively protectable. The biotechnology industry - i.e. the drug developing part of the industry - provides a parallel.

> *'The biotechnology industry has structured an evolutionary model based on massive R&D investments and strong patent positions, and focused in improving the life expectancy of humans first in developed societies, then in the remaining world population, all in the context of monopolistic business models generating large profits for funding future research. Every industry facing large development costs and capital investments must formulate a growth model capable of reducing the level of future uncertainty perceived by investors.'[179]*

For the biochip industry the patent situation is rather unclear. In microarrays, the industry leader Affymetrix has a very broad and strong patent platform, due to its early start with the technology, but the exact reach is very unclear. For microflow systems, the two industry leaders have been involved in legal proceedings with each other, when ACLARA recently sued Caliper for patent infringement, but lost[180]. Almost all of the companies in the first wave of biochip companies - the microarray manufacturers - are into some sort of biotechnology research utilizing the biochips themselves, and have thus extended their activities beyond the development and production of the biochips. These activities include genotyping and other aspects of drug development, and have led to a number of collaborations with the pharmaceutical and biotechnology companies on gene discoveries. The activities are typically attempts at patenting genes or licensing gene discoveries on potential drug targets for royalties. It can be speculated that the biochip companies extend their activities to areas where the commercial appropriation can be better secured by patents, than what is expected or feared from the development and manufacturing of biochips alone, where the situation is more unclear. Following this line of reasoning, the biochip companies may therefore be hesitating to rely on the biochips alone as a sufficient mode for recouping the investments.

The current biochip companies may fear that a second wave of companies enters the fray as the market gets commercially more interesting. For example foundry companies might provide a push towards standardization and commodification[181], as they enter the market with a focus on cheap production technology, making it more difficult for the early technology developers to charge a premium and recoup their investments through this. This may be an obstacle to industry take-off. Still, the number of companies already active in the fragmented industry, and thus the sizable investments made in the industry, indicates that an immense market potential is perceived as tangible and achievable by the investors.

The Future of SMB

NRC's bet is on a cheaper material and production technology that will enable mass production. Apparently, the business concept anticipates a standardization and commodification of the foundry part of the industry in the sense that SMB relies on foundry production based on others' designs. The haziness of the patent situation makes it unclear whether SMB can utilize the technological developments of the industry made so far costless, or licensing or payment of royalties will be necessary. Nevertheless, it is clear from the preceding presentation that a substantial market potential exists, which is only limited by the technological solutions that can be brought forward in terms of cost efficiency and range of applications. The potential outcomes for SMB range from the development of crucial patents for the industry, over acquisition by a larger company in case a consolidation takes place at some point in the development of the industry, to downright failure to establish a competitive technological alternative to the major players, to name but a few possible scenarios that vary widely in desirability from the point of view of NRC. In conclusion, the uncertainties and the potential are very relevant for real option valuation.

5.3 Configuration of the Real Option behind Scandinavian Micro Biodevices

In the application of real option valuation, one of the most important challenges is the configuration of the real option. The configuration is also labeled '*framing the real option application*'[182] and '*mapping the investment project onto the option*'[183]. In short, it is about adapting the business case or the investment project to the concepts of the option pricing techniques. The configuration lays down the guidelines for the following operationalization and quantification.

Given the complexity of corporate investment projects and the flexibility of the option pricing techniques, a number of aspects needs to be considered in the configuration. While the beforehand option pricing techniques enable sophisticated valuation of very complex options, this may not be desirable. Though, it is perfectly possible mathematically to calculate compounded options with many interacting options and to incorporate many risk factors in the stochastic process that depicts the uncertainty, the marginal value of these efforts may be low and even cause loss of tractability and transparency, which reduces the strategic benefits of the framework. The challenge of the configuration is to find the right trade-off between '*a simplicity that preserves intuition and richness* (sic) *that delivers realistic and useful results*'[184]. The configuration will be carried out in the following, looking at the contingent decision, the sources of uncertainty, the expiration mode, and the choice of mathematical solution.

5.3.1 The Contingent Decision

Corporate investment opportunities are generally seen as call options in real option valuation e.g. on operating assets that can be invested in, if the development has been beneficial[185]. In chapter two on the real options literature, it was already established that this also goes for R&D investments[186].

In the configuration and the identification of the contingent decision, the strategic alternatives that NRC has laid down are very helpful[187].

In chapter 2, the notion of R&D as an investment platform was also presented. Following this, it is clear that the research undertaken and the competencies developed may result in options for a broader range of applications, than identified in the strategic alternatives of the business map. This could in particular be related to other medico-technological applications, which is an explicit future research area for NRC as a whole. Furthermore, the option to initiate production at an industrial scale may - if exercised - later lead to new growth options within the area of biochips, or related to the foundry production and the actual use of biochips. Speculation into this kind of derived options (options on options) is very broad and open-ended, and beyond the scope of this paper.

Therefore, the focus will be on the explicitly identified, strategic alternatives outlined in the business map, which arise as a direct and immediate consequence of the research investments in question. For repetition, at the end of year 3, these are:

- '*close down all activities*
- *concentrate on surface technology (microarrays) and close down microflow system activities*
- *concentrate on microflow systems and invest in further development of the technology value chain* (production technology)
- *focus on both product groups and potentially split them into two companies with each their focus areas.*'[188]

In the real option literature, a typology of real options has been established containing various option types with different characteristics[189]. Conceptually, real options on R&D can be seen as options to abandon, time-to-build options (staged investments), and growth options, increasing in complexity in the order mentioned.

The option to abandon is a rather straightforward option type, which holds a clear-cut decision to either continue or abandon the investment project according to the developments. It is as such a single option with focus on the potential in cutting losses through discontinuation.

The time-to-build option is used for staged investments. This option type is sequential in nature with the option to abandon midstream, or to contract or expand scale as the most noteworthy alternatives. This option is a compound option in the sense that options on options are considered in the more complicated cases.

The growth option is used for so-called 'coupon investments', where a relatively small investment is done in order to potentially enable a number of larger investments, depending on the developments. This option type can be both compounded in the sense that options on options or concurrent options are considered in the more complex cases, as well as a multiple option in the sense that parallel advances independent of each other may be incorporated.

Figure 5.8 Compound Options and Multiple Options

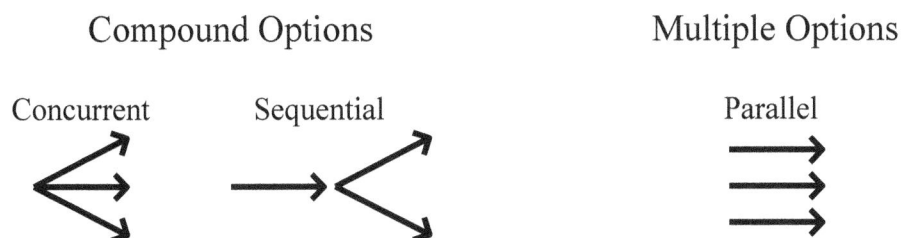

Source: Own construction.

The three option types are identical in the simple case, where the option to either abandon or continue a single project is the only option present. The three option types illustrate well, the different ways SMB can be configured as an option, according to the four identified strategic alternatives.

First of all, the strategic alternatives can be seen as one compounded growth option with four concurrent, alternative outcomes, which are mutually exclusive. SMB as a growth option is illustrated in the figure below. It is the most direct modeling of the SMB business case, which captures the combined research efforts from t_0 to t_3 in the development costs that lead to the four strategic alternatives. Furthermore, it is framed so that the investment required at the time of decision, E_x is one and the same, for the three outcomes that lead to initiation of production. The use of one investment size, E_x regardless of which product technology is initiated, reflects the investment philosophy that NRC will invest in minimum efficient scale, whether it is decided to continue with both kinds of biochips or only one, in order to expand gradually; i.e. to expand as slowly as possible, while still being at minimum efficient scale. This investment at minimum efficient scale is a fundamental assumption of this paper's valuation, and reflects the facts that NRC's has chosen this approach for its subsidiary IONAS[190] and information from NRC, which says that the investment approach and investment size for SMB will be similar to IONAS, if not slightly lower[191].

Figure 5.9 SMB as a Growth Option

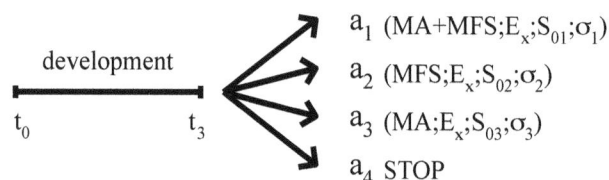

a_1 (MA+MFS;E_x;S_{01};σ_1)

a_2 (MFS;E_x;S_{02};σ_2)

a_3 (MA;E_x;S_{03};σ_3)

a_4 STOP

Source: Own construction.

Practically, this configuration encounters some problems, however. Anticipating next chapter's estimation of the numerical inputs, the only potential for forecasting S_0 is to do so based on E_x. The other approach to forecasting this figure is to estimate SMB's market share of the total market, but since SMB can only be expected to seize a very small fraction, this approach must be expected to provide inaccurate projections. When S_0 is projected based on E_x, the assumption that E_x is fixed regardless of the number of technologies carried forward gives only one activity level, and consequently only one S_0 estimate. Even though it is fair to assume that S_{02} and S_{03} could be of equal size, it makes little sense to enter the same figures for S_{01}, S_{02} and S_{03} into the valuation, because S_{01} should be higher than the two others, simply because it must hold higher combined market potential for the distinction to be worthwhile.

$S_{01} > S_{02} = S_{03}$

From this perspective, there is little reason for undertaking a sophisticated configuration like the growth option, if a differentiation on the outcomes, S_0 cannot be carried out.

Similarly, the volatility estimates would have to be different for the configuration as a growth option, since it is obviously more uncertain that initiation of both product technologies would occur than just one of them. On the other hand, it could be assumed that σ_2 and σ_3 were identical.

80

$$\sigma_1 > \sigma_2 = \sigma_3$$

Anticipating the proceeding chapter, it is sufficiently difficult to come up with just one volatility estimate, based on the business case, to render it close to impossible to capture the subtleties required to differentiate between on the one hand σ_1, and on the other hand σ_2 and σ_3.

In conclusion, the configuration of SMB as a compounded growth option falls apart, due to the character of the business case, which is the foundation for the estimation of various numerical inputs. Since E_x is assumed to be fixed and S_0 forecasts must be based on this, differentiation on S_0 outcomes cannot be done. Since similar differentiation problems can be anticipated for the volatility estimates, it is close to impossible to provide and estimate the numerical inputs that are required to make the configuration as a growth option meaningful. On the face of it, it might appear feasible to uphold the configuration in order to at least do this as correctly as possible, while using simplified estimates anyway. This is not the case however. The crux of the matter is that the estimates on the variables of a_1 must be different, but cannot be estimated so based on the beforehand data from the business case - i.e. more estimates on volatilities and different S_0s. If these variables are not different, then $S_{01} = S_{02} = S_{03}$ and $\sigma_1 = \sigma_2 = \sigma_3$, which would in effect not be a compound option with four outcomes, but a single option with two outcomes, since the three outcomes a_1, a_2, and a_3 could be unified into one then. This would be the single option to abandon, which will be covered later in this section.

Secondly, the strategic alternatives can, slightly simplified, be conceived of as two parallel research focuses, which may wind up with two opportunities to engage in production of two different product technologies. This way, the investment results in a multiple, parallel option to abandon, as illustrated below. By dividing the two product technologies in two, the parallel potential in the investment project is better captured. Concurrently, this configuration facilitates the use of the same volatility estimate for both real options, which it is reasonable to assume, due to the division.

$$\sigma_{a1} = \sigma_{b1}$$

Figure 5.10 SMB as Two Parallel Options to Abandon

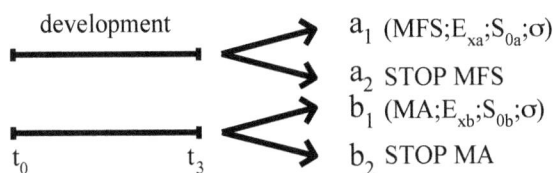

development
a_1 (MFS;E_{xa};S_{0a};σ)
a_2 STOP MFS
b_1 (MA;E_{xb};S_{0b};σ)
b_2 STOP MA
t_0 t_3

Source: Own construction.

Using this configuration, the problems with differentiated volatility estimates and market potential estimates can be avoided, through a simplified use of the same volatility and a division of the one market potential estimate in two somehow. The simplified double use of the volatility estimate is defensible, but the division of the market potential into two S_0 is more questionable. This relates to the main weakness of this configuration; namely its inability to handle the interactions between the two product technologies with regard to the development prior to t_3, the required investment at the time of decision, E_x, and the combined market potential, S_0.

The problems with regard to handling the interactions in terms of E_x and S_0 are quite similar. The required investment at the time of decision, E_x is still assumed to be fixed at minimum efficient scale. Likewise, the combined market potential is consequently one fixed estimate. Both E_x and S_0 could be divided according to some chosen proportions, and this way E_{xa}, E_{xb}, S_{0a} and S_{0b} could be reasonably estimated. Though this would work well for both real options seen in isolation, the situation, where only one of real option is exercised would break with the assumption of fixed E_x and investment in minimum efficient scale, and the S_0 forecasts, based hereon. Opposite, if E_{xa} and E_{xb} both were set equal to E_x, a problem would arise if both real options were exercised concurrently, leading to the double activity level of what is assumed.

Another unfortunate consequence of this configuration is the fact that the combined research efforts during the development must also be split up then (the development costs of the three-year lifetime of the option from t_0 to t_3). This is not possible to do, since the early research efforts are intertwined and focused at shared prerequisites. In this connection, it should be remembered that microflow systems are more complex biochips that integrates the functionality of microarrays as one of the steps in their extended functionality[192]. Hence, the indivisibility of the early research efforts cost-wise and in terms of configuration.

In conclusion, the configuration of SMB as two parallel options is in accordance with the identified potential - as stated in the business map - in possibly making two separate business units and differentiating the investments in the two product technologies. It overcomes the problem related to differentiated volatility estimation, but fails to take into account interactions in the development and the assumption of a fixed investment at the time of decision regardless of the number of product technologies carried through. Furthermore, it would require speculations on the figures on market potential beyond the possibilities of the business map, which leads to S_0 projections based on E_x. Summing up, the configuration of the SMB business case as a multiple, parallel option to abandon is not feasible either. While some inadequacies of the former configuration are made up for, other insufficiencies arise.

In this paper's configuration of the real option that the inseparable R&D efforts provide, the only distinction made is between discontinuation and investment in full-scale production. This way, the combined research efforts of the development are kept united in the calculation, and herein also the synergies in the development. This approach is further motivated by the difficulties in estimating differentiated market potentials and volatilities, based on the business case. In framing the real option this way, the central real option is kept simple. At the same time, the assumption is upheld that NRC will invest in minimum efficient scale, whether it is decided to continue both product technologies or only one, in order to expand gradually; i.e. as slowly as possible, while still being at minimum efficient scale.

Figure 5.11 SMB as a Single Option to Abandon

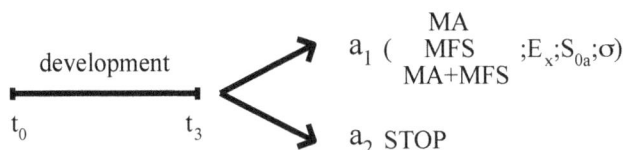

$$\text{development} \quad \begin{cases} a_1 \ (\begin{matrix} MA \\ MFS \\ MA+MFS \end{matrix} \ ;E_x;S_{0a};\sigma) \\ \\ a_2 \ \text{STOP} \end{cases}$$

$t_0 \qquad t_3$

Source: Own construction.

By unifying the development of the two product technologies, this configuration seemingly ignores the event, where one of these is discontinued, or both are initiated separately at different speed at the time of the contingent decision, and the slightly different time horizons. A number of aspects justify this. As was put forward, the benefits and the suitability of working with only one uncertainty profile, σ, the combined research efforts in the development prior to t_3, which takes into account the synergies, and the shared market forecasts, S_0 are the main advantages from this configuration relative to the other two more complex configurations. This way, the data availability sets the limits. The simplification was further motivated by the assumption that the investment required, E_x would be the same whether one or the other, or both product technologies were chosen for initiation of full-scale production. The similarity of the two product technologies implies that some correlation can be expected between successful development of the product technologies, which lends credibility to this simplification. Finally, though more accurate and loyal to the strategic alternatives identified by NRC, the efforts put into more complex configurations that incorporate more options and interactions, may yield little extra value for the analysis. Trigeorgis (1993 & 1996) explains how the marginal value, when adding more options to a configuration is small and diminishing with the number of options[193]. Though every single option is valuable in its provision of flexibility, two options do only add up to the sum of the individual options' value, when there is no interaction among them. When there are interactions, the added value of an extra option is less than if it was appraised in isolation. This is known as the 'diminishing option-value effect'[194].

In the trade-off between '*a simplicity that preserves intuition and* (a) *richness that delivers realistic and useful results*'[195], the outlined configuration was simplified, among other things, due to the increased requirements in terms of data availability that come with more complex options. It was argued that the simplification was reasonable and would provide for a meaningful analysis and data gathering. The emphasis is less on complex options leading to complicated mathematical solutions, than on framing the strategic, contingent decision, and the availability of data. The transparency and tractability ensured through the identification of the central, but simple option, has the advantage of offering a better understanding and exemplification of the critical issues in the real option and the business case, and avoiding a focus on details[196]. These are valid arguments for foregoing the extra precision that might have been achieved through more mathematically, sophisticated analysis[197].

5.3.2 Sources of Uncertainty

The variable that reflects the uncertainty is the volatility. Though, the estimation of the numerical input is a quantitative issue that will treated later, it is appropriate to consider the sources of uncertainty conceptually in the configuration, which establishes the overall guidelines for the operationalization and influences the choice of mathematical solution. The choice of mathematical solution will be presented and discussed in section 5.3.4. In this choice, the modeling of the uncertainty in terms of stochastic process and distribution type is determined.

The sources of uncertainty can be divided in two kinds, namely private risk and market risk[198]. These two kinds of risk are seen as mutually exclusive and encompassing all kinds of risk in this categorization. The private risk is related to the company-specific uncertainties; e.g. chances of successful development and achievement of research targets, patent situation *vis-à-vis* competitors, access to patents and licensing, competitiveness of venture, etc. In other words, the factors of risk that are internal and specific to the company alone. The market risk is related to market payoffs, the chances for industry-wide technological acceptance, commercial breakthrough of the product technology and the industry, etc.; i.e. risk factors that are external to the company in the broadest perception of environmental factors. The private risk is the most challenging to model, since there are no short-cuts to modeling it isolation, such as looking to competitors or comparable companies for data or estimates. On the contrary, market risk per se may be identifiable from exactly those sources, as well as from general, identifiable and quantifiable trends in the environment.

> *'In many cases, direct modeling of private risk can be avoided, because the financial markets have priced the appropriate bundle of risk. For example, consider the value of an option to buy a start-up company, one facing product market and technology uncertainty. A good proxy for the underlying asset for the option is an index of high-tech companies that have recently gone public, companies that face the same bundle of risk as the start-up'.* Amram & Kulatilaka (1999) pp. 61-62.

Anticipating, the next chapter, where the numerical inputs will be discussed and identified, this is the line of reasoning and the approach that will be followed in this paper. Despite of the impression one may get from the above quote, indices cannot be used adequately for this purpose though, since they diversify away private risk. By identifying comparable companies that not only face a comparable market risk, but also have resembling characteristics - in particular from one start-up to another, it is reasonable to assume similarity in private risk too. Consequently, market data can be used as a proxy of both kinds of risk, modeled together. This way many pitfalls can be avoided in the modeling and estimation of uncertainty through stochastic processes. As in the case of the configuration of the contingent decision(s) discussed in the preceding section, complex models can be constructed to take many factors into account.

Corresponding to these configuration issues, the details of very elaborate models may not necessarily provide for a better and clearer analysis.

5.3.3 Expiration Mode

The expiration mode introduces a fundamental distinction from financial options into the real option valuation, namely the one between European and American options. Since European type options are less complicated to calculate, efforts were spend in section 4.7 on determining, when a real option may be seen as European. The thing is that most real options, due to their discretionary nature, may be perceived as American type option, in the sense that for corporate real options, there are rarely contractual bonds that bind the company to await the stipulated maturity. Generally, as in this case, the investment project is carried out within the operations of the company, and therefore the decision to exercise is completely at the discretion of management in terms of authority. In section 4.7, it was demonstrated that if the project duration is known and finite, the real option may be European, but if it is either unknown or infinite, it is has clear American type characteristics. Furthermore, it was shown that if a real option is to be seen as European, it is important that the real option is relatively shielded from external influences. Only so, it is entirely at management's discretion, when to exercise the option. In those cases, the real option is more likely to be European, because it is unlikely to be exercised prematurely or suddenly, because this would disturb the planning of the investment project, as management has originally laid it down or agreed to it. Thus, it was argued that for a real option, where the foundation for the exercise of the option is developed through the investment project, it is reasonable to view this as European. This obviously relates to research projects.

From the way the investment project is planned and budgeted (the business map), it appears that the option can be characterized as having a *finite* and *known* time horizon. Accordingly, the option can be seen as a European option with an expiration time that can be precisely determined. However, this is a common characteristic of budget and investment proposals, which frequently outline an expected scenario, although they obviously incorporate considerable leeway to alter course, if developments are different than expected, at the discretion of management.

Hence, in order to determine whether the option - conveniently - is a European option with an identifiable project duration, a number of issues must be considered.

The project duration cannot be characterized as *infinite* and *unknown*, as SMB does not hold any monopoly relative to the market or other external influences. Since no patent protection does or will create a monopoly situation for SMB, the project duration is finite.

Whether the project duration is *finite* and *unknown* is basically a matter of external or internal factors' influence on the option. The option must be considered so if premature exercise is possible and might be feasible, or if external developments might suddenly render the option worthless. The former would be the situation for SMB, if the technology reached the point where it was ready for market introduction before the three years, and the market was ready. The market must be considered ready given the tangible benefits of the product, but the question is whether it is realistic that SMB has achieved its development target and developed the necessary competencies before the stipulated three-year time frame. It seems rather unlikely that completion will happen long before, since the planning is divided into half-year periods with certain employee recruitment taking place at the end of the planning horizon, and since the time frame is rather short and overseeable. Hence, the project duration takes into consideration both the time needed for achieving the research targets which might happen sooner or later – a highly uncertain process, and the time needed for the training required to build the necessary competencies; i.e. the time horizon is rather predictable. Therefore, it does not appear that developments in SMB is likely to facilitate early exercise, and hence the project duration is not unknown *within* the time frame of the project[199].

Next, the question is whether the project duration can be considered unknown due to external factors that suddenly leaves the option worthless. Even though a competitor comes up with a comparable production method, the complexity of the whole patent situation makes it unlikely that this could block SMB's entrance to the market. Furthermore, the size of the market leaves room for a number of players, and the diversity of the market makes it very unlikely that one player or a few players seize the whole market, due to early entry. Finally, it cannot be ruled out that public debate or developments suddenly make the technology less used and demanded from the market. The risk for the technology being discarded for scientific or medical reasons is not considered big, since the technology to a great extent has proven itself and the scientific community has accepted it. In conclusion, it seems plausible to assume that external factors will not have disruptive effects on the project duration.

Though the investment project does not have a shield from external factors in the shape of patent protection or license contracts, which might lead to a known and finite project duration as suggested earlier, the external factors do not seem to hold the potential to influence the investment project much. Instead, the investment project seems unique in an industry where there might be room for many solutions - i.e. as one of many unique solutions - leaving the development of the foundation of the option and its exercise to the company's discretion, '*enabling a known and finite project duration*'[200].

Summing up, it is reasonable to consider the outlined three-year project duration a reliable and relative accurate figure to use in the calculation, since the characteristics of the investment project does not imply that the time horizon should be considered infinite or unknown. This has the fortunate implication that the option can be seen as a European option, since premature exercise or worthlessness do not need to be considered with regard to estimating project duration.

Though the notion of premature exercise is clearly related to the time span of the investment project, uncertainty in estimating the duration of the real option is one thing, while the desirability of premature exercise is another issue. In particular, because the duration of real options on research projects are by nature not completely predictable in the sense that they may prove shorter, longer, or even unachievable. This is also to say that real options on research projects incorporate a progress in the project, which implies that the ongoing readiness to exploit the research - i.e. liquidate the underlying asset - is non-existing, and completion a prerequisite. Wrapping up, while premature exercise is clearly possible during the course of the project, this possibility is conceptually at odds with the characteristics of a real option on a research project, prior to initiation, where the duration is estimated in order to achieve certain results within the time frame.

In terms of feasibility, the lesson from financial theory that an option is worth more 'alive', than 'dead', due to the remaining value[201] is not applicable, alone because this depends on the tradability of the option, which the established exchanges enable for financial options. Obviously, this is neither a significant, nor a relevant issue for corporate real options. However, this lesson from financial options relies on another assumption, namely the absence of convenience yield; i.e. dividends. This aspect requires some attention with regard to real options.

In the configuration and the operationalization of the real option, it is important to incorporate all cash flows that accrue to the investment project[202]. The primary cash flows are the value of the underlying asset, i.e. present value of expected cash flows, S_0 and the exercise price, i.e. the required investment, E_x. Both are satisfactorily incorporated in the option pricing formula, as independent variables. In the analogy to financial options on stocks, these are respectively the current stock price and the exercise price. However, discretionary cash flows, such as dividends for financial options, must also be accounted for. These can be both positive and negative cash flows that go beyond the variability of the expected cash flows, as modeled in the volatility.

Positive, discretionary cash flows are labeled 'convenience yield'. For real options on research projects, it was argued that appropriation depends on some degree of completion; i.e. the major incoming cash flows only start after the targeted research results have been achieve. Hence, this is not an issue in this case, since extraordinary incomes cannot be expected before the research has been completed. Negative, discretionary cash flows are labeled 'leakage in value'. SMB's investments into the research of the three first years can be seen as an example hereof. These are quite easily incorporated into the framework by subtracting the present value hereof from the present value of the expected cash flows, S_0. All in all, there is no convenience yield making a premature exercise beneficial for SMB, just as there is no leakage in value that can be avoided by exercising the option prematurely. The reason that financial options are sometimes prematurely exercised is not only the often relatively small amount of dividend payouts, but also the fact that upon exercise the value of the underlying asset is also acquired; i.e. both dividend payouts and stock. This further contributes to the difference between financial options and real options on R&D, due to the obstacles to realizing the value of the real option's underlying asset in the course of the investment project, where it is being developed.

One particular kind of leakage in value, which is not directly cash flow related, is the risk that the value of the underlying asset may suddenly drop to zero. This impact is somewhat in between the discretionary cash flows just presented and the stochastic model of uncertainty that the volatility incorporates into the framework. For competitive, proprietary or public reasons, the underlying asset may suddenly be rendered worthless. This could be incorporated into the valuation as a Poisson distribution. The likelihood of a such impact, however, is very hard to estimate, and impossible to predict. Along with the reasons presented in section 5.2.7 on future issues for the industry, this is not expected for SMB or the biochip technology and industry at large, and will not be incorporated into the application. Furthermore, due to its unpredictable nature, this impact has no influence on the determination of the real option's expiration mode evaluated in terms of feasibility of premature, contemplated exercise by management. Based on section 5.2.7, the assumptions drawn are that the biochip technology will not be stopped by public opinion or surpassed by another technology, and that standards and patents will not be a show stopper for SMB. Additionally, it is assumed that the customized and extensive nature of the expected demand in terms of individual designs from customers will leave room for SMB.

In conclusion, there is little reason for complicating the analysis by perceiving the real option as an American-style option. Trigeorgis (1999) describes how senior management is unlikely to continuously adjust their perception of a research project's value, simply for reasons of efficiency. This is only done, when events reach a certain threshold of impact or strategic importance[203]. This reluctance to change course or reevaluate research projects continuously and frequently, further adds to the sensibility of perceiving the real option as European.

The preceding considerations on expiration mode have investigated the potential in exercising the real option on R&D *during* the development; i.e. *within* the time frame, *before* the technology is forecasted to be completed, and have found this event improbable. Trigeorgis (1999) also looks into the issue of postponing the exercise *after* the research targets have been achieved. He argues that also from this perspective, the real option on R&D must be seen as European, based on the first-mover or pioneering advantages that are typically associated with research-based market introductions.

Finally, the difference in the option value between the two kinds of expiration mode is presumably rather insignificant. When appraising an option as European, the result can be seen as the minimum value, since an American option would be slightly more valuable. Thus, the valuation can be seen as a cautious estimate[204].

5.3.4 Choice of Mathematical Solution
The choice of mathematical solution is partially determined by the configuration of the contingent decision and the identified sources of uncertainty. Both of these were configured in

the preceding sections. The contingent decision was laid down as a simple option to abandon and the sources of uncertainty were combined into one that is to be obtained from market data.

One of the main choices with regard to mathematical solution is between an analytic solution and a numeric solution. An analytic solution is a closed-form solution with the Black & Scholes formula as the prime example. Other analytic solutions have also been developed. The advantage of using analytic solution is that a formula is at hand, and once the inputs to the formula have been determined, the result is easily computed. However, as the complexity of the option configuration increases, the availability of analytic solutions quickly becomes exhausted. To appraise more complex options, numeric solutions can be developed. In order to do so, dedicated equations reflecting the option in question have to be derived.

Another choice with regard to the mathematical solution is the choice of stochastic process. The main distinction is between a normal distribution, which is in continuous time (continuous observations) and a binomial distribution, which is in discrete time (discrete observations). For the modeling of complex options, the binomial distribution is the preferred one, because it enables easier modeling of more contingent decisions at discrete points in time in numeric solutions. For example, when decision trees with many decision points can be identified. Normal distributions, on the other hand, are quite difficult to apply in numeric solutions, and again the prime example is Black & Scholes' analytic solution.

The preceding introduction of the real option framework and real option valuation was carried out with reference to the variables of the Black & Scholes formula. This was not done in order to anticipate the choice of mathematical solution. This was done, because this formula is the simplest and the most well-known, and perceived to be the intuitively, easiest comprehensible. Furthermore, the variables in this formula are conceptually the same as the ones used in numeric solutions, only there are more of them in numeric solutions.

In the literature on the real option valuation, the opinions differ as to the optimal solution for real options on R&D. But from the above, it should be clear that this choice depends on the complexity of the option configuration, more than on the nature of the investment; e.g. whether it be in R&D, natural resource extraction, or the construction of a plant. It can also be seen from the below presentation of the positions that the complexity of the option configurations de facto is the crux of the matter.

Faulkner (1996) warns against the shortcomings of using the Black & Scholes formula for real options on R&D. His arguments are that the formula is less understandable, that the log-normal stochastic process of the formula may be inappropriate in certain situations, and that for more complex options, more solutions are available through the use of numeric solutions, which incorporate binomial distributions. Still, he acknowledges that numeric solutions using binomial distributions in certain cases yield the same result as Black & Scholes, and that '(t)here may be cases where use of the Black-Scholes formula is the best approach'.[205]

Brealey and Myers (1988) favor the use of the Black & Scholes formula for the valuation of real options on R&D[206]. According to them, the Black & Scholes formula seen as a shortcut to the more complex binomial calculations, is defensible for research projects.

Trigeorgis (1999) argues that the Black & Scholes formula has its limitations with regard to real options on R&D, because there are no historical time series for estimating the volatility, as would be optimal. If no comparable company can be identified with regard to stock data analysis, the lack of a reliable approach to estimate the volatility in continuous time, makes it far more defensible to use binomial distributions and numeric solutions for the estimates. These estimates would typically be based on managerial judgment or volatility estimates for somewhat comparable historic in-house projects, precisely experienced, it is argued, in discrete time at clearly identifiable points in the development, like the binomial distribution. Furthermore, it is argued against the use of Black & Scholes that sudden drops to zero is easier incorporated with a Poisson distribution into a numeric solution, based on a binomial distribution.

Luehrman (1998a) advocates for a wide use of Black & Scholes as a powerful approach, which provides important qualitative insights in addition to the quantitative valuation, though it may lack in precision for complex options.

It is the position in this paper that the option configuration of the preceding analysis is defensibly simple. This facilitates the use of Black & Scholes' analytic solution. The view that the Black & Scholes formula is less intelligible is not accepted, due to its simple beauty in terms of variables and their interrelations, and the fact that this formula is the limit of most people's option horizon, due to its widespread use and preeminent position in corporate finance. Finally, the objection to the use of normal distributed stochastic processes for real options on R&D, which is seen as primarily suited for modeling stock price volatility by the opponents, is discarded on the grounds of other opposing contributors to the discussion, and the fact that the volatility is specifically going to be found from stock market data, under the assumption that stock prices reflect the actual value and changes in value for a comparable investment and its uncertainty. The integration of a Poisson distribution to take into consideration the risk that external technological developments suddenly render the research of SMB worthless will not be done, since this both add significant complexities to the analysis, is very difficult to reasonably estimate given the low frequency and the hard impact of this event, and considered unlike in the business case.

5.4 Concluding Remarks on the Empirical Focus and the Configuration

This chapter began by pointing to the investment project of Scandinavian Micro Biodevices, as the most appropriate for real option valuation in the light of a rough evaluation of different potential foci relative to the beforehand application. The business case and the revolutionary perspectives of the biochip product technology and the industry were presented. With this in mind the first step of the valuation was carried out; namely the configuration, which led to the choice of mathematical solution. Due to the strategy laid down by NRC and the consequential data availability, along with the nature of the business case, the real option behind SMB was perceived as a simple option to abandon after three years. This can be satisfactory captured by Black & Scholes option pricing formula for European-style options, which consequently was chosen as the mathematical solution. The discussion of the expiration mode revealed complexities that defied direct mathematical modeling, but as it was argued, the choice of a European-style configuration leads to a cautious estimate. In terms of uncertainty and volatility, it was argued that the Black & Scholes formula's incorporation of the normal distribution and the geometric Brownian motion captured the essence of the business case, and could be anticipated to satisfactorily depict and estimate the concrete volatility in the subsequent estimation of numerical inputs. The second step in the valuation is to estimate the numerical inputs of the variables that enter into the final calculation of the valuation estimate. This will be done in the following chapter.

6. Numerical Inputs

This chapter identifies the numerical values of the variables that will be used in the calculations of the valuation in chapter 7. The theoretical context of the variables will be briefly outlined prior to the estimations. The numerical values that will be assigned the variables draw on the data from the presentation and the configuration of the investment project in the preceding chapter. While a number of the numerical values can be inferred rather straightforwardly from the presentation in chapter 5, others are trickier and must be based on assumptions, comparables, or proxies. Following the choice of the Black & Scholes formula, the five variables that will be estimated are:

- present value of the expected cash flows
- required investment at the time of decision
- risk-free interest rate
- project duration
- volatility in the driver of project value.

The volatility is the most radically new variable introduced, compared with conventional valuation techniques. Furthermore, it is relatively challenging to comprehend conceptually. Therefore, the quantification of this variable is done the most extensively and takes up three-quarters of this chapter.

6.1 Time Aspects of the Valuation

In any valuation, it is important for consistency and preciseness to set a valuation date. The valuation date ensures that estimates used are as of the fixed and same day, and delimits the analysis from taking into account developments later than this. The valuation date chosen for this analysis is March 1, 2000 as this was the day, where the business map for SMB was approved by the Project Council, and therefore the date on which the outlined investments were initiated. The time unit for the time-related variables; volatility, the project duration and the risk-free interest rate will be years, and consequently the numerical values will be annual. However, the stock data used for the estimation of volatilities and betas are as of July and August 2000, which is not expected to cause significant discrepancies, given the thorough analysis that is carried out for their validity.

6.2 Present Value of the Expected Cash Flows

The present value of the expected cash flows that SMB can be expected to realize is obviously the most difficult variable to predict. The uncertainties related to this variable makes it possible to imagine a range of values this variable could take, according to the way the industry and the technology develops, the character of demand, SMB's products compared with competitors', the time horizon, and many more factors. Conveniently, the range of possible outcomes need not be taken into account in the estimation of this variable, since the distribution hereof is incorporated into the valuation through the variable of volatility. Instead, an estimate of the average expected cash flows accumulated must be identified.

S_0 is the accumulated cash flows from the projections of the investment project. This is an NPV calculated by the DCF method, using a discount factor, based on a beta identified through CAPM. Also outgoing cash flows are incorporated, except from the large discretionary one time investment, E_x that marks the exercise price.

A starting point for projecting SMB's cash flows could be to look at the way the total market is forecasted to develop. The expectations of various sources were presented in the preceding chapter. Since, it is SMB's intention to go into foundry production, if the technological proof of concept is achieved as expected and the market develops as forecasted, an estimate of expected cash flows could be identified by estimating SMB's market share of the total forecasted market in order to identify a probable turnover. By assessing an approximate cost structure - i.e. a sales to profit ratio - an estimate of net income and expected cash flows could be made, based on the turnover corresponding to the market share.

This approach, however, relies on too many assumptions and uncertain variables to be fruitful in the sense that it is hard meaningfully to come up with exact estimates. First of all, the market projections presented earlier are very rough and range from explosive to moderate forecasts over various time spans. Secondly, the estimation of SMB's potential market share is very difficult, since it initially would be such a small fraction that it would inevitably be inaccurate. Finally, this estimate would assume that SMB could flexibly adjust production, while growing with the market, and that throughout this ongoing adjustment the sales could be translated into profits via a meaningful estimate of a cost structure.

Instead, the approach will be to use estimates of the intended investment in production capacity and the profitability that can be expected. This is done with a view to the investment approach taken by NKT in connection with the industrial production of optical chips recently initiated in IONAS. Here production has been taken from the laboratory stage to industrial scale by investing DKK 100 millions. There are indications that the foreseen investment in SMB might be of the same altitude, or possibly slightly lower[207].

In so doing, the starting point will be the level of activity. The expected profits and expected cash flows will not be derived from the development of the total market. The only thing about the development of the total market that needs to be considered is whether SMB is likely to seize a niche of the market, and whether this share of the market is of appropriate size relative to the rest of the industry.

The investment required to take the technology to industrial scale is estimated to be similar to the recent investment made in IONAS of DKK 100 millions. The point in time where this might be done for SMB is the year 2003. For the sake of estimating the sales and thus the expected cash flows, it is assumed that SMB produces and sells at a stable level as an effect of the initial investment. Furthermore, it is assumed that the DKK 100 millions investment covers the total costs of a five-year period from 2003 to 2007. Hence, these costs are distributed evenly over the five-year period as a basis for estimating the sales that the investment generates.

In order to estimate the sales and the profits - which is equal to the cash flows in the following[208] - based on the costs, a sales-to-profits ratio from a comparable industry is used. The cost structure is implicit in the sales-to-profits ratio in the sense that the relationship between net sales, total costs, and profits can be inferred from it. Unfortunately, no suitable data for a directly comparable company can be found related to foundry production of biochips. A number of American companies with substantial sales of biochips can be identified, but from their reported income statements little can be inferred about the cost structure of the biochip production itself. This is because these companies are actively using the biochips for biotechnological purposes and / or reinvest their earnings in R&D to the extent that they have negative sales to profits ratios. In order to get estimates on the profitability of the foundry production itself, foundry producers from the semiconductor industry are looked at.

The two foundry producers in the semiconductor industry analyzed both have a strong focus on dedicated foundry services. Both are Taiwan-based global players listed on the New York Stock Exchange (abbr.: NYSE). United Microelectronic Corporation (NYSE letter code: UMC) has turnover of USD 930 millions and a sales-to-profits ratio of 31%[209]. Taiwan Semiconductor MFG (NYSE letter code: TSM) has turnover of USD 2.3 billions and a sales-to-profits ratio of 34%.

The rough cost structure can be deducted from the sales to profits ratio, since the residual of the sales to profits ratios obviously are sales to costs ratios, equaling respectively 69% and 66%[210]. The comparable companies were chosen to get figures for pure foundry production. A major drawback for the comparison is that the companies are considerably bigger players that are active in a very consolidated industry and working with a mature technology. Therefore, it is safe to assume that the companies produce more cost efficiently, than SMB will initially, due to their yearlong experience, the economies of scale, and the standardized nature of the products in the semiconductor industry. The motivation for applying the ratios to SMB anyway is that the new biochip technology, because of its novelty and the customization that the differentiated kind of demand requires, might sell at a premium, thereby achieving a similar viable sales to profits ratio.

Table 6.1 SMB Sales Projections

	2003	2004	2005	2006	2007
Net sales	30	30	30	30	30
Total costs	(20)	(20)	(20)	(20)	(20)
Net income	10	10	10	10	10

Source: Own projections, partially based on NRC cost estimates. The costs are the initial DKK 100 millions investment distributed for the sake of the projections. The cost structure applied is the average sales-to-costs ratio – 67.5% - of the two identified, comparable companies, which were respectively 66% and 69%. All figures in DKK millions.

Looking at the projected sales, there should be room for SMB in the market. Throughout the observed period SMB constitutes a decreasing share, going from 1% of the market in 2003 to 1‰ in 2007 with the size of the total market based on SMB's projections presented in section 5.2.5. Though it may seem pessimistic with an expectation of decreasing market share, this is done to simplify the forecasts by assuming a steady activity level[211].

When estimating the expected cash flows, the sales in the five-year period stretching from 2003 to 2007 have been generated by the DKK 100 millions investment. This investment is incorporated in the real option valuation as a one-time investment, E_x. Consequently, the cash flows generated in this period is equal to the sales, since the investment enters into the formula as E_x. In addition to these cash flows generated as 'directly related sales' (2003-2007), the cash flows stemming from the 'development costs' prior to initiation (2000-2003), and the 'continuing value' beyond the forecasted period (post 2007) must be incorporated.

The cash flows labeled 'development costs' are easily identified in the explicit investment plan for SMB presented in section 5.2.6, table 5.2. In the estimation of the cash flows beyond the forecasted period, it will be assumed that the yearly net income continue at the same level infinitely. Though this assumption appears rather farfetched and quite substantial, it is often applied in the determination of the so-called 'continuing value'. This is because the continuing value is rather easily calculated this way, as the net present value of a perpetuity[212]. Since the net present value of the cash flows is the ultimate goal in this estimation of cash flows, it must be discounted to take into account the time-value of money and the investment risk. Due to this discounting, the cash flows projected infinitely have a relatively limited impact on net present value. As a matter of fact, the question is rather whether this approach underestimates the continuing value of the DKK 100 millions investment, when looking beyond 2007. Though, it is more than likely that the continuing value, if commercial introduction has been successful, is higher than this approach will estimate it, it appears reasonable to use it in this case, where focus is on the isolated consequences of the investment in 2003 of DKK 100 millions, and not later reinvestments. Thus, the reinvestments in R&D and business development that most likely will be done continuously subsequently, if the venture is a success, are not taken into consideration.

Table 6.2 Expected Cash Flows for SMB in DKK millions

	2000	2001	2002	2003	2004	2005	2006	2007	Post 2007-
Sales	0	1	4	30	30	30	30	30	
Costs	7	9	11	(100)/(20)	(20)	(20)	(20)	(20)	
Net income (cash flows)	-7	-8	-7	30	30	30	30	30	10

Source: NRC Business Map on SMB and own estimates. The costs in the period from 2003 to 2007 are the initial DKK 100 millions investment in 2003. In the table, they are distributed for the sake of illustrating the approach to the projections for 2003 to 2007. These costs are excluded from the calculation of expected cash flows, since they appear elsewhere in the real option valuation, i.e. E_x. Consequently, the net income is equal to sales for the period 2003 to 2007, but not for the years beyond 2007.

The perpetuity formula is shown below. WACC is the discount factor, which will be explained in the following.

The Perpetuity Formula:

$$CV = \frac{FCF_{T+1}}{WACC}$$

where
CV   = the continuing value
FCF_{T+1} = the normalized level of free cash flows in the first year after the explicit forecast period
WACC   = the weighted average cost of capital.[213]

To get all the cash flow estimates into one present value of expected cash flows, the cash flows must be discounted with an appropriate discount factor in order to take into account the time-value of money and the investment risk. This is done by discounting the cash flows with a discount factor. For the identification of the discount factor, the weighted average cost of capital (WACC) approach is chosen. WACC is the cost of equity and the cost of debt combined into one measure. Since SMB does not have any debt and is assumed (and expected) to be equity-financed throughout the observed period, the only component of the WACC that has to be identified is the cost of equity financing. This is commonly found though use of the capital asset pricing model; a.k.a. a CAPM analysis[214], which identifies the return that an investment with the same risk characteristics receives in the market. This relationship is measured relative to the market portfolio, by seeking out a comparable company with a similar risk profile and identifying its beta, β, which is a measure of the comparable company's return relative to the market portfolio.

The CAPM equation for the cost of equity (k_s) is:

$$k_s = r_f + (E(r_m) - r_f)\, \beta,$$

where
r_f = the risk-free rate of return
$E(r_m)$ = the expected rate of return on the overall market portfolio
$E(r_m) - r_f$ = the market risk premium
β = beta, the systematic risk of equity[215]

The risk-free rate of return has been chosen as the Danish seven-year Treasury Bond to match the maturity of the valuation period, i.e. 2000-2007 for cash flow projections, in accordance with the recommendations in Dallocchio (1997) and Copeland et.al. (1996)[216]. This is 5.47% p.a.

Among four approaches to identify the beta of an unquoted company, Copeland et.al. (1996) mentions one that is convenient and applicable for SMB, namely looking at comparable companies[217]. Most of SMB's competitors are US-based. Fortunately, many of these are on the stock exchange (NASDAQ), and consequently analyzed betas are readily available. SMB has identified two companies as the most appropriate for comparison, as identified in section 5.2.3.

Table 6.3 Betas for Comparable Companies

Company (NASDAQ-code)	Beta	Debt/Equity
ACLARA (ACLA)	2.53	3.7%
Caliper Technologies (CALP)	1.94	14.6%

Source: www.nasdaq.com[218] July 20, 2000.

Before going into more detail with the identification of the beta for SMB, some considerations regarding the expected rate of return on the overall market portfolio have to be done, since the product of $E(r_m)$ and β is the company-specific market risk premium - of course including the earlier identified risk-free rate of return (r_f) in the equation, and consequently these two components have to be chosen consistently.

The market risk premium ($E(r_m) - r_f$) is generally higher in Europe (and Denmark) than in the US, basically due to less effective markets for equity capital in Europe[219]. Copeland et.al. (1996) has estimated it to 5.0% as a geometric average in the period 1926-93 for the US , whereas Danish sources' estimates are in the area of 7%[220]. Though a Danish estimate would be more appropriate for a valuation of a Danish company as in this case, some problems are connected with doing so. This is primarily related to the problem of finding relevant betas. Betas in this case are hard to find in Denmark, since no Danish company is active in the same industry, and the ones that are vaguely comparable (e.g. high-risk profile, R&D heavy, and not yet profitable) are inappropriate for comparisons. The inappropriateness stems from the following characteristics of comparable, Danish companies:
- most are not listed - in Denmark stock-listing is not yet that widespread, and primarily for large, established companies - and
- the volume of stocks traded in Denmark is rather limited, which makes beta estimates less reliable, in the sense that this causes a tendency to undervaluing the systematic risk of companies *vis-à-vis* the overall market portfolio.

Hence, the most accurate betas relevant for SMB can be found in the US market. Likewise, the estimates for market risk premiums are better in the US and more applicable to this case, since:
- the long history of efficient markets for equity capital in the US provides for estimates covering longer periods. So even though the equity capital markets in Denmark and Europe

in general have been greatly improved since the late 1980's and early 1990's, these do not have the same reliability in terms of historical perspective, and

- the beta and the market risk premium have to be consistent, when estimating the company-specific market risk premium, the cost of equity financing (k_s), and the WACC. Applying a US beta estimate to a Danish market risk premium would overestimate this case's company-specific market risk premium.

In summary, US data will be applied to identify SMB's company-specific market risk premium $(E(r_m) - r_f)$ β, primarily due to the difficulties of identifying and estimating reliable betas based on Danish data, which would have been preferable[221], but also because there is a need for consistency between beta (β) and market risk premium $(E(r_m) - r_f)$, and better estimates are available for US market risk premium. Still, the risk-free rate of return (r_f) will be based on Danish data, since r_f rather unproblematicly can be identified, and the global bond markets can be considered very efficient. By taking into account the global market expectations regarding inflationary pressures and exchange rate risks, the T-bonds of the particular country on which the valuation is focused, provides a good level, before adding the specific market risk premium for the cost of equity financing (k_s). The r_f alone is an independent component of the formula indicating the level, compared with $E(r_m) - r_f$ (the market risk premium) that is a product of several variables, which must be consistent.

To get back to the specifics of calculating the cost of equity financing (k_s), the risk-free rate of return (r_f) was identified as 5.47% p.a.[222] following the rate of Danish 7-year Treasury bonds, as recommended by Copeland et.al. (1996)[223]. In comparison, the US 5-year Treasury bond rate was 5.88% p.a. and 10-year Treasury bond rate 5.75% p.a.[224]

The market risk premium $(E(r_m) - r_f)$ was taken from Copeland et.al. (1996) as the geometric average risk premium for the returns on S&P 500 versus the return on long-term government bonds from 1926-93[225]. It amounts to 5.0%.

Finally, two US companies that are listed and comparable were identified by SMB. Their beta values are presented in table 6.3. The two companies are ACLARA ($\beta = 2.53$) and Caliper Technologies ($\beta = 1.94$). These betas cannot be directly transferred to SMB. Each of the two comparable companies has its specific capital structure. The capital structure is basically the composition of the liabilities divided into debts and equity. A measure hereof is the debt-to-equity ratio. The higher the debt-to-equity ratio is, the higher the financial leverage of a company is said to be. This is because debts have to be serviced both in good and bad times, whereas payoffs to the equity - e.g. stock holders - can be adjusted to the level of profits. Hence, debt financing is hard in bad times, where it is an unavoidable cost, but preferable in good times, where only the same fixed amount has to be paid, and the surplus in excess hereof accrues to the company.

Since beta is a measure of a company's specific systematic risk, it also incorporates the effect of the financial leverage. This must be 'unlevered' according to the comparable company's debt-to-equity ratio, and levered back to the target company - i.e. the company of the analysis - applying its particular capital structure (debt-to-equity ratio). The formula for unlevering and levering the beta is shown below. The debt-to-equity ratios for the two comparable companies were presented in table 6.3.

$$beta_L = [1 + (1 - T_c) B/S](beta_u),$$

where

$beta_L$ = the levered equity beta.
T_c = the corporate marginal tax rate
B/S = the debt-to-equity ratio.
$beta_u$ = the unlevered equity beta.[226]

The formula takes into account the tax shield that debt financing provides. The corporate marginal tax rate is assumed to be 34% both in the US and in Denmark. The adjusted betas are presented in the table below.

Table 6.4 Betas for Comparable Companies Adjusted for Financial Leverage

Company (NASDAQ-code)	$beta_u$	$beta_{L \text{ for SMB}}$
ACLARA (ACLA)	2.47	2.47
Caliper Technologies (CALP)	1.77	1.77

Source: Own calculations, based on www.nasdaq.com[227] July 20, 2000.

The beta applied to SMB will be a simple average of the two adjusted betas; i.e. SMB (β = 2.12). The reason that the unlevered betas for the two comparable companies are the same as the levered betas for SMB is that SMB is completely equity-financed.

It is assumed that WACC is the same as the cost of equity capital for SMB, because SMB does not have any debt. For estimating the cost of equity capital, the CAPM was used, with the results presented below.

Table 6.5 CAPM - Components and Calculation of WACC

Risk-free rate of interest (r_f)	5.5%
Market risk premium ($E(r_m) - r_f$)	5.0%
Beta (β)	2.12
Cost of Equity (k_s)	16.1%
WACC	16.1%

Source: Own calculations, based on previously identified estimates.

With the discount factor identified, it is reasonably simple to calculate the present value of the expected cash flows. These include the 'development costs' (2000-2002), 'directly related sales' (2003-2007), and 'continuing value' (post 2007), but exclude the initial DKK 100 millions investment, which comes into the calculation as the exercise price of the option, E_x. As explained earlier, the continuing value is calculated as a perpetuity of the normalized level of free cash flows in the first year after the explicit forecast period, equaling DKK 10 millions / 0,161 or DKK 62 millions. This is the value of the continuing value at the end of the period by 2008. Therefore the continuing value must be further discounted back to the beginning of the period, along with the rest of the yearly cash flows. So even though the assumption of eternal cash flows seemed to hold substantial value, it actually comes down to DKK 19 millions out of DKK 73 millions. This equals 26% of S_0 and is remarkably low given the relatively short time horizon it is discounted at, but stems from the somewhat high discount factor. The present value (abbr. PV) of expected cash flows is all the individually discounted cash flows accumulated.

Table 6.6 Expected Cash Flows for SMB in DKK millions. In Nominal Figures and Present Value

	2000	2001	2002	2003	2004	2005	2006	2007	Continuing value
Sales	0	1	4	30	30	30	30	30	
Costs	7	9	11	(100)/(20)	(20)	(20)	(20)	(20)	
Net income (cash flows)	-7	-8	-7	30	30	30	30	30	62
PV of yearly cash flows	-7	-7	-5	19	17	14	12	11	19
PV of accumulated cash flows	73								

Source: NRC Business Map on SMB and own estimates.

Thus, the present value of the expected cash flows, S_0 is DKK 73 millions.

6.3 Required Investment at the Time of Decision

The required investment at the time of decision, E_x enters into the formula in nominal figures for the time of the decision. Thus, the amount is not discounted, before entering into the calculation, since the time-value of this investment is captured by the option pricing formula. The required investment at the time of decision is the counterpart to the exercise price and can be considered the size of the subsequent investment that will be undertaken, if the development has been favorable.

If SMB at the end of the initial development period by 2003 is technologically mature, and the market is commercially ready, the option to enter the market by investing in chip manufacturing can be exercised. In other words, the exercise price of the option is the investment required to initiate production; i.e. to invest in manufacturing facilities. Even though SMB in effect could sell the technology at this point, and the step from initial development to full-scale production therefore is not the only option at hand if the technology is successfully developed, this does not change the investment required to utilize the technology. Therefore, the value of the option is the same, whether it is exercised within NRC or the underlying asset is sold. Although the required investment in manufacturing facilities might already have been done by a competitor that acquires the technology, for whom the investment can be considered sunk costs and a way to exploit synergies, the value of the option to SMB is unchanged, since SMB would not want to sell the technology cheaper than what it is worth if continued by itself.

The required investment in manufacturing facilities is quite substantial, due to so-called minimum efficient scale concerns[228]. The high threshold for minimum efficient scale in chip production stems from the fact that very expensive equipment that cannot be gradually acquired at a competitive cost must be invested in up-front. Thus to achieve minimum efficient scale, DKK 100 millions must be invested.

6.4 Risk-free Interest Rate

The risk-free interest rate, r_f is taken from government bonds, a.k.a. Treasury Bonds with the same time horizon or maturity as the option in question[229].

The risk-free interest rate that will be applied to the *investment project* analyzed is the effective interest rate from Danish government bonds - a.k.a. Treasury Bonds or T-bonds - with a 3-year maturity as of March 1, 2000. Danish government bonds are chosen because SMB in terms of location is facing Danish conditions. The 3-year time horizon corresponds to the project duration (see below). The interest rate of Danish T-Bonds with a 3-year maturity as of March 1, 2000 was 5.37% p.a.[230]

It should be noted that this choice of risk-free interest rate only concerns the variable of the real option valuation. As will be shown later, when calculating the *implied volatility* of traded options on comparable companies' stocks by applying the option pricing formula, other interest rates for T-bonds might be more relevant. Since the option bids that are used to calculate the implied volatility are traded in the United States, interest rates will consequently be taken from the US context. The same was the case for the calculation of beta in section 6.2, where seven-year T-bonds were used.

6.5 Project Duration

The project duration is quite obviously three years. From earlier discussions on project duration and expiration mode in section 4.7 and 5.3.3, we know that the actual time frame required is uncertain. Nevertheless, it has been argued that the estimate is the best ex-ante estimate available. It is probably close to what might be realized, given the relatively short time frame and the activities that must be carried out, before achievement of the research results or discontinuation.

6.6 Volatility in the Driver of Project Value

The volatility in the driver of project value (σ) is the counterpart to the financial option's volatility of the stock price, which is measured as the standard deviation of returns on stock per time unit, typically per year. Volatility is a measure of how much the underlying asset can be expected on average to deviate from the expected value. This is calculated as a variance (σ^2), which is the square of the standard deviation.

For real option applications, σ^2 is *'the variance of returns per unit of time on (the) project'*[231], and the volatility, σ, the square root hereof. The volatility is the input into the stochastic process that quantifies the uncertainty in terms of the most likely value spread around the expected project value; i.e. the present value of the expected cash flows, S_0.

Ideally, the measure of volatility contains information about how the underlying asset is likely to develop in the future period of the observed option. However, by its ex-ante nature exact data are not available, and instead of subjective estimates, historical data are often used. This is also frequently done for financial options. Even when historical data are settled for, a problem is that many real assets - i.e. underlying assets of real options are not traded, and hence data do not exist. For oil drilling investment projects, relevant, historical data do exist for the underlying asset - i.e. oil, but for most real assets, such as R&D projects, they do not[232]. A viable solution is to find acceptable proxies that are traded, such as data on comparable companies. Still, the identification of a comparable company in the search for a volatility proxy is quite complicated for real options on investment projects that by nature are quite unique.

One way to come up with an estimate on volatility is to find a *similar stock*, either from a comparable company for the investment project[233]. For example, the variance on returns of a biotechnology company's stock is this way seen as reflecting the variance on returns of the underlying asset, which in this case could be a biotechnology research project. The returns on the chosen stock come in the shape of dividends paid and stock price increases, which can then be analyzed for a variance. It is then assumed that the investment project will have the same volatility value. As volatility reflects the uncertainty, and uncertainty can be divided in two; market risk and private risk, it is important to keep in mind that an analysis of an individual stock for a volatility captures both private and market risk, whereas a volatility estimate taken from an index captures only the market risk, since the private risks of the companies in the index are diversified away[234].

A similar method is to utilize the fact that options are traded on quite a number of traded stocks in the US. By analyzing the bids on the options of the comparable companies, the so-called *'implied volatility'* can be identified[235]. This approach utilizes the fact that numerical values for all variables but the volatility can be observed in the market. In other words, by processing the values of the options offered in the financial markets in the option pricing formula, the volatility that has been used can be calculated.

For companies that have a history of similar investment projects, *in-house data* might be available that have a close resemblance to the project in question[236]. Finally, *managerial judgment* might be a way to establish an estimate, drawing on management experiences[237]. Summing up, there are basically four ways to identify the volatility:
- managerial judgment,
- historical in-house project data,

– historical stock data on a comparable company or relevant industry index, and

– implied volatility based on traded options on stocks of a comparable company.

Of course, the final numerical input into the calculation may very well be found by taking the results of more than one of these methods into consideration.

The figure below illustrates the approach taken to estimating the volatility in the following sections. Managerial judgment and in-house data are both approaches that rely on internal data, whereas historical stock data and implied volatility approaches rely on exchange data from comparable companies. This paper only makes use of external stock data; i.e. the two approaches based on comparable company data. Therefore, a few sections have been devoted to discuss the use of comparable companies. The two approaches are applied separately, and at the end of the chapter, the volatility estimate, which is to be carried forward is established as a weighted estimated of the two approaches, weighted in the light of the analysis.

Figure 6.1 The Approach of the Analysis to the Volatility Estimation

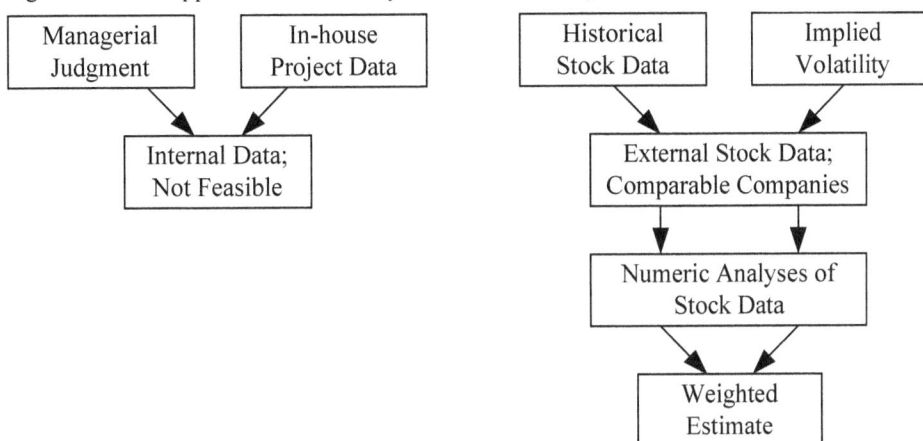

Source: Own construction.

6.6.1 Managerial Judgment

Though management most often has the best and most concrete perception of the uncertainty[238] related to a given research project, a prerequisite for using managerial judgment as the method is some sort of experience by management with translating the uncertainty perceived into the quantitative concept of volatility, and a familiarity with real option valuation. Though some of this could have been achieved by introducing management hereto, resources in the shape of management time were not available.

6.6.2 Historical In-house Project Data

Historical data on similar projects were not available in-house, since

– The range of projects historically has been very diversified. Hence, there are no previous projects in this field within NRC,

- Few projects have been concluded. It is not possible to make an estimate on total returns before - at the earliest - at completion of the research phase and early market introduction phase, which has only happened to few of NRC's portfolio of research projects, and
- Efforts are not tracked and measured, and data not produced in NRC on the relevant aspects. Even if this was attempted, it is very difficult to identify the extent of returns attributable to specific research carried out in NRC.

6.6.3 Historical Stock Data and Implied Volatility

The two first approaches discussed were internally focused. They were not evaluated to hold much potential. The two last-mentioned methods both rely on the existence of comparable companies or relevant stock indices that are either listed, or both listed and with options traded on their stocks. Hence, the data applied will be based on stock data external to NRC. In the following section, the notion of comparable companies and its use will be presented and discussed.

6.7 Comparable Companies

The discussion of comparable companies will look into the reasonability of using these, both comparable companies at large, as well as the use of American ones, before presenting the comparable companies actually chosen.

6.7.1 Reasonability of Using Comparables

The main argument for using data on comparable, listed companies to appraise investment projects is simply availability, or rather the lack of better suited data. Since the listed companies are closely followed by analysts, and obliged to disclose quite extensive information to the market, the information processing is quite significant. The professional investors and the analysts do follow the industry and the respective companies closely. For research-intensive companies with few profits realized, but with a high potential, it is quite common that rough, scheduled research plans are presented. It is then reported to the market - in particular the analysts following the stock - whether the overall research targets in the shape of milestones have been met, as well as findings ahead of schedule or unexpected, extraordinary findings.

Thus, it is fair to assume that, even though the companies active in the industry of SMB have not shown any profits yet, the expected future returns at any given point in time, and the way these expectations have changed, reflect the best estimates given the information available. The stock price incorporates this information and reflects the expectations of future profits. This means that even though no returns in the shape of company profits have been obtained, the volatility of the returns on the stock value can be measured historically. Since it is not unreasonable to assume that the changes, which have occurred ex-post, are of the same kind as those to come - for lack of better knowledge about the future - the historically observed volatility is applied to future-related option pricing. Therefore, both the volatility measures found through analysis of historic stock data, as well as the volatility measures calculated as implied volatility of the options offered, rely on ex-post information that are used to establish realistic expectations by professional investors. These realistic expectations are either incorporated in the stock price - expected future earnings - or in the option price - expected future volatility - and captured for volatility estimates respectively through historical stock data or implied volatility.

Hence, the stock prices and the option prices ultimately reflect investors' expectations to the companies' future profit-earning potential, both at a given point in time, as well as over time, when looking back at the developments. Therefore, the volatility both measured ex-post by analyzing stock performance, and ex-ante by calculating the implied volatility of the options offered in the financial markets can be applied to option pricing.

An aspect that makes the use of comparables problematic, is the extent to which the comparable company and the investment project are similar. The target is a so-called twin asset. The question is whether the comparable company and the investment project actually face the same conditions and have similar properties, and thus can be assumed to exhibit the same volatility with regard to the realized and expected returns. In essence - it might be objected that - what the use of comparables provides for in terms of data, it might lack in comparability.

6.7.2 Reasonability of Using American Comparables

Since American exchanges are the most advanced in the world in terms of activities and coverage - respectively the use of financial instruments such as options on stocks, and the number of listed companies - it is very fortunate that the majority of companies active in the biochip industry is American. SMB has identified the two most comparable, listed American companies, which will be used in the estimation of volatility. A number of European comparable companies were also pointed out. Though they were more like SMB in terms of research focus and nature of relations to academic institutions, they were like SMB not listed on any exchange. The fact that the European counterparts are not listed is most likely due to their small sizes and the lesser use of exchange listings for small, hi-tech companies in Europe, compared with America.

Though the use of American comparables is a step further away from the ideal twin asset with regard to the properties of and the conditions facing the two assets compared with, it can be defended.

First of all, the target is to identify a volatility that is applicable to the three-year time horizon of the investment project. The focus in this stage of the development is on own competencies and the achievement of the research targets set. This kind of research is international in nature, and as such the challenges and the uncertainty somewhat comparable. From the research nature of the project, it seems that there is little locational difference between Denmark and America with regard to expected volatility. Though, there are of course individual differences from company to company, the dependence on international research and international commercial breakthrough of the technology is shared.

Secondly, on the product side, companies active in this industry need a global perspective. Partly due to the scale advantages that must be exploited, and partly because the requirements of the market presumably are the same, given the universal nature of biological focus; i.e. molecular structures. Since the critical suppliers and buyers are global in nature, market and competitive conditions do not seem to inhibit the use of American comparables for a Danish company. Though legislation may be asymmetric with regard to what is allowed, if this is different and distinctively restrictive in one country, this can easily be circumvented technically by choice of placement.

Finally, the international financial markets can be seen as somewhat efficient. Hence, the financial conditions facing the competitors are globally alike and converging, making the implications of the financial conditions for volatility and variance on returns much alike. Also the resemblance between the respective financial markets make the transfer of ratios such as volatility quite reasonable. This is so, because this variable is not related to the absolute level like interest rates are, which might differ internationally due to differences e.g. in currency rates and inflation. Instead volatility is related to the proportions, i.e. the relative level, by explaining the fluctuations of the asset in terms of variations in returns.

6.7.3 Comparable Companies in the Analysis

In the following determination of volatility, the focus is on two American companies that have been pointed out by SMB as being the most similar ones[239].

ACLARA Biosciences Inc. and Caliper Technologies Corp. are both California-based companies active in the most sophisticated biochips, the microflow systems, also known as the so-called 'lab-on-a-chip' concepts or microfluidics. Both companies were established in 1995, and went public with listings on NASDAQ approximately four years later. Caliper had its IPO on December 15, 1999, whereas ACLARA's IPO was on March 21, 2000[240]. None of the companies have launched any products yet[241].

The concept of volatility is the most extraordinary introduced by real option valuation. Consequently, few people are familiar with the quantification of the concept. Therefore, two other companies have been included in the analysis to establish a benchmark to relate the quantification to. The two companies with which most business interested people are familiar, are rather different from the biochip companies. The biochip companies are quite often young and rely almost solely on profit potential to convince investors, compared with the two companies that are included for reference. These differ in terms of establishment and proven commercial track-records. The companies chosen are Intel (among other things microprocessors) and Coca Cola (soft drinks).

106

The companies were chosen because they are more widely known and were expected to be less volatile than the biochip companies. Their beta[242] values (Coca Cola 0.57 and Intel 1.5) indicate that they fluctuate less with the market portfolio, than the biochip manufacturers in question (ACLARA 2.53 and Caliper 1.94)[243]. The market portfolio ideally contains all companies, and in this case it contains a large number of companies[244]. By combining a large number of companies, the market portfolio tends to even out large parts of the fluctuations; i.e. diversification. Therefore, the higher the beta is, the more fluctuating a company's stock price is.

6.8 Implied Volatility

When data on traded options on stocks is used to find an estimate on volatility, the analysis utilizes the fact that all factors in the option pricing formula are known, except the volatility[245]. However, for mathematical reasons the equation cannot be inverted, so that the volatility is expressed as a function of maturity, option price, exercise price, current stock price, and risk-free interest rate. Therefore, an iterative search procedure must be applied[246].

The formula used is the Black & Scholes formula for European-style call options. Obviously, the data fed into the formula, when calculating implied volatilities, is taken from the quotations on call options too. The quotations on most of the options analyzed here, however, are on American-style options. One of the significant insights from option theory is that an American-style option on an asset, which does not pay out dividends in the lifetime of the option should never be exercised prematurely, i.e. before the expiration date[247]. Therefore, American-style options on stocks can be evaluated using the formula for European-style options, as long as the stocks do not pay out any dividends. Though, this would be an invalid assumption in general as many stocks do pay dividends, it does make sense anyway in most contexts, since the dividend payouts are frequently small and insignificant compared with the option value. Furthermore, the option pricing formula for European-style call options can be applied even when dividend payouts can be expected with a few moderations of the underlying data, when stocks are analyzed. Since, this formula is far simpler to work with, this is very fortunate.

6.8.1 Dividends

Dividends introduce two problems, when applying the European option pricing formula to American options that pay dividends. These are how to handle the reduction in value that is caused, and how to determine the optimal timing of the exercise.

Reduction in Stock Price

First of all, dividend payouts reduce the value of the stock on the ex-dividend date[248], and thus the stock price. That is, the value of the call option's underlying asset decreases, and consequently - presumably - the stock price[249]. The value of the call option decreases because its value depends on the difference between the stock price, S_0 and the exercise price, E_x, in a such way that the higher S_0 is, the higher the chance that exercise at E_x is feasible. Fortunately, the loss of value caused by dividend payouts can be handled within the European option pricing formula by subtracting the expected dividends from the stock price, S_0 before inserting it into the formula[250]. The expected dividends must be discounted at the risk-free interest rate, before they are subtracted[251]. Since a tax shield is created for the company, when paying out the dividends, the stock price is not decreased with the whole dividend payout per share, but with a smaller amount reflecting the tax effect, a.k.a. pull-through[252]. The size of tax shield depends on the corporate tax levied on the company.

Optimal Timing of Exercise

Whereas the first problem was related to the reduction in value caused by dividend payouts, the second problem is related to the timing. Here the question is, whether it is beneficial to exercise the option prematurely to capture the dividend payouts, or to forego the expected dividend payouts for the remaining value of the option; i.e. the value of the option 'alive'. If the option is to be exercised prematurely, this must be done as shortly before the ex-dividend date as possible, to appropriate as much of the option's value as possible. In other words, the second problem caused by dividend payouts with regard to the application of the European option pricing formula to American-style options is to determine whether it is optimal to exercise the option '*at a time immediately before the stock goes ex-dividend*'[253] to capture the expected dividend payouts, or to hold the option for its remaining value.

Dividends' Impact on the Analysis

For ACLARA and Caliper no dividends have been paid, while they have been listed; respectively since March 21, 2000 and December 15, 1999 - at the time of writing 5 and 8 months. Since these companies are under development in the sense that they are developing the technology and awaiting the commercial breakthrough, it seems a valid assumption that no dividends can be expected within the next 6 months[254], due to lack of earnings and, if earnings should arise, due to reinvestment needs. The same assumption is made for the other biochip and biotechnology companies that will be presented and analyzed later. None of these 11 companies have ever paid out dividends, and only two of them have sporadically shown insignificant earnings; namely Aurora Biosciences and Incyte Genomics. For Coca Cola and Intel however - both of them large established companies compared with the biotechnology companies and active in mature industries, with a history of paying out dividends - the above line of reasoning cannot be applied. Instead, the dividends have been considered individually in the two cases. For a thorough analysis of the projection, timing and impact of dividends for these two companies, please refer to appendix 6. In the analysis, the results will be presented without further treatment of this issue.

6.8.2 Risk-Free Interest Rate and Implied Volatility

In the identification of the interest rate for the real option on NRC's investment project the interest rate of Danish Treasury bonds with a three year maturity was used. For the calculation of the implied volatility of options traded on American exchanges however, the American risk-free interest rate in the shape of the interest rate of American Treasury bonds will be applied. The maturities of the T-bonds are matched with the options in the following way. For options with maturities of 1 day, 1 month, and 3 months, the 3-month interest rate has been applied, which equals 6.15% per year. For 6 month maturities, the 6-month interest rate has been applied, which equals 6.29% per year[255].

6.8.3 Numerical Analysis Presented

The options that will be analyzed for implied volatilities are traded on NASDAQ, the American Stock Exchange (abbr. AMEX), or NYSE. The data for the analysis is gathered at the end of July and in early August 2000. At this time, regular options on the stock in question were on offer with expiration in July, August, October 2000, and January 2001, and LEAPS options with expiration in January 2002 and January 2003. Regular options are traded on almost all stocks at AMEX, NYSE and NASDAQ. LEAPS options however, are on offer for less stocks. LEAPS is short for Long-Term Equity Anticipation Securities. The expiration day in a given month is the Saturday following the third Friday of the expiration month for both regular and LEAPS options[256]. Most of the analyses are done as of July 19-20, 2000, and the corresponding maturities are 1 day, 1 month, 3 months, 6 months for the options. The notation and exact number of days used in the analysis are shown in the table below.

Table 6. 7 Expiration Data

Option names	Option expiration date	Number of months	Number of days
JUL 2000	22-07-00	0MM	2
AUG 2000	19-08-00	1MM	29
OCT 2000	21-10-00	3MM	91
NOV 2000	18-11-00	4MM	91
JAN 2001	20-01-01	6MM	180
FEB 2001	17-02-01	7MM	207
MAR 2001	18-11-00	8MM	237
JAN 2002	20-01-01	18MM	539
JAN 2003	17-02-01	30MM	898

Source: www.nasdaq.com.

The market makers offering options are required to both put forward ask and bid prices, i.e. how much they respectively sell and buy the options in question for. The ask and bid prices are not the same[257], since there is a so-called bid-ask spread giving the market makers a profit potential. This analysis is done on the ask prices for call options, though these are the highest of the two. The ask prices are chosen because the market makers must be expected to be more interested in issuing and selling call options than acquiring them - and thus in effect canceling them. Also the market makers do not make money holding the options. Therefore, market makers are more likely to influence the pricing of bids to make them less attractive, than strictly looking to price the options as precisely as possible.

The primary focus of the analysis is the determination of the implied volatilities of ACLARA and Caliper, since these have been pointed out as the most comparable companies to SMB. To better understand the findings, similar analyses of other options are made in order for similarities to support the analyses and peculiarities to be investigated and explained. It would be optimal for the estimation of a volatility that the analysis must come up with for SMB, if an option was offered on one or both of the two companies with a three-year maturity in the shape of a LEAPS option. Unfortunately, this is not the case. The longest maturity for Caliper and ACLARA is 6 months. Hence, the implied volatilities of Caliper and ACLARA can only be the basis for some sort of estimate extension, e.g. extrapolation. The companies with LEAPS options traded can help facilitate this.

The presentation of analyses is split into three.

First, the approach is applied to Caliper and ACLARA, which are cross-analyzed to test the approach and to evaluate the preciseness. For this purpose, Coca Cola and Intel are analyzed too.

Hereafter, the level of the estimates identified are evaluated in terms of appropriateness. This is done by analyzing implied volatilities of competitors also active in the biochip industry.

The analysis of the LEAPS options is the last part of the analysis. LEAPS options are traded on Intel and Coca Cola's stocks and the chosen biotechnology companies, so the findings and the comparison from the first part on Intel and Coca Cola can be utilized, when the estimates from Caliper and ACLARA have to be extended. Though, the biotechnology companies are not comparable, they can also be utilized for the long-term analysis of LEAPS options to identify tendencies with regard to extended maturities for more volatile companies, than the benchmark companies.

The data and the calculations behind the calculation of implied volatilities and the historical data that will be introduced later are on the diskette attached at the back of the booklet containing the appendices.

6.8.4 Technical Test of Approach; Preciseness of Estimation

When utilizing stock exchange data to calculate implied volatilities, it quickly becomes clear that there are variations in the implied volatilities calculated depending e.g. on exercise price and maturity. However, certain patterns in the way that the options are priced can be observed. The patterns can be seen by plotting various sets of data graphically, along the significant variables. These graphs help disclose and understand the price setter's underlying perception of volatility. Through this understanding, the volatility estimate that must be considered to be the most correct and appropriate for the application at hand can be identified among the various estimates of implied volatilities.

The reason that the implied volatilities as measured with the Black & Scholes formula vary with different maturities and exercise prices is basically because the price setter has a different perception of the way that the stock price is expected to vary, than is illustrated by this formula.

110

The Volatility Smile

One of the graphical presentations of the data is to plot the calculated volatilities as a function of the exercise prices. The result is the so-called volatility smile.

Figure 6.2 The Volatility Smile

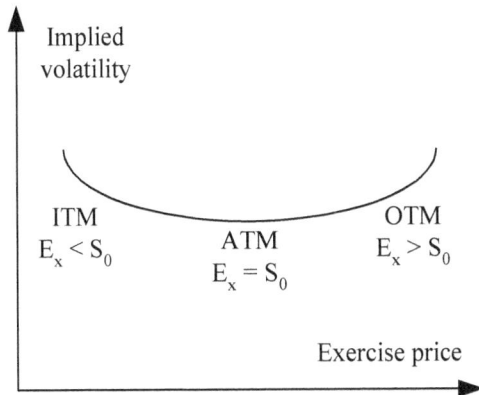

Source: Hull (1997) p. 503. ITM, ATM and OTM indications added.

The graph shows the lowest volatility at-the-money (abbr. ATM) and increasing volatilities the further out-of-the-money (abbr. OTM) or in-the-money (abbr. ITM), the exercise price is[258]. This pattern is typical for foreign exchange options[259]. Here, the Black & Scholes formula would have underpriced[260] the OTM and ITM options, if the ATM volatility were to be applied to the whole range of exercise prices. This distribution could be approximated by applying a so-called jump diffusion model that would add a Poisson distributed component to the distribution[261]. Conceptually this would be a sudden and abrupt event that triggered a high decrease or increase in stock price or currency exchange rate with equal probability.

For options on stocks however, the volatility smile typically turns into more of a volatility grimace[262]. For this pattern, the high-exercise-price options (OTM) have lower volatilities, than the options with a lower exercise price (ITM).

Figure 6.3 The Volatility Grimace

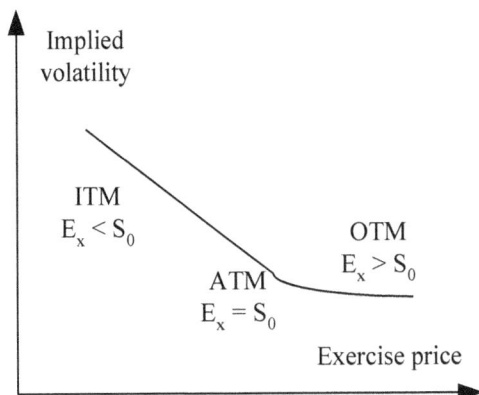

Source: Hull (1997) p. 504.

This pattern basically reflects a negative correlation between the stock price and the volatility. For this relation a number of explanation models have been proposed that mostly see the volatility as a function of the stock price with different causal explanations of the latter. Conceptually seen - from a trading point of view - the rationality behind the negative correlation is that when '*the stock price increases, the volatility tends to decrease, making it less likely that really high stock prices will be achieved. When the stock price decreases, volatility tends to increase, making it more likely that really low stock prices will be achieved*'[263].

An economics-based explanation of this is that when the stock price decreases, the value of the equity, and the equity to debt ratio, decreases too. This increases the leverage of the company, and thus the financial risk, resulting in higher volatility[264]. The opposite holds for stock prices increases[265]. This fundamental explanation aside, the causality behind the correlation could be superficially interpreted as embodying respectively a panicked reinforcing downward movement[266] and a contained, saturated upward movement of the stock price.

Though, the described pattern clearly breaks with the assumption of the Black & Scholes formula of one volatility within the lifetime of an option and across all exercise prices[267], observations do support the pattern. Still, Hull (1997) investigates a number of models and wraps up various research contributions to conclude that '*(a)t present, there do not seem to be any really compelling arguments for using any of the models introduced ... in preference to Black-Scholes for stock options*'[268]. Amram & Kulatilaka (1999) also concludes with specific reference to the corporate context, i.e. real options that '*the payoffs to most real options are virtually unaffected by unexpected changes in volatility, known as stochastic volatility*'[269].

One of the questions is whether to take the implied volatility estimate from an OTM, ATM or ITM option. This choice reflects the perception of the influence of the stock price, S_0 on the volatility, i.e. stochastic volatility. Underlying this discussion is the fundamental difference between real options and financial options that the latter are traded and have prices derived from the market, making it possible at all to talk about the state of the options in terms of the current stock price, S_0 versus the exercise price, E_x. Thus, for financial options it makes sense to postulate causal relations between the stock price and the volatility, σ, since both can be observed and reacted upon in the market. Especially to argue for the stock price's influence on volatility, since new information is continuously incorporated into the stock price causing and reflecting volatility, and because the changes in volatility for different values of stock prices may be observably dissimilar.

For many real options however, the price of the underlying asset, i.e. the present value of the expected cash flows cannot be continuously monitored, as is the case for SMB. Here it does not make sense to talk about the status of the option in terms of immediate exercise (OTM, ATM, ITM) during the investment project, since the prices are not continuously available. The only change in the underlying asset that can be precisely measured along the way, is in case the investment project is rendered worthless, e.g. by the technology reaching a dead-end, a competitor patenting the technology researched for, another superior technology seizing the market, etc., which basically means sudden termination and worthlessness[270]. This kind of development could be incorporated into the option pricing formula in the shape of a jump diffusion model based on the Poisson distribution, as it was discussed in section 4.6, 5.3.2 and 5.3.3. Still, this extension of the model has no implications for the exercise price at the point of initiation, and as such for the determination of the initial state of the option (ATM, ITM, OTM), which is the difference between the value of the underlying assets and the exercise price. Since, the value change or price change that can be monitored this way is a post-initiation drop to zero that leaves exercise of the option unfeasible and the exercise price unimportant no matter how low[271], it cannot be used to determine what state the option is in at initiation, when an implied volatility has to be chosen.

The development in the market potential of the research target might be monitored through extensive efforts put into ongoing market surveillance and market intelligence, thereby providing a proxy for some of the underlying asset's value. Still, this would only be related to the market potential, and not the changes in the value of the research project itself, as it moves closer to completion of the technology. On top of that, the value of the underlying asset cannot be said to follow a continuos process in the development of its value, since its value depends upon the achievement of the research target, i.e. full completion through perfection of the technology to the extent that it is applicable. In other words, the investment project's underlying assets does not have a price before it is completed, since its value can be said to be immeasurable until it is done. Thus, the company-specific uncertainty component of the volatility is best approximated by a discrete distribution, because it is immeasurable while under development.

In summary, the implied volatility to choose with regard to the financial option's state of the comparable company - i.e. which exercise price in terms of OTM, ITM, ATM to choose the corresponding volatility from - for the use in the real option valuation cannot be identified unambiguously by looking to a stochastic volatility explanation. The lack of continuos measurement of the value of the underlying asset makes it unreasonable to apply stock price-dependent models for the volatility of the SMB real option. Thus, it will be assumed that the SMB real option has the same volatility during investment project's three-year explicit planning horizon. Still, a discussion of other more qualitative features of the real option may give an indication as to the state of the option in order to determine whether to take the implied volatility OTM, ITM or ATM.

In the prioritization between potential investment projects in NRC, research areas and research projects with huge future market potential are selected, to improve the chance of adding significant value. The choice of research target this way becomes unproved technologies, where big leaps forward can be expected and aimed at. The ambitious goals with corresponding high technological and market uncertainties, but a huge profit potential if successful, implies a deep out-of-the-money option through a high-risk, high-return profile. Following this perception, the uncertainties regarding market development and technological challenges induce high variation that is beneficial for the deep OTM option's chances of ending ITM. This perception suggests that the implied volatility estimate should be taken OTM. This way of perceiving the investment is also supported by the earlier presented estimate on the present value of the expected value (S_0 = DKK 73 million), which was significantly lower than the investment required (E_x = DKK 100 million).

On the other hand, the above trade-off between the profit potential and the uncertainties has somehow been considered and found suitable by the management of NRC prior to initiation implying that if the scenario unfolds as expected, the value of the underlying asset is higher than the cost, which would be an ITM option. In this perception the private risk of not achieving research target, or the risk of the market developing disadvantageous is put into the model as a high variation that is threatening for an ITM option at the time of initiation.

All in all, a number of arguments can be proposed for perceiving the real option of SMB different ways. In the estimation of implied volatility in this context, the estimate will be the volatility corresponding to the ATM options. The rationale behind this choice is as follows. First of all, the volatility of an ATM option for stocks is taken at the median value of the underlying asset. From here the volatility covers stock price changes both upwards and downwards from the current price, i.e. the prices from this point can be both decreasing and increasing in value. Secondly, the ATM option is conveniently placed in the middle of the perceptions of the real option as an OTM option with a high volatility and high upside potential and the real option as an ITM option with the realization made uncertain by a high volatility. Thirdly, by choosing the ATM implied volatility, the analysis does not need to take into consideration the different stock price-dependent models for the volatility - i.e. the volatility's dependence on the value of the underlying asset, when extracting the implied volatility from the options on stock and applying it to the real option. It is simply assumed that the investment project has it own unmeasured and 'unpriced' life, which value during the project does not effect the volatility. Thus, the progress in research that can be expected at a given time is unaffected by the valuation at that time. In other words, the company-specific uncertainty, i.e. the private risk component of the volatility, is unaffected by the value of the underlying asset during the project. Concurrently, the market potential of the completed investment project is unaffected by the continuous achievement of gradual research results, and so is the value of SMB's research target upon achievement. Put another way, the market uncertainty, i.e. the market risk component of the volatility, is unaffected by the value of underlying asset. Both of these observations against a S_0 dependent volatility make good sense in connection with the identification of a volatility estimate for SMB. Finally, the determination of the option value ATM by the market makers is far more sensitive to changes in volatility, and must therefore be assumed to provide more accurate information[272].

The volatility smiles of Caliper Technologies (abbr. CALP), ACLARA Biosciences (abbr. ACLA), Coca Cola (abbr. KO), and Intel (abbr. INTC) have been plotted in the diagrams on the following page, based on the stock options with the longest maturity / latest expiration traded[273].

The graphs of the four companies' implied volatilities plotted against the exercise prices do show the described volatility grimaces that are typical for options on stocks. ACLARA is the only one that stands out with a curve shaped as a 'W', though it is decreasing over the whole observed range of exercise prices as the rest. The volatility smile of ACLARA as depicted for other, shorter maturities (August 2000 and October 2000) show the same jagged curve, as do a volatility smile plotted on more recent data as observed on August 21, 2000. The deviation from the expected downward slope is unexplainable through the models presented on stochastic volatility in Hull (1997), but since the deviation is rather small in terms of percentage points, the issue will not be further investigated.

The implied volatilities of the ATM options are presented in the table below:

Table 6.8 Implied Volatilities from Volatility Smile Analysis for Options At-The-Money

Company	Current Stock Price	Implied Volatility at Current Stock Price (ATM)
Caliper	47.88	144.6%
ACLARA	49.94	120.6%
Coca Cola	60.31	33.4%
Intel	141.50	45.3%

Source: www.nasdaq.com, based on own calculations. Note: Maturity - 6 months (Coca Cola 7 months).

Figure 6.4 Volatility Smiles for Selected Comparable and Benchmark Companies

Figure 6.4a

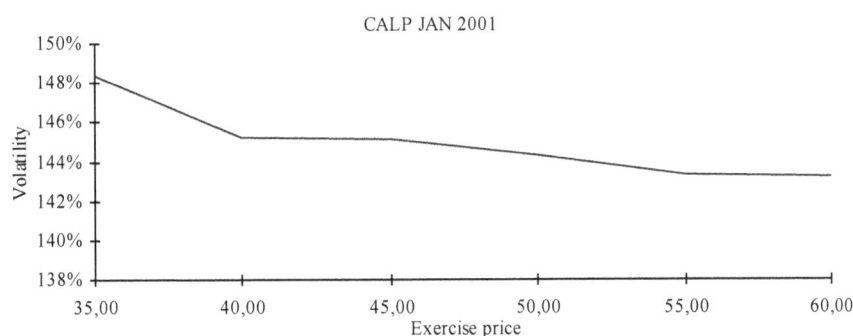

CALP JAN 2001

$S_0 = 47.88$
$\sigma = 144.6\%$

Figure 6.4 Volatility Smiles for Selected Comparable and Benchmark Companies (continued)

Figure 6.4b

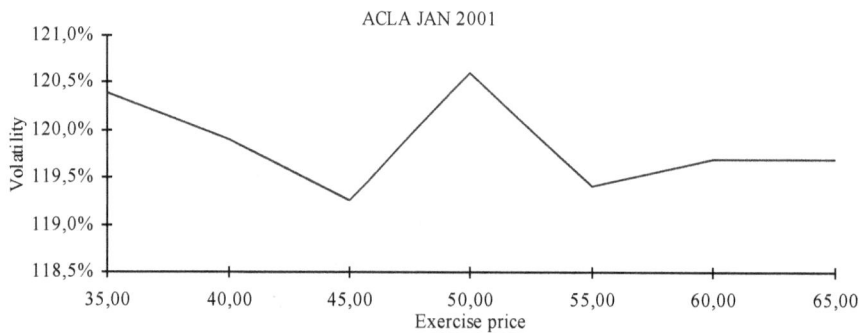

ACLA JAN 2001

$S_0 = 49.94$
$\sigma = 120.6\%$

Figure 6.4c

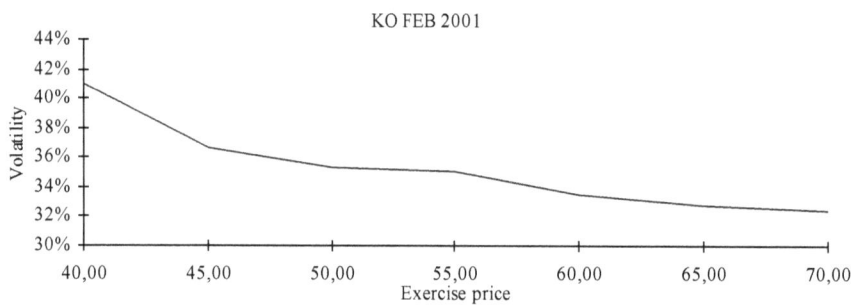

KO FEB 2001

$S_0 = 60.31$
$\sigma = 33.4\%$

Figure 6.4d

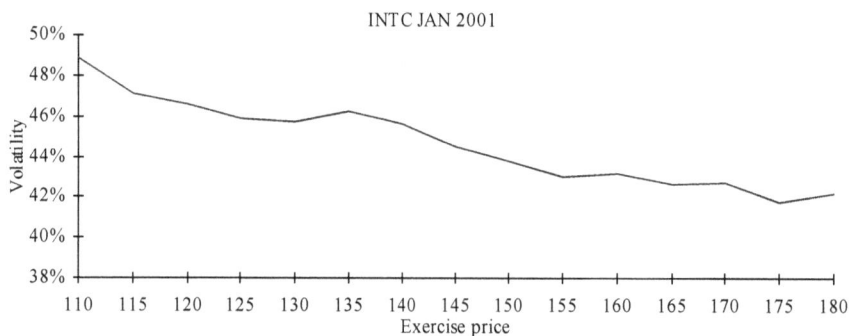

INTC JAN 2001

$S_0 = 141.50$
$\sigma = 45.3\%$

Source: www.nasdaq.com and own calculations. Volatility in percentage on the vertical axis and exercise price in USD on the horizontal axis. All data as of July 20, 2000. Expiration as indicated above graphs (JAN 2001 equals January 20, 2001 - FEB 2001 equals February 17, 2001). Company abbreviations explained in text.

To find the exact ATM value, interpolation has been used to find the corresponding volatility value. The options are typically traded on the exchange in exercise price intervals of USD 5.00. If volatility estimates for stock prices in between these intervals are required, it is reasonable to interpolate linearly between the observations[274]. For Caliper, the implied volatilities with the exercise price closest to the current stock price were (45.00; 145.1%) and (50.00; 144.3%). By linear interpolation the ATM estimate was found to be (47.88; 144.6%).

116

The implied volatilities of the two comparable companies are significantly higher than for the two companies used for benchmarking. Hence, the assumption that the two established companies would be more stable, based on their beta values seem valid. The numeric values for Coca Cola and Intel are much in line with Luehrman's (1998a) observation that manufacturing companies typically have yearly volatilities in the area of 30% to 60%[275].

The Volatility Term Structure

The volatility term structure is the implied volatilities plotted against the maturities of the options. An important part of this analysis of implied volatilities is to estimate a volatility for a three-year maturity as the SMB real option is. Therefore, tendencies in the way implied volatilities change over different lengths of maturities are relevant, when implied volatilities for ACLARA and Caliper are to be extended maturity-wise in order to be applied to the real option of SMB.

However, the graphs do show different developments. Caliper has increasing volatilities for increasing maturities, whereas ACLARA shows the opposite development. In an examination of research contribution, Hull (1997) finds no clear cut causality between implied volatility and maturity, though for OTM call options, a relation has been established that shows that short term maturities tend to have higher implied volatilities than long-term maturities, i.e. the volatilities decrease with increases in maturities[276].

Figure 6.5 Volatility Term Structures for Comparable Companies

Figure 6.5a

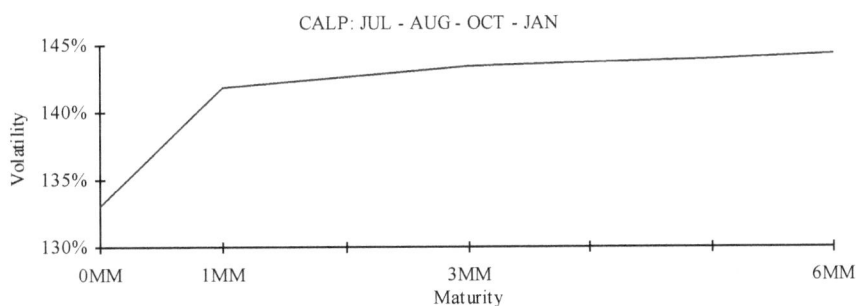

CALP: JUL - AUG - OCT - JAN

$E_x = 50.00$
$S_0 = 47.88$

Figure 6.5 Volatility Term Structures for Comparable Companies (continued)

Figure 6.5b

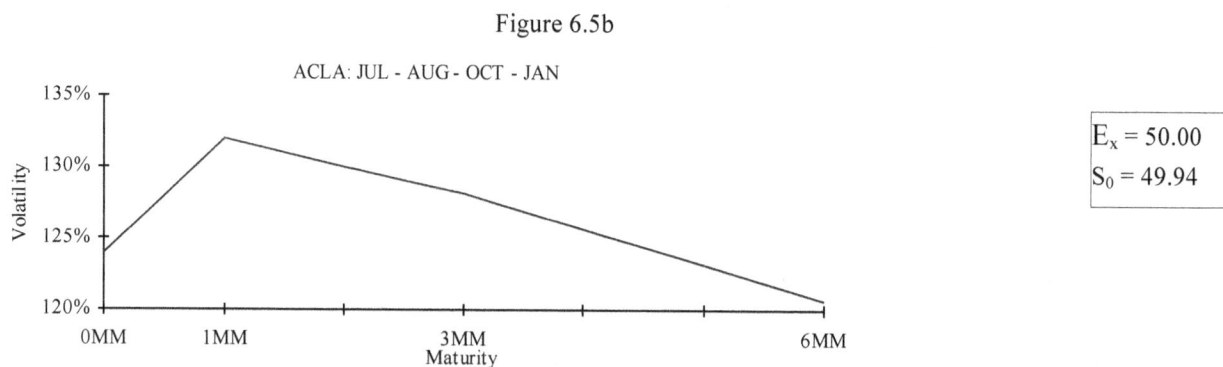

ACLA: JUL - AUG - OCT - JAN

$E_x = 50.00$
$S_0 = 49.94$

Source: www.nasdaq.com and own calculations. Volatility in percentage on the vertical axis and maturity in months on the horizontal axis. Expiration as indicated above graphs (JUL equals July 22, 2000 - AUG equals August 19, 2000, etc.). Exercise price (E_x) and current stock price (S_0) in USD as of date of analysis indicated next to the graphs. All data as of July 20, 2000. Company abbreviations explained in text.

The volatility term structures in figure 6.5 have all been taken as closely at the money as possible following the conclusions of volatility smile analysis, so the presented correlation for OTM exercise prices' effect on volatility is of little significance to this analysis.

The Volatility Matrix

When implied volatilities are identified in order to be applied to other options, a problem can be that the exercise prices or the maturities are not identical from comparable company to target company. This can be somewhat overcome by establishing a volatility matrix. A volatility matrix contains implied volatilities tabulated with exercise price and maturity on each dimension. The matrices are presented for ACLARA and Caliper below. The tables basically contain the same information as the volatility smile and the volatility term structure combined. The tables are more exact numerically, but lack the graphically insights.

In case the option that is to be analyzed do not have the same exercise price or maturity or both as the traded options from which the implied volatilities have been identified, the appropriate estimate can be found by interpolation[277]. As the word says, interpolation can primarily be defended within the limits of the matrix. Opposite, extrapolation for values higher or lower than the tabulated exercise prices and maturities; i.e. outside the span of the panel, cannot be done only based on the matrix without looking further into the issue. Since 6 months maturity data are all that is available for the comparable companies, it is necessary to look into the way other companies' implied volatilities develop, when maturities increase, before the volatility estimates from the comparable companies can be extended.

Table 6.9 Volatility Matrices for Comparable Companies

Option name	Maturity	35.00	40.00	45.00	50.00	55.00	60.00	
CALP JUL 2000	0MM	306%	180%	133%	133%	152%	205%	
CALP AUG 2000	1MM	148%	148%	141%	142%	141%	139%	
CALP OCT 2000	3MM	146%	146%	145%	143%	143%	142%	
CALP JAN 2001	6MM	148%	145%	145%	144%	143%	143%	

Option name	Maturity	35.00	40.00	45.00	50.00	55.00	60.00	65.00
ACLA JUL 2000	0MM			108%	124%	131%		
ACLA AUG 2000	1MM	132%	132%	131%	132%	132%	132%	133%
ACLA OCT 2000	3MM	126%	128%	126%	128%	127%	125%	126%
ACLA JAN 2001	6MM	120%	120%	119%	121%	119%	120%	120%

Source: www.nasdaq.com and own calculations. Expiration as indicated in the option names and explained in table 6.7 in section 6.8.3. Current stock price for Caliper USD 47.88 and ACLARA USD 49.94. Exercise prices in USD. All data as of July 20, 2000. Company abbreviations explained in text.

Since the focus of this analysis is to extend the estimates for ACLARA and Caliper in terms of maturity, the following sections of the analysis will look into maturity aspects and comparison on the longest maturity available or appropriate for comparable and benchmark companies. The most appropriate analysis approach to implied volatility and time-wise extension of estimates is considered the volatility term structure, which precisely depicts the development over different maturities. This analysis will focus on ATM options as decided earlier.

6.8.5 Industry Participants; Level of Estimates

To evaluate the level of the implied volatility estimates identified for Caliper and ACLARA, a number of listed competitors active in the biochip industry[278] that were not pointed out as the most comparable companies by NRC have been analyzed in terms of implied volatility. The results have been plotted as volatility term structures and are presented for all companies in one diagram below. Before, that the companies are briefly presented with some characteristics. For the sake of the comparison, the same characteristics for Caliper and ACLARA are presented.

Table 6.10 Competitors Active in the Biochip Industry

Company name	NASDAQ abbreviation	Revenues 1999. USD millions	IPO date	Time listed. Months	Volatility ATM
Sequenom Inc.	SQNM	0.18	01-02-00	6	137%
Nanogen Inc.	NGEN	8.12	14-04-98	28	110%
Incyte Genomics Inc.	INCY	156.96	17-10-96	45	110%
HySeq Inc.	HYSQ	6.40	04-11-98	21	98%
Affymetrix Inc.	AFFX	96.86	27-05-97	38	90%
Aurora Biosciences Corp.	ABSC	50.32	14-04-98	28	91%
Caliper Technologies Corp.	CALP	12.09	15-12-99	8	144.6%
ACLARA Biosciences Inc.	ACLA	2.94	21-03-00	5	120.6%

Source: www.nasdaq.com. Implied volatilities are estimated for the longest maturities available ranging from six to eight months.

Three of the competitors have implied volatilities higher than 100%, which is at the level of Caliper and ACLARA. These are Sequenom, Nanogen, and Incyte. The level of Caliper and ACLARA is not so high that it must be dismissed compared to the competitors, but it is very clear that the two companies chosen as comparables are in the upper end of the biochip industry in terms of implied volatilities. Under the assumption that the degree of technological maturity and market acceptance, and hence volatility, is correlated with the turnover, and that the point in time when an IPO can be carried through indicates that technological proof of concept to a certain extent has been reached, the presented characteristics of the competitors might somewhat explain the findings. Sequenom, which has the most similar volatility, has a smaller turnover than ACLARA and Caliper, and has been listed equally short time, i.e. about half a year. Nanogen has revenues at the same level, but has been listed longer. Incyte is one of the heavy competitors with a long history on the exchange and the highest turnover among the competitors observed. The two with the lowest implied volatilities, Affymetrix and Aurora are in the same class as Incyte, whereas HySeq share many characteristics with Nanogen, Caliper and ACLARA.

All in all, the level of the estimates on implied volatilities for Caliper and ACLARA seem appropriate compared to the competitors, since there seems to be a vague tendency towards small revenues and short time listed being related to high volatilities. Furthermore, it seems reasonable that the comparable companies pointed out are in the higher end of the implied volatility estimates, since they are going to be applied to a newly established company as SMB, which is not as established as any of the listed competitors. SMB is only projected to reach the turnover level of the smallest of the competitors, Sequenom, in 2001[279].

Figure 6.6 Volatility Term Structures for Competitors Active in the Biochip Industry

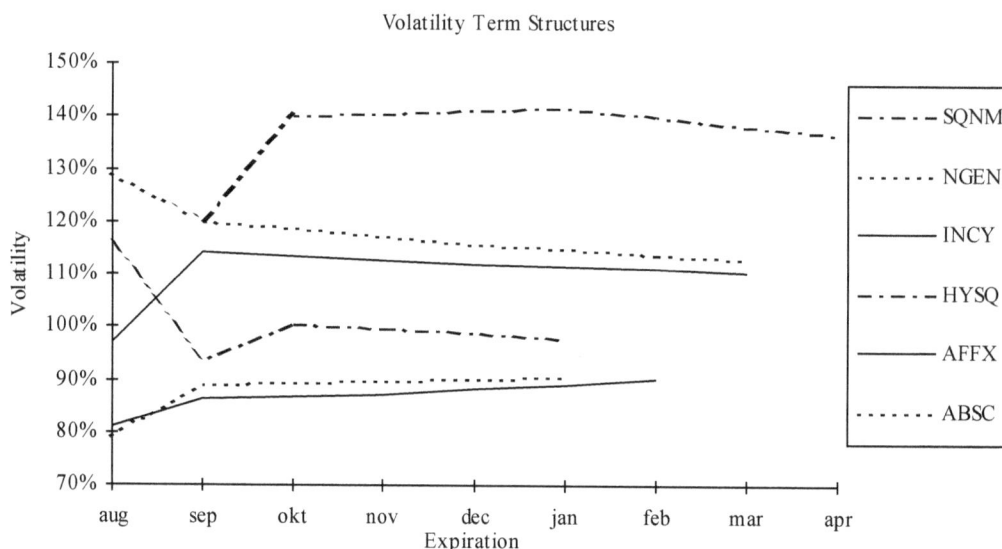

Source: www.nasdaq.com and own calculations. Volatility in percentage on the vertical axis and expiration months on the horizontal axis. Expiration dates as outlined in table 6.7. Exercise price (E_x) taken as the closest to the at-the-money price. The current stock price (S_0) as of date of analysis. All data as of August 15, 2000. Company abbreviations explained in text.

6.8.6 Long-term Analysis; Extension of Time Horizon

The final part of the analysis is related to the extension of the estimates on implied volatility for ACLARA and Caliper, to match the maturity of the SMB real option. That is from a maturity of 6 months to a maturity of three years.

Fortunately, LEAPS options are traded with maturities of up to three years, but unfortunately not on the direct biochip competitors that are the companies most similar to Caliper and ACLARA. Of companies from the preceding analysis, LEAPS options are traded on Intel and Coca Cola. Five biotechnology companies will be analyzed to look into extensions for more volatile companies.

The analysis of the LEAPS options on Intel and Coca Cola focuses on the consistency of the approach and the results, as compared to the 'regular' options with shorter maturities. This might give an indication of what happens to the implied volatilities, when the maturities are increased manifold, and whether the approach applied in the preceding analysis can be reasonably extended to longer maturities. The graphical presentation will be the volatility term structure which can be seen in the figure below, where implied volatility estimates for both the regular and the LEAPS options are presented.

Figure 6.7 Long-term Volatility Term Structures for Benchmark Companies

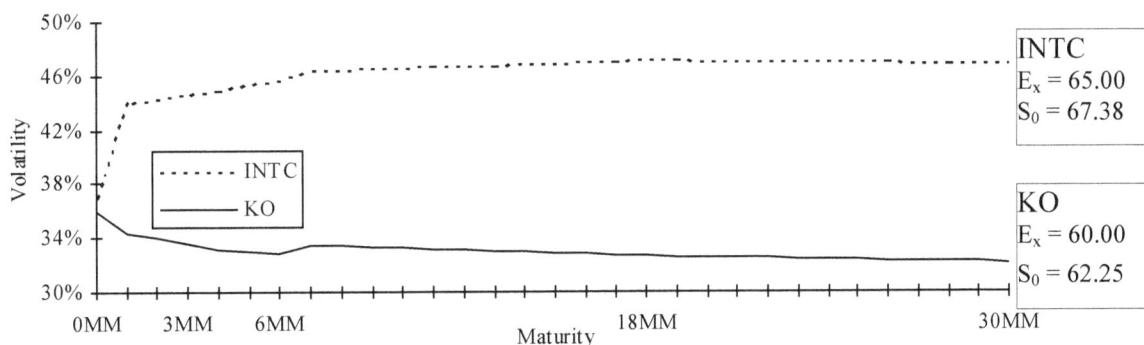

Source: www.nasdaq.com and own calculations. Volatility in percentage on the vertical axis and maturity in months on the horizontal axis. Expiration dates as in table 6.7 with additional implied volatilities for January 2002 and January 2003[280]. Exercise price (E_x) and current stock price (S_0) in USD as of date of analysis indicated next to the graphs. Please note that Intel's stock price is radically less than earlier figures. This is due to a stock split of July 30, 2000[281]. Data for maturities of 7 months and less as of July 20, 2000. Data for maturities of 18 months and beyond as of August 15, 2000. Company abbreviations explained in text.

The introduction of the long-term LEAPS options does seem to even out the curves that appear very stable from maturities of 6 months to 30 months. The numeric values are shown in the table below.

Table 6.11 Long-term Volatility Term Structures for Benchmark Companies

	Jul-2000 0MM	Aug-2000 1MM	Sep-2000 2MM	Oct-2000 3MM	Nov-2000 4MM	Dec-2000 5MM	Jan-2001 6MM	Feb-2001 7MM	Jan-2002 18MM	Jan-2003 30MM
INTC	37,0%	44,0%	*44,3%*	44,7%	*45,0%*	*45,3%*	*45,6%*	46,4%	47,1%	46,9%
KO	36,0%	34,4%	*34,0%*	*33,6%*	33,2%	*33,1%*	32,9%	33,5%	32,7%	32,1%
INTC Absolute change		18,9%	0,7%	0,7%	0,7%	0,7%	0,7%	1,6%	1,6%	-0,6%
INTC Monthly change		18,9%	0,7%	0,7%	0,7%	0,7%	0,7%	1,6%	0,15%	-0,05%
KO Absolute change		-4,4%	-1,2%	-1,2%	-1,2%	-0,5%	-0,5%	1,7%	-2,4%	-1,6%
KO Monthly change		-4,4%	-1,2%	-1,2%	-1,2%	-0,5%	-0,5%	1,7%	-0,22%	-0,13%

Source: www.nasdaq.com and own calculations. For background data, see above graph. Some of the values presented for the short-term maturities are found by linear interpolation (written in italic).

In the table, the percentage changes can be seen both absolutely from observation to observation regardless of the interval between observations, as well as the compounded, average monthly changes . The changes between the long-term maturities spanning approximately a year are of the same size as the changes between each month for the short-term maturities. When the changes are calculated on a monthly basis, it becomes clear that the implied volatilities are quite stable. Thus, the long-term implied volatilities of Coca Cola and Intel are very consistent with the longest short-term estimates, and seem to be a straightforward extension of the results of the preceding analysis.

In conclusion, the analysis of the LEAPS options on Coca Cola and Intel indicates that the implied volatilities for the longest regular options, i.e. 6-month maturities, can be extended without changing the level of the estimates.

To further test the extent to which the estimates of the short-term maturities can be unproblematic extended, the five biotechnology companies will be analyzed with regard to their long-term volatility term structures, as Coca Cola and Intel have just been. In so doing, it will be revealed whether the time-wise extensions are as stable for the more volatile biotechnology companies, as they are for the more established companies. None of the five companies are active in biochips, but among their activities are drug development for disease treatment of various kinds, such as diagnostics and drug development, and traditional equipment for medical purposes; i.e. medico-technology. The companies are all a lot bigger than the comparable companies and their competitors from the preceding section. None of these companies has a turnover of less than USD 500 millions. The results of the analysis are presented graphically below.

Figure 6.8 Long-term Volatility Term Structures for Selected Biotechnology Companies

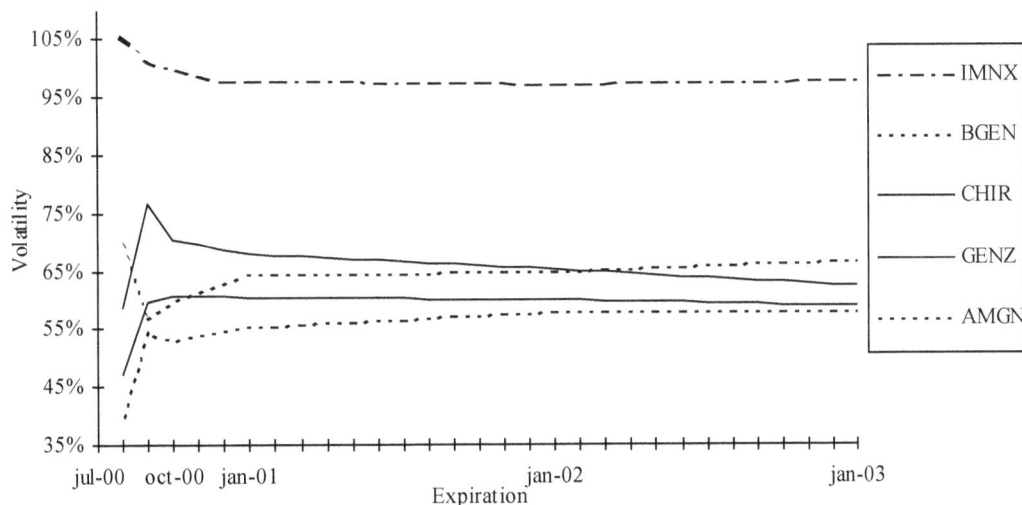

Source: www.nasdaq.com and own calculations. Volatility in percentage on the vertical axis and expiration months on the horizontal axis. Expiration dates as in figure 6.6 with additional implied volatilities for January 2002 and January 2003[282]. Exercise prices (E_x) and current stock prices (S_0) as of date of analysis are indicated in table below. All data as of August 15, 2000. Company abbreviations explained in text.

As can be seen, the implied volatilities of the biotechnology companies seem to follow the same pattern as the two benchmark companies. Since the figure is a bit more compressed, it is hard to see how much the deviation is. Therefore, the long-term development has been put in numbers in the table below.

Table 6.12 Long-term Implied Volatilities for Selected Biotechnology Companies

| Company name | NASDAQ abbreviation | Exercise price | Current Price | Volatility ATM[283] | | | | |
				jan-01	jan-02	Monthly change 2001-02	jan-03	Monthly change 2002-03
Immunex Corporation	IMNX	50,00	47,63	98%	97%	-0,07%	98%	0,05%
Biogen Inc.	BGEN	65,00	67,19	65%	65%	0,04%	67%	0,25%
Chiron Corporation	CHIR	45,00	45,88	68%	65%	-0,34%	62%	-0,37%
Genzyme Corporation	GENZ	70,00	68,44	60%	60%	-0,06%	59%	-0,16%
Amgen Inc.	AMGN	70,00	68,00	55%	58%	0,38%	58%	0,00%

Source: www.nasdaq.com and own calculations. For background data, see figure above.

Here it becomes clear that the deviations, measured as monthly changes, are equally small. As in the analysis of the benchmark companies, there is no clear indication whether the small change in implied volatility generally is upwards or downwards.

In conclusion, it seems defensible to extend the longest of the short-term maturity estimates on implied volatility to the longest maturities of up to 3 years' maturity, or actually 2½ years from August 2000 to January 2003. The small changes that can be observed do not point unambiguously to any directional change, i.e. increase or decrease, so the conclusion is that the comparable companies' estimates on implied volatility, for the short-term maturities of six months and below, can be extended without changes.

6.8.7 Concluding Remarks on Implied Volatility

The focus of the analysis was to estimate implied volatilities for the two comparable companies pointed out, namely ACLARA Biosciences and Caliper Technologies. The patterns that appeared from the calculations of their exchange data corresponded at large to the expectations, and the findings for other companies, both established ones in mature industries, companies in the biotechnology industry, and direct biochip competitors. Thus, the approach to the estimation and the level of the estimates were judged to be valid. The main problem encountered was the need for a three-year maturity estimate, which could not be matched by the longest options traded on the two comparable companies; namely 6 months. It was found that the volatility term structures[284] seemed to show a tendency to smoothen out and stabilize as the maturities increased. For the longest short-term maturities of regular options and in particular for the long-term maturities of the LEAPS options, the implied volatilities appeared very stable.

Therefore, the estimates on implied volatilities that will be carried forward in the paper are the ones identified in figure 6.4. The estimates are the exact at-the-money values found for the January 2001 options with a 6-month maturity. For Caliper Technologies the implied volatility was 144.6% and for ACLARA Biosciences it was 120.6%. For the final estimate on the implied volatility, a weighted average of the two companies will be constructed[285]. Since, there is no reason for assigning more weight to one, than the other, this becomes a simple average of the two implied volatilities. Therefore, the implied volatility identified through the analysis is: (144.6% + 120.6%) / 2 = 132.6%.

6.9 Historical Stock Data

The use of historical stock data to estimate the volatility is rather straightforward. The volatility is as previously mentioned the standard deviation on returns. To calculate this, the variance is calculated, and the standard deviation is hereafter known to be the square root of the variance. The formula for the variance (abbr. VAR) as known from fundamental mathematics is shown below:

$$ VAR = \frac{n\sum x^2 - (\sum x)^2}{n(n-1)} $$

'n' is the number of observations and 'x' is the continuously compounded return, i.e. the change in value from observation to observation, e.g. not necessarily annualized unless data have been chosen only to be represented on a yearly basis[286].

A rule of thumb, when choosing the historical period analyzed is that it should equal the project duration[287], over even exceed it if possible[288]. The line of reasoning behind this is the fact that the higher the number of data points are, the more accurate the estimate will be, and that by matching the historical period with the future project duration, the infrequent, but significant periodical effects that are likely to influence the underlying asset over the time horizon in question will be captured. Speaking against the use of long time horizons is the fact that older data might not be relevant for future projections, since volatility changes over time. Hull (1997) suggests a compromise of 90-180 days based on daily data[289].

In this analysis, the choice of historical period is made by the availability of data. As has been mentioned, the stocks of the two comparable companies have only been traded for respectively four and seven months. Thus, the analysis is somewhat capable of following the suggested compromise of 90-180 days by incorporating all data available. Estimates of the most recent 3-month and 6-month periods will be presented and commented on in order to investigate the analysis' sensitivity to the choice of historical period. Bridging the recommendations to use time periods equivalent to the project duration, while refraining from using time periods that go back more than half a year, 6-month estimates are considered the most appropriate in this analysis. Stock data on two biotechnology industry indices will also be included in the analysis. These are included to investigate the impact that the observed disparate periods have on the estimation of volatilities.

Before the data are put into the calculation, they need to be cleaned for extreme observations. First of all, dividend payouts need to be considered. When stock data are analyzed for the variance on returns, this is done to find the volatility of the underlying asset. Since dividend payouts are liquidation of some of the underlying asset's value, and does not reflect a change in the actual value of the underlying asset, they can be considered irrelevant for volatility analysis. Therefore, the drop in the stock price that dividend payouts cause due to the liquidation of value, should not be included in the calculation of the variance on returns. This can be avoided simply by taking out the days of dividend payouts, the so-called ex-dividend dates[290, 291]. Though, the formula for calculating the variance on returns could be adapted to incorporate dividends, taking them out of the analysis is the recommended approach[292]. Since the two comparable companies have not paid any dividends yet, this is not a problem for their estimates. For the benchmark companies, the ex-dividend days have been taking out, whereas corrections could not be done for the biotechnology indices, due to their compounded nature, making a such maneuver extremely difficult.

Since all events from the historical period that influence the returns, which are unlikely to be reoccurring in the future time horizon observed, should be excluded, the IPO days have also been taken out. These days have an opening price that is not determined by the market, and the stock price might change quite dramatically as the market responds to the new stock and the price it is offered at, and the stock's price level is subsequently set. Therefore, the IPO days have been taken out for ACLARA and Caliper[293].

The time unit of the volatility estimate that is calculated depends on the intervals between the data points. In the analysis daily data are used. Therefore, the volatility estimate is daily too.

Since the time unit of the real option valuation is yearly, the estimate is converted by multiplication to a yearly level. A question that has been debated in the academic field is whether trading days or adjusted calendar days should be used to convert to yearly estimates[294]. This appears to be more of a principal and conceptual discussion, than a matter that has a strong impact on the end-result. Following, the recommendations of Hull (1997), trading days will be used in this paper[295]. Though an average of 252 trading days have been suggested, here the exact number of trading days observed for each year in the data set will be used.

Table 6.13 Volatility Estimates for Comparable Companies

	Volatility 3-month estimate (April 20 - July 19)	Volatility 6-month estimate (January 20 - July 19)	Volatility full period traded	Full period length in trading days
ACLARA	129%	n/a	154%	82
Caliper	150%	174%	170%	148

Source: www.nasdaq.com and own calculations. Volatility as standard deviation on returns based on historical stock price data, converted to yearly estimates.

In order to get an overview of the stock price developments behind the volatility estimates, the stock prices are illustrated graphically.

Figure 6.9 Stock Price Developments for Comparable Companies 1999-2000

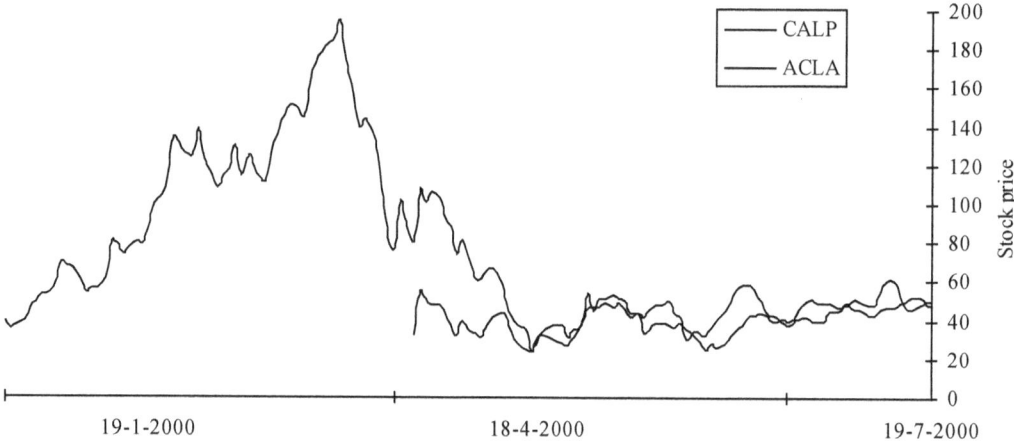

Source: Own construction, based on www.nasdaq.com.

From the graphs it appears that the development of Caliper's stock price has been more volatile than ACLARA's, because of the first half of the observed period, prior to ACLARA's IPO on March 21. If the full-period volatility estimate of Caliper, i.e. seven months is compared with the full-period estimate of ACLARA, equal to four months, Caliper's is 16 percentage points higher than ACLARA. It is tempting to interpret this difference, as the graphically depicted strong rise and fall of the stock price in the two months up to April 18, 2000, especially since the volatility of Caliper in the three months prior to the 3-month estimate (January 20- April 19) can be calculated to 194%.

Yet, the difference is even more outspoken when the two companies' most recent 3-month estimates in the period up to July 19 are compared. Here Caliper is at 150% and ACLARA at 129%, which corresponds to a difference in percentage points of 21. Therefore, the difference in the estimates of the two companies do not seem to be decreased by a shorter time horizon of the comparison, even though the apparently volatile period from mid-March to mid-April, where data is available for both companies, have been left out.

However, by setting the period shorter at the most recent three months and thus leaving out of the calculation the large changes observed prior to April 18, the level of the estimates becomes lower than the full-period estimates. The question then is whether the estimates should be taken for the comparable three months periods for both companies, or the 6-month estimate should be taken for Caliper and the shorter full-period estimate of four months for ACLARA. The choice basically depends on which level is considered the appropriate, and how important identical time periods and the length of the time periods are.

At the end, when the analysis has to come up with one estimate to be carried forward in the paper, the time intervals have to be identical, if the estimates of the two companies are to be given equal weight. Therefore, everything else being equal, the preferable solution would be identical time periods. Still, in terms of time period length, the preceding theoretical discussion set six months as the most appropriate. Before deciding whether to include the 6-month estimate for Caliper, along with a shorter time period for ACLARA, and potentially adjusting the weights of the two companies in the analysis, the industry's development in the same period will be analyzed. This is done to test whether Caliper's notably higher 6-month estimate is specific to the company, or the industry has been through the same development, with a difference in the level of volatilities between the most recent three months and the last half a year. For this purpose two biotechnology indices will be analyzed. Industry indices have been chosen in order to investigate the market risk in isolation, since - as it will be remembered from section 5.3.2 - the company-specific private risks have been diversified away in indices. The preferred industry index would have been one for the biochip industry, but this is not available. Therefore, biotechnology indices have been chosen. In the following, the two indices will be indexed for the last three years, and volatility estimates corresponding to the time horizon of the SMB real option and the comparable companies will be calculated and presented. The indices are the BTK Index which consists of 17 biotechnology companies listed at AMEX, and the IXBT Index which is NASDAQ's biotechnology index. It consists of more than 100 biotechnology companies.

Figure 6.10 Indexed Stock Price Development for Two Biotechnology Indices 1997-2000

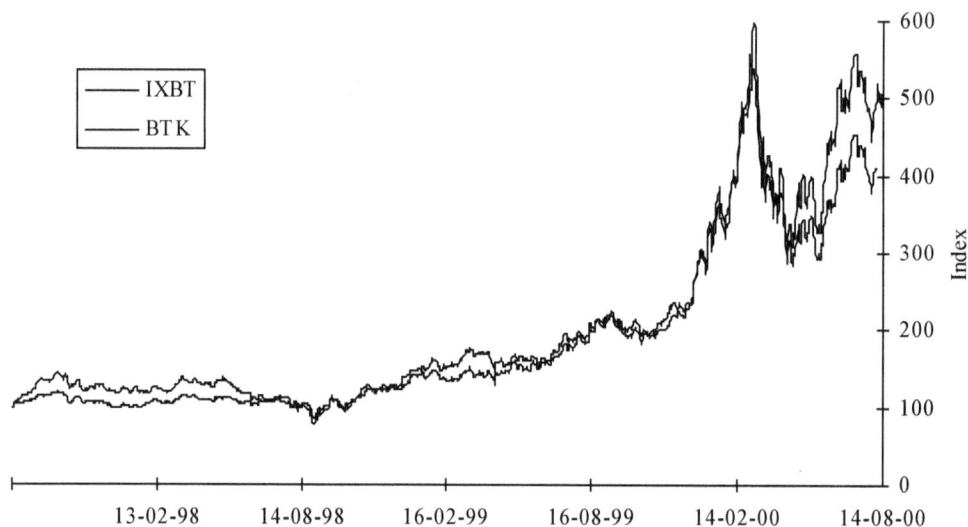

Source: Own calculations, based on www.nasdaq.com. Index 100 = August 15, 1997.

From the indexed stock prices for the last three years, it appears that the development since the year-end of 1999 has been more volatile than the years before. But as can be seen from the table, this does not translate into that big an increase in the numerical values shown in the table below. From the graph on Caliper in figure 6.9, the same observation was made, namely that an apparently volatile development as seen graphically did not make that big a difference in the numerical values. This reason is that the returns, which the volatility calculation is based on, are daily returns. Since it means little for the calculation of the standard deviation, as opposed to the graphical presentation, whether the change day after day is predominantly upwards or downwards, the long-term trends that make a visual impression of high volatility might in reality represent equal daily changes, but primarily in one direction.

Table 6.14 Volatility Estimates for Biotechnology Indices

	3-month	6-month	1 year	1½ years	2 years	2½ years	3 years
IXBT	51%	68%	56%	50%	47%	43%	40%
BTK	63%	79%	64%	56%	53%	50%	47%

Source: Own calculations, based on www.nasdaq.com.

From the analysis of the biotechnology indices, it can be seen that the level of the 6-month estimates is notably higher than the most recent three months and the level of the longer time periods. Thus, it appears reasonable to assume that ACLARA most likely would have gone through the same as the industry and Caliper, before March 2000. The extreme rise and fall of the stock prices in the first months of 2000 that Caliper went through along with the industry cannot be considered an isolated event though, when the development of the last three months since May 2000 is looked at. Consequently, there is nothing in the illustrated development to indicate that the developments in the early months of 2000 could not happen again, and that they should consequently be excluded from the volatility estimate of Caliper by only looking at

128

the time period after April 20. In conclusion, the estimate on the volatility based on historical data for Caliper will be taken from the six months time period, and for ACLARA for the longest period available, i.e. four months.

Like in the estimation of the implied volatility figure to carry forward in the analysis, a weighted average will be constructed. But as earlier touched upon, the short time period available for ACLARA appears to be a disadvantage, since, although turbulent, the months before ACLARA's IPO - in particular January to mid-March 2000 - cannot be ignored as abnormal, as concluded from the analysis of the biotechnology industry as a whole. Therefore, the estimate of ACLARA's volatility from the historical stock data at 154% will only enter into the one final figure with one third. Consequently, the estimate for Caliper at 174% will be two-thirds. The final estimate on volatility to be carried forward from this analysis of historical stock data thus becomes 167%.

6.10 Estimate on Volatility

The preceding analysis resulted in two different estimates on the volatility that is to be applied to the real option of SMB. The first was found by extracting the so-called implied volatility from the traded options on the stocks on the comparable companies. The estimate identified this way was 132.6%. The second estimate was found through analysis of the historical stock prices, as the standard deviation on the returns on the stock of the comparable companies. This estimate amounted to 167%.

Surprisingly, the implied volatilities were lower than the historical stock data volatilities. This was not only the case for the comparable companies, but for the majority of the companies investigated in the analysis. This finding was surprising, since some sort of brokerage or safety margin for the market makers could be expected to increase the implied volatilities on the options offered, as compared to the historical volatility that the analysis of the historical stock prices gives. In this case, it should be kept in mind that the option prices analyzed even were the ask prices.

Figure 6.11 Comparison of Historical Stock Data Volatilities and Implied Volatilities

Figure 6.11a

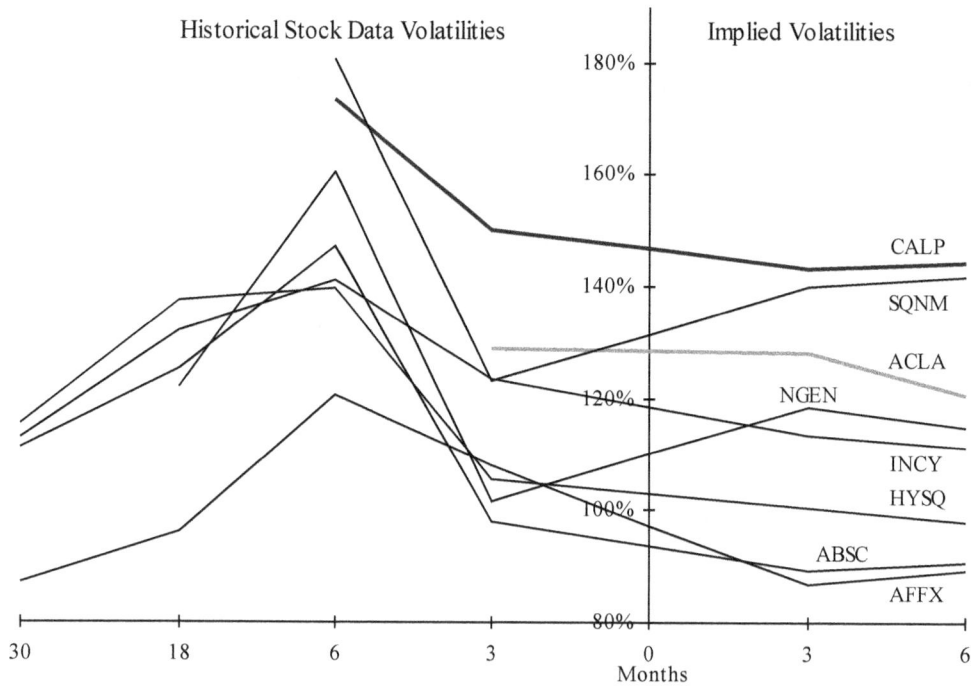

Figure 6.11b

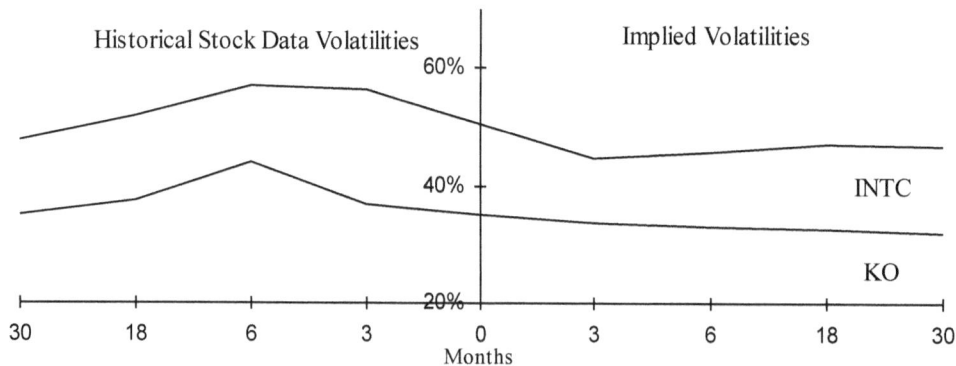

Source: www.nasdaq.com and own calculations. Unification of data presented in preceding analysis.

The above figures depict on the one side, the implied volatilities calculated for the options on the time horizons into the future, and on the other side, the volatilities identified through analysis of the time periods before the date of the analysis[296]. The first figure shows that the expectations of the market is for a lower volatility in the 6-month period to come, than was the volatility in the preceding 6-month period. If a trend is to be spotted, it is that the level of the implied volatilities are similar to the volatilities calculated on the longer historic periods.

Though these also include the last 6 months, their weight in the estimate is obviously only partial. Though not as clear, the same trend can be seen at a smaller scale in the second figure.

From this, it must be concluded that the market makers offering the options do not expect as high a level of volatilities in the immediate future, as was observed in the last 6 months, but rather expect the historical level from before the 6 months.

The theoretical literature is rather divided and indecisive on the question of which is the better source for estimating volatilities. The research that has compared historical stock data volatilities with implied volatilities in terms of preciseness evaluated ex-post shows mixed results. Some research says that one is the better, while other research says the opposite[297].

Nevertheless, given the well-accepted assumption of a semi-efficient market, all historic information must be incorporated in the market estimates. In other words, it must be assumed that the price setters, among other things, base their estimates on historical developments. Hence, the lower implied volatilities must be seen as an expression of the market expectations, saying that the development of the last 6 months will not repeat itself within the following 6 months. These expectations are in accordance with the notion that the continuos decrease in stock prices on NASDAQ listed stocks in the month after April 14, 2000 - that in particular hit the so-called new economy stocks - in particular Internet stocks, but also the biotechnology stocks - was merely a correction that does not reflect a radical change in the business conditions of the stocks listed on NASDAQ.

Still, in this paper no 'preference' over estimates based on historical data is given to the implied volatilities in terms of explanatory value, though the latter have the appealing feature of attempting to forecast the future. The two approaches are attributed equal importance, and the concluding estimate of volatility that will be taken from the analysis and applied to the real option, will be a simple average of the two estimates, following the line of thought that perceives the best estimate to come from a mix of approaches[298]. Thus, the volatility estimate becomes (132.6% + 167%) / 2 equaling 150%.

6.11 Concluding Remarks on the Estimation of Numerical Inputs

This chapter has established the quantitative inputs to the variables of the formula for the valuation to come. Given the configuration and the choice of mathematical solution in the chapter preceding it, it was rather straightforward to estimate the numerical inputs. The two most problematic variables were the expected cash flows, S_0 and the volatility, σ. The estimation of S_0 touched the very core of the uncertainty related to valuation, which is, based on projections of the future cash flows, to incorporate the value-generating potential in the valuation estimate. On the other hand, the estimation of volatility was primarily made difficult, when it came to relating its abstract theoretical content with practical and quantitative measures. The following chapter will use the numerical inputs to conduct the valuation itself. After this is done, the chapter will go on to evaluate the sensitivity of the valuation by looking into the precision and uncertainty related to the estimation of the numerical inputs to each of the variables. Thus, the final evaluation of the findings of this chapter will be done in the light of the valuation, and the variables' respective impact on the valuation estimate.

7. Valuation

After having operationalized and estimated the elements of the real option in details, this chapter presents the calculation, which ends up in the valuation estimate. In the beginning of the chapter the value of SMB as an investment project is appraised. Following this, a sensitivity analysis is carried out on the numerical inputs of the variables, and their impact on the valuation. The sensitivity analysis reveals among other things that the present value of expected cash flows, S_0 is a problematic variable to estimate in this valuation.

Hence, an alternative use of the formula is proposed, in which S_0 is made into the dependent variable, and C_0, which is usually the value of the option that has to be paid upfront, is perceived as the initial investment undertaken - i.e. the 'development costs' in the terminology of section 6.2 - before the potential investment at the time of decision, E_x. This way, S_0 depicts the minimum that the present value of expected cash flows must be forecasted to hold, if initiation of the investment project is to be considered feasible. This may be an easier task for management, who presumably is used to think in terms of present value of expectable cash flows, and the market shares required to capture these cash flows.

The chapter ends with a brief outline of the findings from the valuation. The overall conclusion on the application and applicability of real option valuation is presented chapter 8 containing a critique of the entire quantitative application of the real option framework; i.e. the financial perspective on real options.

7.1 Processing the Numerical Inputs

With the configuration identified in chapter 5 and the numerical inputs estimated in chapter 6, the value of SMB as an investment project as of March 2000 can be calculated. Especially, the estimated cash flows of table 6.2. are relevant for illustrating the option profile in terms of cash flows. It was decided in the configuration to use Black & Scholes' option pricing formula, which was presented in chapter 4.

Figure 7.1 Estimated Nominal Cash Flows

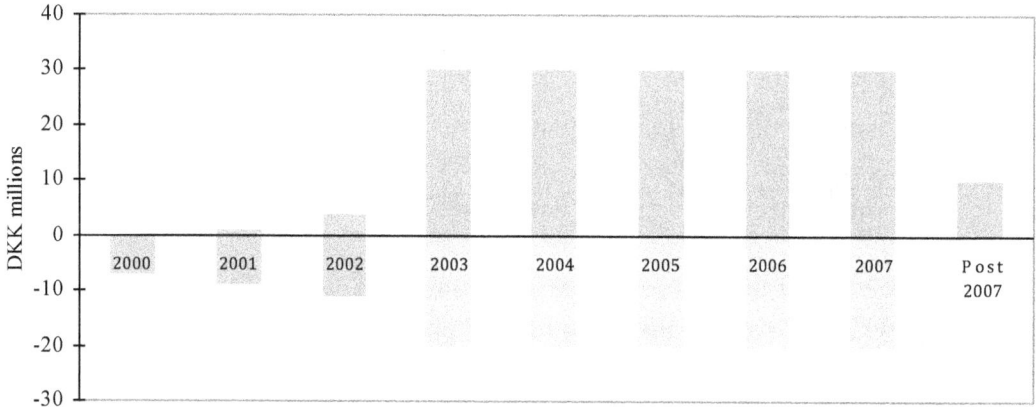

Source: Table 6.2. Post 2007 is the level of yearly net income in the shape of net cash flows from year 2008 and onwards.

As outlined in chapter 6, the required investment, E_x of DKK 100 million is for illustrative purposes distributed over five years, and consists of the light gray columns. The sum of all the dark gray columns enters into one estimate of the expected cash flows, S_0. The above figures are nominal, undiscounted values. The consolidation of the cash flows for the option calculation is shown graphically below in the same colors.

Figure 7.2 Estimated Discounted Cash Flows

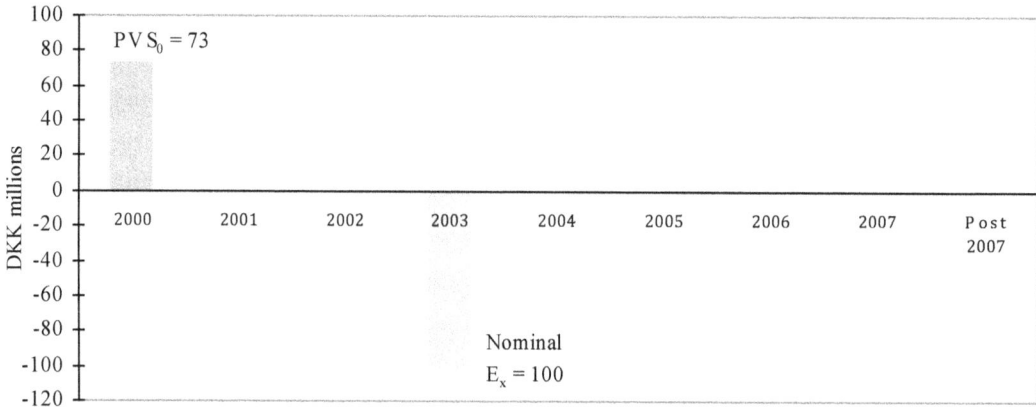

Source: Table 6.6. PV S_0 is the present value of the accumulated expected cash flows, including the continuing value after year 2007.

With the above data in hand, it is fairly easy to calculate the net present value of SMB following the Discounted Cash Flow method. The only thing left to include into the estimate of S_0 is E_x, which has so far been kept separated from S_0 in order to prepare for the option calculation. This is done by discounting the nominal value of E_x back to the year 2000 at the discount rate of WACC, and subtracting this from S_0. In so doing, one arrives at an estimated

DCF NPV of **DKK 9 millions**, as of March 2000. According to this estimate, the investment project is worthwhile, tipping slightly to the positive side.

The data put forward in NRC's strategic plan facilitated the calculation of a simple DCF method. In contrast, a Decision Tree Analysis was not enabled. An attempt to link the strategic alternatives with specific market payoffs had not been undertaken in the business map, and the issue was not further pursued, due to the requirement of detailed scenarios. This was considered too resource-demanding in terms of interview time required to establish it in cooperation with NRC, and too problematic with regard to establishing it based on own assumptions.

For the option calculation, the inputs identified are presented below.

Table 7.1 Estimated Numerical Inputs

S_0	E_x	σ	t	r_f
DKK 73 m	DKK 100 m	150%	3.0	5.37% p.a.

Source: Chapter 6 on numerical inputs. The volatility (σ) is measured annually, the duration (t) in years, and the risk-free interest rate (r_f) per year. S_0 and E_x in DKK millions.

Inserting the estimated numerical inputs into the option pricing formula, the value of SMB as of March 2000 is **DKK 58 millions**. This estimate is sometimes labeled the Expanded Net Present Value (abbr. ENPV). The estimate is clearly a recommendation to initiate the project.

The difference between the DCF valuation (abbr. DCF
NPV) and the real option valuation (abbr. ENPV) is striking, with the latter being decisively in favor, as to whether the investment project should be undertaken. The difference between the estimates is labeled the real option value, since the difference in value is basically the added value of integrating real options in the valuation. The difference of DKK 49 millions between the estimates has two components as illustrated below.

Figure 7.3 Real Option Value; The Difference between Real Option Valuation and DCF Valuation

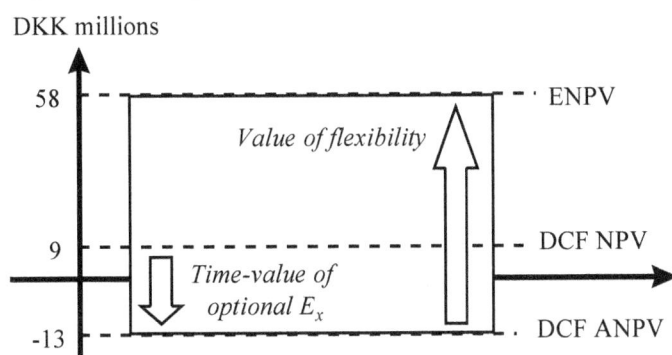

Source: Own construction.

First of all, the required investment, E_x was discounted at the discount factor WACC in the DCF valuation. One of the things the real option valuation does is to discount E_x at the risk-free interest rate, because the investment is optional. In other words, even in the DCF approach, management would be capable of abandoning the project before year 2003's large discretionary investment. Management would probably consider doing so, if the developments were against the project. Since management is not committed completely to do so by initiating the project, this investment is less risky before the time of commitment. Therefore, the DCF NPV could be adjusted to take this particular aspect into account by discounting E_x at the risk-free interest rate. This could be labeled the DCF Adjusted NPV (abbr. DCF ANPV) and amounts to **DKK - 13 millions**. This minor adjustment alone makes the investment project appear unfeasible by simply keeping the option to abandon open, yet without adjusting the contingent cash flows after the year 2003 accordingly.

Thereby, additionally DKK 22 millions are added to the difference that the flexibility value accounts for by itself. The value-added by the flexibility therefore amounts to DKK 71 millions, which is the difference between the positive DKK 58 millions and the negative DKK 13 millions. This can be explained by a different discount factor, which applies a different time-value of money for the required investment at the time of decision, E_x. It reflects the fact that the opportunity costs for optional investments should be lower, since the risk does not enter until the investment has been done. In other words, the costs of E_x should not be discounted and devaluated as much, as they were in the pure DCF approach (DCF NPV).

Summing up, the sheer flexibility value incorporated in the real option valuation is even higher than the difference between the DCF NPV and the ENPV, since the real option valuation discounts the required investment at the time of decision differently.

The composition of the estimate was illustrated in the figure above.

7.2 Sensitivity Analysis

As is evident from the preceding chapter on the estimation of numerical inputs, some of the variables could not be identified precisely, and a number of simplifying assumptions had to be made. Therefore, this section is devoted to recapturing the uncertainty on the estimation of each variable, and its impact on the valuation. An error margin will be identified for each variable and the consequences calculated individually. Before this is done, a table from chapter 4 on the directional impact of changes will be presented again.

In the following table, the effect on the value of the option (C_0) of an increase in the other factors of the formula is depicted:

Table 7.2 Effects of Increases in Variables for the Option Value

An increase in ... :	S_0	E_x	σ^2	t	r_f
... has this effect on C_0:	↑	↓	↑	↑	↑

Source: Own construction, based on Black & Scholes (1973) p. 644, Trigeorgis (1996) pp. 82, 91-92 and Levy & Sarnat (1994) p. 636. Identical with table 4.1.

136

As was explained earlier, the maturity (t) is only present in the formula multiplied with the interest rate (r_f) and the volatility as a variance (σ^2). Therefore, equal percentage increases in maturity, interest rate, and volatility (σ^2) have the same effect on the value of the option (C_0)[299].

The uncertainty on the variable S_0 and the range of values this may take is substantial. The estimation of the incoming cash flows generated from an investment is probably the crux of the matter for all valuation-related projections. The fact that this is an R&D investment only makes matters more difficult. The estimation of this variable was the most arbitrary. Still it should be kept in mind that it was only intended to be an average value[300], around which the variable volatility takes into account the variation, which is substantial in this case at 150%. Another mitigating circumstance is the fact that the estimation hurdle is not a question of sales projections alone or costs projections alone, but related to the level of profits that can be expected. Anyway, this is the least valid numerical input on any of the variables. Since it is an average and the uncertainty is depicted in the volatility, it makes little sense to look at the error margin of this variable, exactly because the uncertainty is incorporated in the shape of the volatility to a wide extent.

The required investment at the time of decision, E_x is rather predictable, given the short time horizon. Since this investment was used to project the sales, and thus the net income, the proportions can be assumed to reasonable. An error margin of a ± 20 % will be used for sensitivity calculations. The calculation relies on the assumption that the level of sales generated is unchanged within the error margin.

Table 7.3 Impact of Change in the Required Level of Investment within the Error Margin

E_x	80	100	120
C_0	59	58	56
Change in C_0 in percentage	+3%		-2%

Source: Own calculations. Figures on C_0 in DKK millions.

As can be seen, the impact of a change in E_x is rather insignificant.

E_x was used as a basis for forecasting net income by applying a sales-to-costs ratio from a comparable industry. It was assumed that the sales-to-costs ratio was 3:2. This was an optimistic estimate since the level inarguably is rather high. If the sales-to-costs ratio proves to be 5:4, this is equal to a fall in profit margin from 33% to 20% on revenues. This decrease of 13 percentage points in profit margin, equal to 40% fall in profit margin, leads to a valuation estimate of DKK 39 millions, corresponding to a decrease of 33% in real option value.

The volatility estimates identified in chapter 6 for the two comparable companies Caliper and ACLARA spanned volatility values from 121% for ACLARA estimated as implied volatility, to 174% for Caliper based on historical stock data analysis.

Table 7.4 Impact of Change in the Volatility within the Error Margin

Volatility (σ)	121%	150%	174%
Error margin in percentage	-19%	-	+16%
C_0	50	58	63
Change in C_0 in percentage	-14%	-	+8%

Source: Own calculations. Figures on C_0 in DKK millions. Volatility as standard deviation.

Evidently, the error margin encountered in the estimation is quite significant, and so is its impact on the valuation.

Though it was mentioned that equal, percentage increases in project duration (t), risk-free interest rate (r_f), and volatility (σ^2) have equal impacts on the valuation, this is only technically in terms of the calculation with the option pricing formula. Increases in e.g. project duration (t) in fact have other more practical implications. An increase in project duration will in reality add to the prior-to-decision costs ('development costs'), and implies foregone profits and vice versa for decreases in project duration, of course. Both of these influence S_0 in rather intertwined and unpredictable ways, which are beyond the scope of the paper.

The only change in project duration that will be calculated in this sensitivity analysis is an isolated change, ceteris paribus. The likelihood that the targeted research results will be achieved within the time horizon, t is captured by the volatility, which depicts the stochastic process of the investment project, and thus its chance of success. Therefore, in this view, the question of whether the forecasted time horizon is reasonable is only related to whether the uncertainty regarding proof of concept can be resolved within the project duration. Since, the forecasted time horizon is only three years, it is reasonable to assume that this target can be achieved, approximately on the stipulated time. Therefore, the sensitivity analysis will only calculate on an error margin of ± 6 months, equal to ± 16.6 %[301]. Hereby is not meant that the desired research results have necessarily been achieved, but rather that the target of resolving the uncertainty has been met. This may of course reveal that the results cannot be achieved.

Table 7.5 Impact of Change in the Project Duration within the Error Margin

Project duration	2½ years	3 years	3½ years
C_0	54	58	60
Change in C_0 in percentage	-6%	-	+5%

Source: Own calculations. Figures on C_0 in DKK millions.

Paradoxically, the longer the project duration, the higher the value. This is in conflict with the intuitively appealing in completing an R&D project before scheduled, and thus reaping strategic first-mover advantages, minimizing development costs and generating extra revenues by extending the lifetime of the product. The findings are, of course, a result of the logic of the option pricing formula, where longer maturity increases the chances of an upside, as well the potential magnitude of the upside. Nevertheless, as earlier mentioned, it is beyond the scope of the paper to go so far beyond the projections of NRC, as to predict the cost and revenue implications hereof.

Finally, the variable of risk-free interest rate (r_f) must be analyzed. Under the assumption of efficient financial markets, this is the most well-estimated variable, as of a given valuation date. In other words, it cannot be estimated more precisely. Of course, this does not mean that it cannot change. In fact, it does change continuously. Hence, a range from 4% p.a. to 8% p.a. will be considered.

Table 7.6 Impact of Change in the Risk-free Interest Rate within the Error Margin

Risk-free interest rate	4.00%	5.37%	8.00%
C_0	57	58	58
Change in C_0 in percentage	-1%	-	+1%

Source: Own calculations. Figures on C_0 in DKK millions.

As it will be remembered from section 4.2 and 4.3 increases in r_f leads to increases in C_0, because only E_x is discounted in the formula, where S_0 enters into the formula as a present value. For real options, r_f has been used to calculate S_0 too. The results that come from processing S_0 with r_f within the error margin are notably different.

Table 7.7 Composite Impact of Change in the Risk-free Interest Rate within the Error Margin

Risk-free interest rate	4.00%	5.37%	8.00%
S_0	81	73	61
Change in S_0 in percentage	+13%	-	-17%
C_0	65	58	48
Change in C_0 in percentage	-1%	-	+1%

Source: Own calculations. Figures on C_0 and S_0 in DKK millions.

This impact shows even more the critical issue surrounding the estimation of S_0. But as argued there is no better way to estimate the interest rate, than to use the market values. On a side note, the strong impact can be seen as reinforcing the pseudo truth from macro economics that a low level of interest rates leads to a high investment level, which DCF is a strong proponent for.

Ignoring the problems with the present value of the expected cash flows, S_0 for a moment, the variable with the most significant error margin was the volatility. Not just because it had a high relative impact on the valuation, but also because the estimation was more troublesome and imprecise. Therefore, the sensitivity of the estimation will be further looked into. For this purpose, the value estimate of the investment project can be related to the values of the volatility variable. This can be done graphically as in the figure below.

Figure 7.4 Real Option Valuation Estimate depicted against Volatility

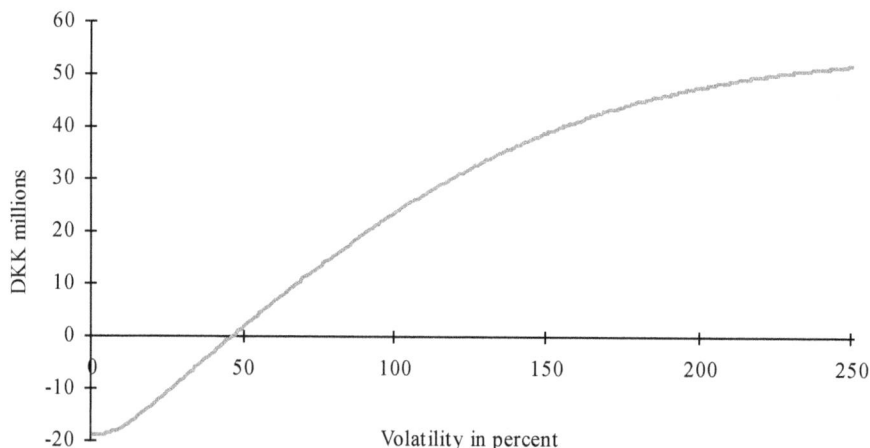

Source: Own construction.

The figure illustrates the value of the investment project compared with the size of the volatility. The 'development costs' up until the time of decision - i.e. sales and costs in the period from 2000 to time of the decision in 2003 - have been subtracted the value of real option. These costs amounts to DKK 19 millions, as present value as of 2000. These costs are subtracted here, because they are considered sunk costs from this perspective, which means that the real option is broken up conceptually from a go / no-go decision point of view. Though, the development costs are included in S_0 in the calculation - the real option itself does not change - the break-up of the real options gives an indication of the overall potential. This means that the investment project will only be considered worthwhile, if the real option valuation with the development costs comes up with estimates beyond these costs.

As can be observed, this is the case for volatility values above 50%. To put this into context, this corresponds to the volatility measured for Intel. In other words, an investment project with this real option profile - apart from the volatility - is only significantly interesting as an investment, when its volatility is higher than Intel.

7.3 Alternative Use of Option Pricing Formula

The biggest problem with this valuation, and I dare say valuations in general, is the difficulty of forecasting the future income-generating potential, i.e. the expected cash flows. If these were known, the exercise would be almost strictly academic, and limited to processing the data according to theories. Nevertheless, this is a fact of life for valuation that cannot be surpassed. However, there is an opportunity to circumvent the problem of having to estimate these directly, inherent in the option pricing formula.

By reversing the approach to the formula, the expected cash flows, S_0 can be seen as the unknown variable. Instead, the value of the option, C_0 is interpreted as the amount that is paid to create the option; i.e. the 'development costs' of section 6.2. In the graphical presentation of the mathematical principles labeled 'The Cone of Uncertainty' in section 2.4 (p. 20) and 4.3 (p.

140

48), the 'development costs' were illustrated as P_0, defined as the investments undertaken prior to the contingent decision. This illustration gives a clear picture of what is focused at in this exercise. By reversing the use of the formula, there is only one unknown variable in the formula, namely S_0. Though, the solution of the formula changes to a numerical one, since S_0 cannot be isolated, this is easily solved through iteration in a spreadsheet[302]. This approach has been proposed as particularly relevant for R&D projects[303].

Through this reversed use, the option value of the investment project today is obviously not found, but instead the present value of the expected cash flows, S_0, which are required to break even. In other words, the minimum current value of the underlying asset required to make the 'purchase' of the option financially viable is estimated. When this is known, it can be evaluated whether the predicted market potential leaves room for activities of this magnitude, and the market share that is needed to achieve this level of sales and profits. For experienced management this should be intuitively appealing. For this paper's application of real option valuation, the advantage is that the quality of the data that are entered into the option pricing formula increases substantially.

The required present value of the expected cash flows, S_0, when processing the numerical inputs this way, becomes DKK 28 millions, or close to half the earlier estimate. Again, it should be emphasized that this is the accumulated net income required in the shape of the present value of expected cash flows, excluding the required investment at the time of the decision. If these cash flows were to be distributed, as was done in the projection that was undertaken earlier the other way around, sufficient cash flows to reach a present value of DKK 28 millions and thus break even would be achieved by the end of 2005, assuming the same sales-to-costs ratio.

The levels of expected cash flows, S_0 that different sizes of 'development costs' - here C_0 - would require to ensure break-even can be illustrated graphically, as done below.

Figure 7.5 Required Level of Expected Cash Flows relative to Level of Development Costs to Ensure Break-even

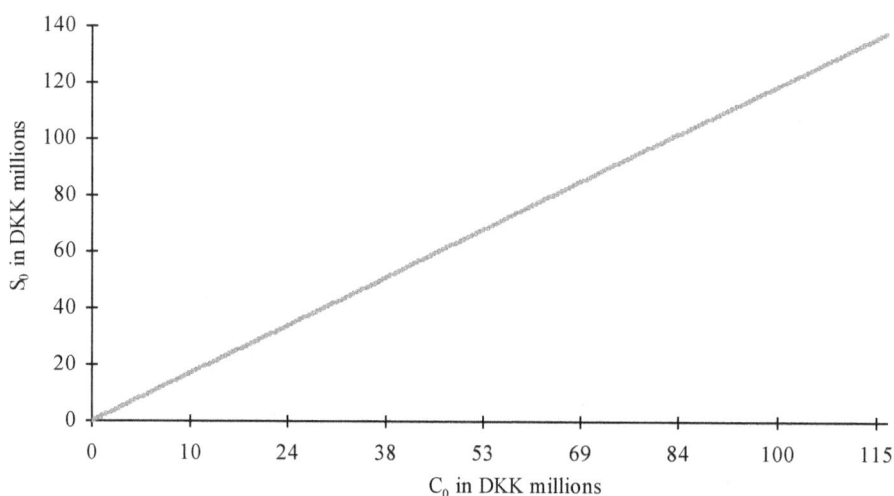

Source: Own construction, based on own calculations. All figures in present value.

From the graph, it can be seen that the relationship between S_0 and C_0 is linear. Furthermore, it can be seen that in order to stay above break-even, S_0 has to be slightly higher than C_0. The required level of S_0 becomes relatively smaller in percentage difference relative to C_0, as C_0 grows. In other words, C_0 and S_0 converge. For C_0 around DKK 10 millions, S_0 has to be 64% higher than C_0. This figure decreases steadily to 18% for C_0 at a level of DKK 120 millions.

7.4 Concluding Remarks on Real Option Valuation

The processing of the numerical inputs in connection with the calculation of a valuation estimate showed that SMB is worth DKK 58 millions in net present value, as a real option. This was DKK 49 millions more than according to the DCF approach, which appraised SMB at DKK 9 millions. Though both approaches were in favor of initiating the investment project, the real option approach was most clearly so. In the face of scarce resources on behalf of NKT and NRC, the investment project might hypothetically have been discarded for investment projects with higher net present values according to the DCF approach, but lower NPVs according to the real option approach, if investment projects were only evaluated using the DCF method without taking into account the option value. The DTA method was not carried out, due to lack of empirical data in the business map of SMB and NRC resources available.

The sensitivity analysis showed that the two most problematic inputs were the present value of the expected cash flows, S_0 and the volatility, σ. Though the uncertainties for S_0 were somewhat justified, as S_0 must only depict an average value, whose variation the volatility captures, the error margin was considered too intangible for further treatment and consequently not calculated. The error margin for the volatility was known from the analysis to range from -19% to +16% leading to a slightly lower impact on the valuation estimate of respectively 14% to +8%. A graphical presentation of various sizes of volatility plotted against the corresponding calculated values of the investment project revealed that for the investment project to break-even in terms of real option valuation, given the rest of the numerical inputs - particularly the investment outlays - the volatility had to be higher than approximately 50%. For comparative purposes, this reflects a level of uncertainty equal to that of Intel.

Due to the difficulties related to the estimation of S_0, an alternative use of the option pricing formula was undertaken at the end of the chapter. This transferred S_0 from an independent variable to the dependent variable, while C_0 in this context is interpreted as an independent variable - usually the dependent variable - consisting of the 'development costs' before the contingent decision is to be made; i.e. before the option is to be exercised at the time of decision. This approach gives valuable information on the minimum net present value that S_0 must hold for the investment project to break-even. This amounts to DKK 28 millions, which is approximately one third of the actually estimated amount for S_0. If the sales generated are distributed according to the forecasts of the valuation with the same sales-to-costs ratio, the cash flows generated up until 2005 would be sufficient to break-even.

In the next chapter, the application and the applicability of real option valuation to the case of the paper is concluded upon.

8. Conclusions

The conclusions are divided in two. The first part concludes on the financial perspective side of the gap in the shape of the real option valuation. This part focuses on the applicability. The conclusions herein are subsequently used in the conclusions on the real option framework's capacity for bridging the gap between financial theory and strategic theory.

8.1 Conclusions on the Financial Perspective

A great number of aspects has to be considered when conducting a real option valuation. Compared with the conventional Discounted Cash Flow method, the number and complexity of the variables are higher. Of course, the preceding analysis has been more elaborate on the theoretical presentation of the theoretical framework and the operationalization, than need be for the DCF approach, where a higher degree of background knowledge can be anticipated, and the theoretical and empirical foundation is more well-grounded through its widespread use. Though, this familiarity obviously lends credibility to the practical application in the perception of the users, it is equally obvious that the DCF approach has its shortcomings, and that it may very well be worthwhile to apply the real option approach in a number of cases. Precisely, the lack of familiarity with real option valuation may be one of the main obstacles for a broader use. The dissemination of the necessary background knowledge is made difficult by the complexity of the framework. Therefore, it is in place that the use of real option valuation is initially evaluated compared with conventional valuation techniques such as DCF.

8.1.1 Similarities and Distinctive Features vis-à-vis Conventional Valuation Techniques

The first step in the application of the financial perspective on real options was to place it theoretically. It was shown that real option valuation is more of a complementary approach to conventional valuation techniques, than a radical break with the existing theories and approaches to valuation. As such, real option valuation is a method within the prevalent NPV approach to valuation.

The approach to determining the quantitative impact of uncertainty - respectively risk and volatility - is also similar between DCF and real option valuation in the sense that both aims at estimating the value of the investment as if the assets in question were traded; i.e. detached from individual preferences. Theoretically, the real option approach could identify this without looking to the market - e.g. through historical data on comparable, in-house projects or managerial judgment, whereas the DCF approach's use of beta[304] specifically links the valuation to the expected returns on the market portfolio. Practically, as was seen in this analysis, the two approaches rely on the identification of 'twin assets' in the shape of comparable companies to determine the value as if the investments were traded. Consequently, the real option approach does not deviate from conventional approaches to appraising investments by looking at a constructed market price, and doing this through identification of comparables. The tradability assumed this way is parallel to one of the main assumptions behind the Black & Scholes formula, namely that the underlying asset - for financial options

144

frequently stocks - can be sold at any time with no transaction costs. Thus, it seems conceptually reasonable to appraise the value of the investment on an 'as if' basis with regard to tradability and the use of comparables.

The theoretical framework behind real options itself is based on elegant mathematical principles, which are internally consistent. The primary challenge to the theoretical consistency is posed by its relations to the empirical field; i.e. in the application of the principles in the corporate setting. As explained, real option valuation depends on the existence and identification of at least one contingent decision. Consequentially, it captures flexibility value in the contingent decision that conventional valuation techniques do not. This shift denotes the most characteristic additional feature of real option valuation compared with other NPV methods, namely the treatment of uncertainty as holding both upside and downside potential in *lieu* of treating it entirely as value-decreasing.

Furthermore, the more subtle modeling of the dispersion of potential outcomes has its advantages over DCF and DTA in terms of very dynamic uncertainty profiles. On the other hand, the dependence on a contingent decision and the complexities of the framework limit its use to somewhat homogenous investment projects with well-defined time spans, thus effectively delimiting its applicability from valuation at the company level.

8.1.2 The Reality of the Business Case Interpreted as a Real Option

The unit of analysis was chosen for its anticipated suitability, and it can be speculated whether the valuation had succeeded equally well, if a less suitable focus had been investigated. The translation of the fundamental, theoretical principles from financial options into the corporate setting of real options was remarkably smooth operationally. As it was explained, the configuration of the reality of the business case into a real option may be the most important challenge in the application of real option valuation. But with the option pricing techniques developed, the extent of complexities that can be incorporated is almost exclusively limited by one's mathematics and statistics skills. Though, it was argued that the optimal level of accuracy and complexity that should be sought after in the configuration may not be the most detailed, the real option approach to valuation was explained to hold the promised potential with regard to the development of mathematical solutions to a wide range of real options.

The characteristic feature of the real option framework is the flexibility to shape an investment project through the course of the project, as the future unfolds, by exercising active management. Clearly, this is not remote to the activity of strategic planning, where contingencies are likely to be incorporated in strategies on investments under uncertainty. The integration of optional features was seen in NRC's explicit strategy on SMB. Here strategic options had been identified *without* any intentions to use these in a real option analysis.

Still, the reality of the business strategy of SMB did deviate from the real option configured in some aspects. The real option configured in the business case was a simple option to abandon a research project in case developments over a three-year time horizon turned against it. As was argued the configuration was kept simple for reasons of data availability, the nature of the data, the similarity between the two distinguishable option-containing technologies, and an overall weighing of simplicity versus complexity. A major obstacle to introducing more detail into the analysis was the meaninglessness of dividing some of the estimates. These were all reasons for not pursuing looser estimates from the case company in an attempt to sophisticate the analysis by further dividing the estimates.

For the operationalization and the valuation, the configuration had the effect that most of the projected cash flows were coupled into the estimate of S_0, with only E_x standing out. It could be argued that some of these cash flows could have been split up, since they differ in time horizon, and thus are optional to different extents. This is a fair critique, if all flexibilities were to be evaluated, but nevertheless it may be the most important point to simplify in the application of the real option approach. As was discussed above, it is simply an unfeasible and almost impossible ambition to attempt to incorporate all subtleties into the valuation and thus the configuration. The crux of the matter is to distinguish between discretionary and non-discretionary spending, or the spending which is routine versus extraordinary[305]. The extraordinary spending is basically determined by looking at the size of the cash flows. The motivation for the distinction in the preceding analysis, and the corresponding coupling of cash flows, is easily grasped, if one looks at the figures of section 7.1, which illustrate the cash flows, where E_x stands out.

The critique of the configuration has so far defended a simplification compared with the ideal, but unachievable incorporation of all nuances. If the perspective is turned, the simplification nevertheless captures the value of significant degrees of flexibility.

The diminishing option-value effect[306] of adding additional options into the configuration was an important reason for not enhancing the complexity of the configuration. Especially in the case of SMB, where there is a strong correlation between the two technologies which contain potentially, alternative options, little extra value could presumably be identified by choosing one of the more complicated compound or multiple options discussed in section 4.3.1.

8.1.3 The Quality of the Numerical Inputs

The estimation of the numerical inputs was rather straightforward once the mathematical solution had been determined. At the same time, some variables were difficult to satisfactorily estimate, due to their character.

The sensitivity analysis of the preceding chapter has already somewhat anticipated the critique of the numerical inputs. The variables E_x (required investment at the time of decision), r_f (risk-free interest rate), and t (project duration) were rather straightforward to estimate within the given constraints at the time of the valuation. Conceptually, the estimates provide reasonable, numerical inputs, for which better estimates are simply not at hand, before the fact. Therefore, the main critique of these three variables lies in their ex-ante nature, which cannot be said to be more problematic, than the activity of forecasting in general; e.g. in comparison with the DCF approach.

The variable containing the present value of the expected cash flows, S_0 was seen in isolation the most dubiously estimated. Conceptually, the variable is obviously relevant and the content clearly outlined. The ability to generate future cash flows is simply the corner stone of valuation. Still, it is by nature difficult to predict, which is basically a fact of life for NPV valuation techniques.

The estimate from the analysis could have been more sophisticated, by taking into account more aspects. Yet, the level of detail does not ensure a better aggregated estimate; it may even induce more degrees of uncertainty. The main line of reasoning behind the estimate was that the investment would be profitable, and that the profitability corresponded to the level of activity estimated. The profitability estimate was taken from foundry production of microchips, and the activity level from the activity level of a similar investment in optical chip production, made in another NKT company. Given the fact that the decision to initiate production is made at a point in time, when the commercial consequences can be more precisely anticipated, it is reasonable to assume that the investment will indeed be profitable, if undertaken. But regardless of the reliability of the proxies used, this is the most uncertain variable.

Therefore, it was shown that through an alternative use of the option pricing formula, this variable could be altered from being an independent variable to becoming the dependent variable. This way, the data quality of the numerical inputs into the valuation was significantly improved, while important insights were learned.

Still, bypassing the problem like this, does not test real option valuation satisfactorily.

The difficulties encountered were very similar to the ones that are characteristic for the DCF approach, due to the fact that the same inputs must be forecasted in the DCF approach and that S_0 is in effect estimated applying DCF techniques.

There are important differences though. Most significantly, real option valuation only needs a numerical input on the average value of projected future cash flows, which is evidently easier. This is so, because the volatility captures the uncertainty and thus the fluctuations that can be expected. In other words, the division in two of the value level, S_0, and the expected distribution, the volatility, provides for a more sophisticated analysis of uncertainty per se. Through a separate and systematic treatment that enables modeling of the uncertainty as a stochastic process, the real option approach captures the value-increasing potential of uncertainty through the ability to actively respond to the future, as it unfolds. In comparison, the DCF approach incorporates a more static and simplified proxy for the uncertainty, which only perceives it as a risk that destroys value. At the same time, a number of individually projected scenarios would have to be calculated, if a distribution of likely outcomes should have been forecasted.

In conclusion, the real option approach may be said to have an advantage here relative to the other NPV methods in the sense that it only need to identify an average, since the volatility depicts the range of outcomes the value of S_0 may take.

The volatility reflects the driver of project value. This variable is the most extraordinary one introduced by the real option approach relative to conventional approaches to valuation. The process of estimating the numerical input of this variable and the quantitative sensitivity analysis that followed, revealed that this estimate had a high error margin.

The volatility had to be estimated based on comparable companies. This was an approximation that was accepted for the lack of a better method. Though there were also valid motivations for this, a significant number of insufficiencies were related to the application too. Despite of the fact that the use of comparable companies is quite similar to the way that betas and discount rates are identified in the other NPV methods on the face of it, the fact is that the discount rates and the betas are explicitly, theoretically related to the market returns, and thus more directly empirically measures the theoretical content. Here real option valuation is at a disadvantage in its use of market proxies for the volatility, which is significantly more abstract and detached from what is actually intended to be measured.

In many ways, the volatility proved to be the cornerstone of real option valuation. Though the uncertainty can be subtly modeled, there are still nuances of uncertainty that need to be investigated further. In addition, the estimation would benefit much from a larger number of practical applications and more theoretical contributions, along with more reliance on in-house estimates, which presumably better capture the uniqueness of a specific corporate investment project. This would definitely be improved, if the familiarity with the real option framework was spread more widely to the level of management and practitioners in general. This way, the non-optimal reliance on comparable companies could be adjusted to a more subtle estimation approach.

One of the breaches in using comparable companies is the obvious difference between the companies. Here the differentiated capabilities across companies imply that important parts of the private risk are ignored, though it is obvious that some companies will do better, while some will do worse in the competitive struggle ahead. This uncertainty, which depends on the interdependencies and interactions between the industry participants, is however, extremely difficult to predict. Another breach is in the speculation that volatility might change over time, which is relevant, since the estimates are taken from companies that are listed and have come further in their development towards commercial introduction.

A number of reasons for drawing the parallel were presented, and as a proxy the use of comparable companies was defended. In this regard, it is important to keep in mind that the value and size difference between the comparable companies and the investment project is not the major issue. Rather, the core of the matter is whether they can be expected to have similar variation patterns, and as such share drivers in project value. To the extent that the variation is caused by the state of the technological development across companies within the industry and the uncertainty related to being a company with products under development and no commercially introduced products yet, this may not be as farfetched, as the differences from investment project to comparable companies may indicate at the first glimpse. The challenge of a changing volatility throughout a company's development is harder to conclude upon, but for the application in this paper, the basic assumption of most real option valuation techniques of a fixed volatility will be upheld. This qualification is overcome reasonably, due to the fact that the estimates on volatility are not derived from immediate and momentary observations, but rather taken from an extensive period of time.

Summing up, the variable of volatility has some conceptual shortcomings in terms of estimation. The content of the variable is difficult to measure directly, and the proxies at hand from comparable companies are conceptually further away from the theoretical definition, than e.g. beta in the DCF approach, which theoretically aims explicitly at estimating an asset's correlation with the market portfolio, which is also what is practically measured. These conceptual flaws of real option valuation are somewhat mediated by the fact that the comparable companies are not compared with for an estimate of value, but rather the variation in value. Once the conceptual shortcomings are taking into account, the ex-ante difficulty of estimating the future uncertainty are less profound, due to the explicit and systematic treatment of uncertainty. The estimation process itself is straightforward, and as the analysis showed, the numerical input is identifiable. Though, the analysis showed the highest error margin among the variables - leaving aside S_0 - the present value of expected cash flows for a moment - ranging from -19% to +16%, the sensitivity analysis showed that the impact on value was slightly less, respectively ranging from -14% to +8%. Though the spread is a little higher than desirable, it does not challenge the exactitude of the valuation markedly.

8.1.4 The Valuation Estimate

Following the configuration and the estimation of the numerical inputs, the calculations of the valuation were carried out. According to the strategy laid down by NRC, the investment project was appraised to be worth DKK 58 millions, compared with the DKK 9 millions estimate from a simple DCF valuation. In other words, the flexibility value of the option was shown to be quite substantial.

The value estimate was for a unified option to abandon that somewhat followed the original strategy of NRC and SMB, but simplified the options laid down in the strategy by combining them. This strategy might of course be changed through the course of the investment project. Nevertheless, the estimate represents the value from the point of initiation, under the constraint that information about the future is not at hand. As such, the value estimate is obviously as of a given point in time; i.e. the valuation date. Furthermore, it can be said to express the minimum value of the investment project in the sense that the simplifications undertaken reduce the amount of option value. First of all, the real option was configured as a European-type option, despite of the fact that most real options - including the one of the paper - might be seen as American-type options, due to their - for management - discretionary nature. Secondly, the simplified configuration only focus on one growth option; i.e. the option to abandon one growth opportunity, when there may in fact have been more options, each presumably adding some value. These could be concurrent growth options at the point of decision (as identified in the business map of NRC in the shape of four options in total) or subsequent growth options in medico-technology or other biochips-related applications of the research carried out in SMB. Though it was explained that the diminishing option-value effect may render the extra value marginally low, the above aspects nevertheless add to the underestimation of the value. All in all, when the valuation estimate is perceived as a cautious estimate, it is remarkable that so much option value is uncovered in the valuation anyway, namely DKK 58 - 9 millions = DKK 49 millions.

Though the estimation of numerical inputs in some cases were problematic, the sensitivity analysis showed that the error margins and their impacts were bearable and did not critically undermine the valuation results. Through alternative uses of the option pricing formula, it was even possible to avoid the use of the most problematic numerical input, S_0, and use the real option approach to valuation to forecast the potential in present value that was required for the investment to be worthwhile. This alternative use significantly improved the quality of the inputs to the valuation. Even when applying the numerical inputs (including S_0), the insights of the valuation were usable. For example, the determination of the volatility, which ceteris paribus would lead to break-even, gave a concrete contribution to the understanding of the value aspects of the investment project; i.e. in this case the necessity that the expected volatility is higher than it is for Intel.

In the following quotation, Luehrman (1998a) very precisely wraps up the essence of the above presented conclusion on the applicability:

> *'the real limitation is not the framework but rather the data or our knowledge of the project's parameters. Even when we know that we lack necessary data, the framework can help by showing us what the effect on value would be if the data were one thing or another'.* Luehrman (1998a) p. 66.

8.1.5 General Remarks relative to Conventional Valuation Techniques

The fact that valuation is aimed at quantifying complex, future phenomena makes it a discipline of best approximation, which does not pretend to provide monolith and exact measures of value, whose assumptions and forecasts will pass the test of time. Thus, in comparison with other valuation methods, some of the problems appear less invalidating for real option valuation per se, but much more related to the activity of valuation instead. Compared with the DCF method, the inadequacies related to estimating S_0 are very similar. Even the use of comparable companies can be identified in this comparison, though it is somewhat more appropriate in the DCF approach, due to the theoretical contents of the concept of beta and discount rates.

8.1.6 Major Shortcomings and Benefits

Seen in isolation, some of the major problems related to the real option approach to valuation are the modeling and estimation of volatility, and the forecast of the expected cash flows, S_0. In terms of volatility, an important question is whether it can be reasonably estimated using comparables; i.e. do variance in market returns as incorporated in the stock prices of comparable, listed companies approximate the volatility in the value driver of the investment project. The problems related to S_0 are rather evident.

Of course, there are some caveats in the application of real option valuation and the complex framework around it. Though a number of insights appear readily applicable, there are reasons to be careful, when using these insights operationally. Two counterintuitive insights were that longer project duration (t) and more uncertainty (volatility, σ) enhance value. In connection with project duration, the validity of the insights depends on the absence of competitive disadvantages from longer time horizons - i.e. slower reaction time - and on the initial costs not to increase as a consequence of the extended period. In the case of volatility much emphasis has been put on demonstrating what is and what is not meant by this. To outline two of the most important qualifications to this insight, the uncertainty is not desirable if it is only a risk; i.e. a higher probability of negative developments. Additionally, higher volatility is not beneficial, if it is beyond the company's capacity to respond to. Especially the latter deserves further comments with regard to this application of real option valuation.

As presented in section 2.7, Huchzermeier & Loch (1997) discuss companies' shortcomings with regard to exploiting the asymmetric upside potentials for different kinds of uncertainty, which can be seen as factors causing different kinds of volatility. A company's capacity to respond to certain kinds of uncertainties (i.e. to utilize the higher potential outcomes) may be inadequate, even to the extent that the option value is reduced. Examples hereof could be that a company is unable to keep up with technological progress or to fulfill changes in customer demand. Huchzermeier & Loch (1997) raise an interesting discussion, which does not apply as much to this paper's financial application of real option valuation, as to the strategic perspective. Since the real option valuation of SMB made use of a proxy from comparable companies' market returns, this volatility estimate is directly related to market payoffs, and according to Huchzermeier & Loch (1997) explicitly causing an uncertainty for which the principle of more volatility leading to higher value prevails. With regard to strategic analysis and strategic planning, this contribution nevertheless highlighted the danger of blindly chasing uncertainty, while calling for more research into the different kinds of uncertainty and volatility. Yet, the issue has not been treated further in the subsequent literature.

All in all, through increased familiarity and practical use, the estimation and use of volatility could be greatly improved. Though there are some qualifications and - to a certain extent - some questionable estimation techniques and wanting data quality, even a rough and simplified application of real option valuation, as in this paper, uncovers significant value. Thus real option valuation must be seen as a step forward for valuation. One of the important things to keep in mind may be not to strive for exactitude given the focus on the future, and instead aim at simple option configurations that capture extra value implications, but not as such all contingencies, imaginable as well as unforeseeable.

8.1.7 Real Option Valuation and R&D

The focus of the application in this paper has been a research investment project. Technically, most of the lessons learned are probably applicable to other types of investment projects. As such the approach would probably not be very different. Still, some of the challenges encountered in this application may be surpassed in connection with other kinds of investment projects.

Basic requirements are that a contingent decision and a fixed time frame can be identified. Apart from that the major challenges, where different kinds of investment projects may be foreseen to vary, are the configuration of the business case in terms of mapping the options and the estimation of volatility. The R&D nature of this paper's business case complicated these two issues in two ways.

First of all, the wide applicability of the basic findings from R&D implies a potential, which is hard to capture completely in the configuration. The options may simply be too numerous. In this aspect, other kinds of investment project may be easier to configure by being in a context, which is more clear-cut in terms of contingencies and potential developments. Nevertheless, as was argued in this case, this is not a reason for refraining from the use of real option valuation, since significant value may still be captured, even if the configuration is not exhaustive.

Secondly, the unique and distinctive character of most R&D investment projects makes the estimation of volatility through the identification of 'twin assets' problematic; e.g. the use of comparable companies. The core of the matter is to approximate the volatility in the driver of project value. In this regard, investment projects with measurable drivers of value have a clear advantage. Commodities such as natural resources and other standardized goods traded on global markets (e.g. paper, oil, cacao), energy supplies and other utilities, and real estate may be examples of underlying assets, which are measurable / priceable and where historic prices may provide good and relatively direct proxies. Opposite, investment projects where such drivers are unavailable, even in the shape of comparable companies, the real option approach to valuation may be close to impossible to apply.

8.1.8 Summing Up

In summary, the real option approach to valuation provides additional insights into the activity of valuation by capturing extra dimensions of value, most notably flexibility, compared with conventional valuation techniques. The investment projects that can be analyzed must exhibit real option characteristics, which does not limit the applicability of the approach as much as could be anticipated; neither in terms of configuration, nor mathematical solutions.

The technical challenges of applying real option valuation is not that difficult to overcome, and the primary qualification and problem is the extent to which the numerical inputs capture the realities of the business case. In other words, whether the estimates of some of the variables actually measure the content as outlined theoretically. Nevertheless, it is the position of this paper that real option valuation shows new indicative approaches for incorporating more aspects of value into the activity of valuation.

Though the application of this paper focused on research investments, the real option approach may very well be more readily applicable to other kinds of investment projects. As such R&D appears to be a complex unit of analysis, due to the unique and compounded nature of most R&D.

With these conclusions on the applicability of the financial perspective on real options in mind, the next section concludes the paper by addressing the main thesis related to the real option framework's capacity for bridging the gap between financial and strategic theory.

8.2 Conclusions on the Gap

The strategic perspective on real options puts forward the notion that uncertainty might be valuable, when the commitment of resources can be adjusted to as the future developments unfold. This responsiveness to contingencies resembles the capabilities view's notion of a capability as *'a capacity to act in certain ways in a certain range of circumstances'*[307]. This shared focus provides for the integration of the strategic perspective into one of the predominant positions in strategic theory. While the capabilities view is particularly suited for an encompassing analysis of competitive advantage, the strategic perspective extends it by establishing a dynamic and forward-looking perspective on the aspects of capabilities that hold the highest value and the approach to utilizing these capabilities. For knowledge-based capabilities such as research capabilities, the integration of the two perspectives is particularly relevant. In a joint analysis, the capabilities required are perceived as investment platform, designed to enhance the creation of growth options. In a such analysis, research capabilities are pregnant with option value, due to the wide applicability of the fundamental principles and knowledge, the uncertainty related to achieving desired research results, and the ability to decide on the commercial exploitation along the course of the research as the uncertainty is resolved.

Though the strategic perspective contributes to strategic theory by adding a dynamic and forward-looking perspective to the capabilities view, and thus somewhat overcoming its retrospective character, even both perspectives in this fruitful unification do not deal with the introverted and distinctively internal focus that is stated as one of the major shortcomings of the capabilities view by itself.

NRC lend itself well to an analysis of competitive advantage in the capabilities view. An illustrative presentation of its resource base suggested that it could be seen as an investment platform with a corporate venturing capability applicable to both internal and external research results. In NRC, investment policies could be understood through real option lenses. In the face of uncertainty, NRC was shown to apply an incremental investment approach in certain cases presented. Though preemptive investments or optimal production capacity planning could be speculated to require early commitments of full investments, it was shown that gradually increasing investments were pursued. In a real option perspective, it could be argued that the value of awaiting future developments in the face of substantial uncertainty made this the more valuable approach. In summary, the strategic perspective was shown to be theoretically compatible with a predominant position within strategic theory, namely the capabilities view, extending the analysis of competitive advantage with directions as to the nature of competitively strong capabilities. This was shown to be particularly relevant for knowledge-based capabilities, such as research competencies.

The solid theoretical positioning of the strategic perspective on real options in the field of strategic theory and the illustrative presentation of NRC at a rather holistic level of strategy was as far as the strategic side of the gap was outlined in the analysis.

In terms of bridging the gap, it must be remembered that valuation fundamentally must serve strategy. As it was established, it makes little sense to simplify the strategic analysis or the strategic planning in order to accommodate a real option valuation hereof. Hence, the primary challenge in bridging the gap is to explicitly analyze and quantitatively estimate the value-impact of identified strategic alternatives.

With regard to the analysis of competitive advantage, the real option approach to valuation most notably depends on the identification of a contingent decision or more, and a fixed time frame. As it has been explained, the major benefit of real option valuation is the incorporation of the value of management's option to alter course in the face of uncertainty, and to await the development as the future unfolds.

Meanwhile, the strategic perspective on real options as an extension of the capabilities view appears to be more concerned with creating options that are exposed to uncertainty and awaiting the resolution of uncertainty, than identifying the contingencies and specifically incorporating contingent decision points, where flexibility may be required. In other words, the strategic perspective's contribution to the capabilities view is more concerned with developing latent options in the shape of an investment platform with valuable growth options, than looking to identify the exercise of them.

In conclusion, the inherent flexibility demands of strategic analysis, which must cope with contingencies and complexities at the most holistic level of the firm and provide broad directional guidelines, are too far removed from real option valuation's demand for a clearly demarked investment profile, as to facilitate quantitative analysis of competitive advantage.

That said, parts of the strategic planning may however benefit from the incorporation of real option valuation. As in NRC's corporate venturing set-up, the strategic choice among potential ventures to enter into - the choice among business maps - may be supported by real option valuation. At this more concrete level of strategic planning, it may be very beneficial with comparative valuation in order to prioritize, and value-based considerations on the strategies laid down on the individual ventures seen through real option lenses.

In terms of bridging the gap for research investments, the strategic perspective on real options was demonstrated to be in excellent concord with the capabilities view. However, the real option valuation of the business case revealed that certain aspects of research investments complicate the operationalization. The wide applicability of ongoing research efforts and the difficulties of forecasting explicit scenarios given the substantial technological and market uncertainties make research investments complex to configure. This was particularly true for the contingent decision, but also for the effects of the expiration mode. Furthermore, the estimation of certain numerical inputs were difficult. Most notably the present value of the expected cash flows, which had to be based on dubious assumptions. Though the volatility was found problematic to estimate too, one of the main improvements was found to be combined treatment of future cash flows and volatility. This way of forecasting cash flows deriving from research - which in any event is problematic - may be more appropriate than through conventional valuation techniques. Though the analysis came up with cautious estimates and important insights on the value-impact of uncertainty, it is very likely that other kinds of investments would make more suitable objects of analysis. The preeminent example in the literature hereof is natural resource extraction.

In conclusion, the real option framework may not fulfill its alluring promises entirely in terms of bridging the gap between financial valuation and strategic analysis and planning at the most holistic level of firm strategy. The prerequisites and foci simply appear to be too divergent. Nevertheless, the framework does hold a significant potential for strategic decisions, when investment projects become more concrete at the lower levels of strategic planning. The practical implementation of the framework, and in particular the financial perspective, is still not that widespread among practitioners, which is probably due to the lack of familiarity with the framework, most notably the volatility, but maybe also the intuitive and mathematical barriers. Since the theoretical underpinnings are well-established, the obscurity that the framework suffers from could presumably be helped through more practical applications in the literature. As Flyvbjerg observes when he paraphrases Kuhn '*a research area without many and good cases is a research area without systematic production of examples, and a research area without examples is a weak research area*'[308].

Given the well-developed nature of the theoretical principles on both the strategic and the financial of the gap, it can be argued that the biggest immediate steps forward towards utilizing the undeniable potential of the real option framework should be taken in applications and efforts put into relating it to the realities of strategic analysis, strategic planning and financial valuation. Due to the unique context of the individual company in terms of strategic complexities and uncertainty, the main potential might very well lie with practitioners, and not in further development of the already very instrumental theoretical framework. Through the active use of the framework's insights and tools, practitioners may think value-creation through real options lenses into strategy formulation, while testing, monitoring and evaluating volatility estimates and other quantitative aspects. Forecasting contingent decisions through the real option framework helps identify critical targets or events, which have value-impact, because the framework's focus is on those decisions that go hand-in-hand with further resource commitment. As such the primary benefit is not just the emphasis on forecasting contingencies - which all serious strategic analysis and planning must be assumed to investigate - but more so its explicit treatment of the value-impact related to the timing and extent of the resource commitment. The division of the uncertainty into market risk (events) and private risk (targets) may facilitate more systematic evaluation of the events and targets that actually trigger further or terminated resource-commitment. Since uncertainty is related to the company-specific capacity to adapt to it, capabilities across firms with regard to achieving targets and responding to events can aptly be considered differential in the sense that an opportunity for one company may be very well be unexploitable to a competitor. Thereby is also said that there are limits as to how much uncertainty can be theoretisized, which may only be transcended by practitioners with hands-on feel of the particular uncertainties a company is facing. In that sense, the real option framework can only provide the methods for the analysis, not the substance that must go into it.

This paper's division of the framework in two perspectives that are both demonstrably applicable, though disparate, may better facilitate attempts at bridging the gap by highlighting what aspects of the gap are the most critical, and thus showing how wide or narrow - depending on the perspective and the application at hand - the gap actually is. The first step towards an alignment is to identify the desirability of doing so and developing the heuristic mindset to approach it with.

There is no doubt that the real option framework addresses the issue of greatest concern to the firm; namely the future. Though hard to predict, its attempt at systematic treatment of uncertainty is hard to ignore, as is its dictum that uncertainty can be a guiding light.

9. Perspectives

As touched upon in the conclusion, the need for further research may not be as pressing, as the need to devise ways of actually applying the framework. The literature on the real option framework lacks detailed case applications that exemplifies and demonstrates that the technicalities are not a big barrier. Unfortunately, the few case applications to R&D that can be found surpass this, presumably due to reasons of confidentiality. This is probably due to the sensitive nature of the data. The rest of the literature presents unconvincing stylized examples which almost all contains simplified business cases, where the DCF method show negative NPVs and the real option approach positive NPVs. For the dissemination of the techniques behind real option valuation. It can be hoped that more detailed case applications will be put forward.

Of suggestions for further research, many aspects have already been covered by research. As such the theoretical framework must be considered very sophisticated. In this regard, this paper has not tested the limit of the framework in many contexts, but more introduced aspects of the existing sophisticated analytical framework behind, which is capable of capturing very complex configurations and uncertainty profiles. One aspect of uncertainty must be pointed to though, as an area that need further research, namely the extent and limit of the value-impact of uncertainty. As was explained in the paper, it has been demonstrated that certain kinds of uncertainty in the shape of volatility do not exhibit quite the unequivocal value-enhancement for options, as has otherwise been conceived of as the cornerstone. These results should be further investigated with a view both to the direct quantitative implications, as well as to nature of uncertainty, when utilizing the strategic perspective on real options.

Notes

CHAPTER 1

[1] Børsen (March 21, 2000), Frankfurter Allgemeine Zeitung (May 8, 2000), Business Week (June7, 1999), The Economist (August 14, 1999), Harvard Business Review (Jan-Feb 1994), (Jul-Aug 1998), and (Jan-Feb 1999).

[2] These advances have been carried out in what is known as the Human Genome Project, which has just been concluded in February 2001.

[3] The consequences of the advances within genetics outlined here are far from exhaustive, but among the most notable. A more thorough presentation can be found in the paper.

[4] Copeland (1996).

[5] Andersen (1999) p. 19.

[6] Ibid. p. 163.

[7] Ibid. p. 235. Own translation.

[8] Ibid. p. 168.

[9] Flyvbjerg (1991) p. 148.

[10] Andersen (1999) p. 165.

[11] Flyvbjerg (1991) p. 151. Own translation.

[12] Since NKT Holding is publicly listed, stock exchange regulation on information disclosure pertains to the provision of data.

[13] Andersen (1999) pp. 39-40.

CHAPTER 2

[14] Cox, Ross & Rubinstein (1979) p. 229.

[15] Amram & Kulatilaka (1999) p. 36.

[16] Black & Scholes (1973).

[17] In 1997, Myron Scholes and Robert C. Merton were awarded the Nobel prize in Economics for their work in that context. Fisher Black had died in 1995. Robert C. Merton had worked closely with Black and Scholes on the arguments in seminal article published in 1973. Amram & Kulatilaka (1999) pp. 31-31.

[18] Cox, Ross & Rubinstein (1979) pp. 229-230.

[19] Ibid.

[20] as is known from statistics, by letting delta / the subintervals go towards zero.

[21] Faulkner (1996) p. 54, Amram & Kulatilaka (1999) p. 6, and Hearth & Park (1999) p. 2.

[22] Myers (1984).

[23] Myers (1984) p. 127.

[24] It can be argued that since the late 1980's and throughout the 1990's, financial theory through value-based management as presented by e.g. Copeland (1995) has had a significant impact on strategic thinking in the business enterprise sector. By assessing restructuring opportunities, and actively expanding the firm value through divestment and M&A, information policies, financial engineering initiatives, this line of financial theory has in some ways bridged the gap, though at an overall (corporate) level, which holds no promise for business strategy; i.e. how to compete in a given market or industry.

[25] By using the word 'functional', no normative meaning is intended, even though Chandler's definition is one of the most cited, and thus predominant in the field ofd strategy. Instead the word is used in the sense that the definition points to a number of activities included in the formulation of strategy, which is suitable for outlining the field of strategy investigated in this paper.

[26] Grant (1996) p. 15 and Ghemawat (1999) p. 1.

[27] Trigeorgis (1996) p. 23.

[28] Myers (1984) p. 128.

[29] The DCF technique and the differences between it and real option valuation will be treated in more detail in chapter 4 and chapter 5.

[30] Real option valuation is specifically excluded from the term referred to as conventional valuation techniques. By this term, the discounted cash flow approach to valuation can be kept in mind in the following. This approach will be presented in the paper.

[31] See also Amram & Kulatilaka (1999) pp. 63-64 and Trigeorgis (1996) pp. 7-8.

[32] Trigeorgis (1996), Mitchell & Hamilton (1988), Faulkner (1996), and many more.

[33] A more thorough presentation of the impact of the strategic perspective on real options on strategic theory can be found in appendix 1.

[34] Foss (1998).

[35] Grant (1996) p. 122.

[36] Ibid. p. 106.

[37] Hamel & Prahalad (1996) p. xx (page numbers in preface).

[38] Foss (1998) p. 7.

[39] To be a core competence, a capability must have certain characteristics in terms of competitor differentiation, extendability, and customer value. Hamel & Prahalad (1996) pp. 223-228.

[40] Competitive advantage is analyzed in terms of the extent, the sustainability, and the appropriability of the competitive advantage according to Grant (1996) pp. 128-133.

[41] Hamel & Prahalad (1996) pp. 172-193 and Grant (1996) p. 126.

[42] The limits of the capabilities view presented here draws heavily on Foss (1998).

[43] Foss (1998) pp. 12-15.

[44] Ibid. p. 12.

[45] Ibid.

[46] Ibid. p. 12.

[47] Ibid. p. 8.

[48] Black & Scholes showed that the formula conceptually was particular applicable to the valuation of warrants, which share many characteristics with financial options in being contractually laid down with fixed time horizons, and related to an observable and predefined stock price, but also to the analysis of common stock and bonds. For strategy formulation, the focus on the valuation of common stock is the most relevant of the proposed uses in Black & Scholes (1973). The line of reasoning is that the stockholders hold an option on the company's assets with the right, but not the obligation to buy them. This they will do if the value of the assets is higher than the debts in the company. 'In effect, the bond holders own the company's assets, but they have given options to the stockholders to buy the assets back. The value of the common stock ... will be the value of the company's assets minus the face value of the bonds, or zero, whichever is greater.' Black & Scholes (1973) pp. 649-650. In other words, the stockholders, due to their limited liability, hold the option to default on the debt payments to the bond holders in case of bankruptcy or liquidation at a point where the value of the assets is less than the value of the debts. This application is of limited practical use, because of the complexity of the valuation unit in terms of estimated cash flows and volatility, the continuous distribution of dividends, and in particular the undeterminable time horizon. Therefore, at the corporate level, the real option valuation is relatively useless with regard to a value estimate of a going concern.

[49] Grant (1996) p. 110.

[50] For a more thorough presentation of the different kinds of real options, please refer to section 4.3.1 Types of Real Options.

[51] Growth options and option to abandon can under certain circumstances been seen as two sides of the same option. C.f. section 4.3.1

[52] Kogut & Kulatilaka (1994), Foss (1998), Kulatilaka & Perotti (1998), Amram & Kulatilaka (1999).

[53] Kogut & Kulatilaka (1994) pp. 54, 61.

[54] Foss (1998) p. 12.

[55] Foss (1998) p. 12.

[56] Kulatilaka & Perotti (1998) p. 1022.

[57] Amram & Kulatilaka (1999) p. 66.

[58] Ibid. p. 21.

[59] Kogut & Kulatilaka (1994) p. 61.

[60] Faulkner (1996) p. 54.

[61] Amram & Kulatilaka (1999) pp. 27, 69.

[62] Kulatilaka & Perotti (1998) p. 1022.

[63] Myers (1984) p. 135, Dixit & Pindyck (1995) p. 107, and Smit & Ankum (1993) pp. 241-243.

[64] Herath & Park (1999) p. 3.

[65] The contributions are of course limited to the ones to my knowledge. I cannot pretend to be familiar with all contributions on real options and R&D, but hope to have found the most quoted and important through my research.

[66] Myers (1984) p. 135.

[67] Faulkner (1996) p. 54.

CHAPTER 3

[68] From the first discovery of superconducting materials in 1911, the fundamental problem had been that in order to achieve the frictionless transmission that superconducting materials facilitate, these had to be cooled down to minus 269 degrees Celsius - the boiling point of Helium, which is a quite troublesome process, dependent on vacuum, making the practical application highly unfeasible. Basically, more energy was used to cool down the superconducting materials, than was saved through the elimination of energy losses in connection with the transmission itself. In 1987-88, discoveries in the international research community showed that ceramic superconductors would work at a higher temperature (minus 196 degrees Celsius - hence the name High-Temperature Superconducting materials, which made it possible to use liquid nitrogen to cool down the ceramic superconductors. This reduced the energy required to cool down the superconductors with a factor 100, and likewise also the costs associated with the use of superconductors.

[69] Ingeniøren, December 16, 1988.

[70] Some of the research results stem from the time before the unification of NKT research into NRC, e.g. the four companies listed in the note below. The distinction is not central and will not be upheld. Thus when referring to NRC's value-creating capacity, parts hereof may originate from the time before the consolidation of NKT research; i.e. the actual establishment of NRC.

[71] NKT Elektronik sold 1994, Lycom sold 1994, Draka-NKT sold 1996, GIGA sold 2000. GIGA was the most valuable (DKK 9.4 billions). The total proceeds from the four divestment are estimated to be in the area of DKK 11-13 billions. Interview June 5, 2000 with Søren Isaksen, CTO, NKT Holding.

[72] NKT 'Vision 2005'.

[73] The 'NKT Company Package' includes various non-operational, administrative activities, such as legal services, human resource procedures, patent applications, etc.

[74] Grant (1996) p. 123.

[75] Keil (2000) p. 5.

[76] To be a core competence, a capability must have certain characteristics in terms of competitor differentiation, extendability, and customer value - Hamel & Prahalad (1996) pp. 223-228.

[77] Amram & Kulatilaka (1999) p. 69.

[78] The cost budget figure of DKK 50 millions neither takes into account the costs incurred in connection with the decentralized research efforts in NKT before 1990, nor other revenues or benefits, e.g. from intra-company assignments. It therefore presents a simplified and indicative estimate on the value-creation, which nevertheless must be perceived as significant and disproportionate to the costs.

[79] section 2.7 & 2.8.

[80] section 2.8.

[81] Interview June 5, 2000 with Søren Isaksen, CTO, NKT Holding.

CHAPTER 4

[82] Trigeorgis (1996) p. 23.

[83] section 1.2 'Theoretical Perspective'.

[84] Copeland et.al. (1996) & West & Jones (1999).

[85] The formula is taken from Friedl & Hansen (1999) p. 8, but can also be found with other notations in Levy & Sarnat (1994) p. 38 and Trigeorgis (1996) p. 32.

[86] By the use of the term 'linear' is meant that for each point in time of the cash flows observed, only one observation prevails, and not that the cash flows systematically follow a straight (linear) line graphically.

[87] Copeland et.al. (1996) p. 156.

[88] Levy & Sarnat (1994) p. 635.

[89] The time factor is obviously not the earlier described time-value of money, but the time the investment project is exposed to the uncertainty / volatility.

[90] Amram & Kulatilaka (1999) p. 29.

[91] Levy & Sarnat (1994) pp. 637, 640.

[92] Black & Scholes (1973) p. 644, Trigeorgis (1996) pp. 82, 91-92 and Levy & Sarnat (1994) p. 636. Please note that s2 (variance) and s (standard deviation - square root of variance) both are measures of the volatility and both enter into the formula. The s is the one that will be identified in chapter 6 on numerical inputs to the variables.

[93] Black & Scholes (1973) p. 644.

[94] Black & Scholes (1973) p. 646, Trigeorgis (1996) p. 211, and Levy & Sarnat (1994) pp. 627-628.

[95] Cox, Ross & Rubinstein (1979) pp. 250-251.

[96] Trigeorgis (1993) p. 6.

[97] The presented outline of the development is inspired by Trigeorgis (1993) and Trigeorgis (1996).

[98] Leslie & Michaels (1997) p. 7.

[99] Trigeorgis (1996) p. 124.

[100] In fact, real option valuation may be applied to real options that are tied to contractual agreements, such as government-granted, time-restricted licenses. However, this is not the rule.

[101] The risk-free interest rate also enters into the calculation of the discount rate with which S0 is discounted, e.g. through the use of the CAPM model to determine the discount factor.

[102] Robbins-Roth (2000) pp. 111-123.

[103] Trigeorgis (1993) p. 6 & Trigeorgis (1996) p. 227.

[104] Trigeorgis (1996) p. 252. See also section 6.3.1.

[105] Amram & Kulatilaka (1999) and Luehrman (1998a) p. 51.

[106] Trigeorgis (1996) pp. 127-129.

[107] Ibid.

[108] This kind of stochastic process is a so-called Ito's process, and the kind of processes that will be treated in this paper.

[109] Friedl & Hansen (1998) pp. 28-29.

[110] Ibid. p. 34.

[111] Ibid. p. 21.

[112] Trigeorgis (1996) p. 125.

[113] Friedl & Hansen (1998) p.19-20.

CHAPTER 5

[114] Matthews (1997) in ATV (1997) pp. 117-119.

[115] Respectively the exercise price and the value of the option in the option pricing formula of Black & Scholes.

[116] 'To lay golden eggs in an incubator ' to paraphrase recent news paper articles - Børsen 16/03/2000, Politiken 22/03/2000, and Børsen 24/08/2000.

[117] section 3.3 and 3.4.

[118] This presentation of Scandinavian Micro Biodevices draws heavily on NRC's business map. Specific references are only made in connection with direct quotes.

[119] chapter 3.

[120] Genomics: The branch of molecular genetics concerned with studying the organization of genomes and determining the nucleotide sequences of the component genes. Source: A Dictionary of Science, Oxford University Press © Market House Books Ltd 1999 at www.xrefer.com.

[121] Genetics: The branch of biology concerned with the study of heredity and variation. During the 20th century … important advances in biochemistry and microbiology have led to clarification of the chemical nature of genes and the ways in which they can replicate and be transmitted, creating the field of molecular genetics. Source: A Dictionary of Science, Oxford University Press © Market House Books Ltd 1999 at www.xrefer.com.

[122] Fortune (1999).

[123] Microfluidics can be defined as: 'The manipulation of small quantities of fluids on a chip to perform chemical reactions of measurements'. Lehman Brothers (1997) p. 116.

[124] It is known that Japanese companies are also active in the field, but so far without commercial introductions. Thus, little is known of the Japanese level.

[125] Micro as a prefix indicates 10^{-6} , which e.g. for distance means 1/1000000 of a meter or 1/1000 of a millimeter (milli is equal to 10^{-3} .

[126] NRC's Business Map for SMB.

[127] www.nkt.dk.

[128] D&MD (1999) p. 392.

[129] Microflow systems are also known as labs-on-a-chip.

[130] A more detailed introduction to the product technology of biochips and the difference between microarrays and microflow systems is attached in appendix 4.

[131] The presentation of the fundamental genomical concepts draws on U.S. Department of Energy (1992) - 'Primer on Molecular Genetics'.

[132] The complete map of a human genome that is established can be thought of as the genome of one particular human being, though the complete map is based on pieces of several individuals genomes gathered into one.

[133] A comparison or benchmark functionality.

[134] The sequencing of the humane genome was concluded in February 2001 and was published in its entirety in Science of February 15, 2001. The map of the human genome is remarkably known as The Book of Life by the researchers working on it.

[135] Department of Energy (1992) p. 5.

[136] Ibid.

[137] The use of the term translate is different from the way the term 'translation' is used in connection with the protein synthesis that the genes cause - see later.

[138] While some diseases are entirely genetically determined, many diseases are acquired from factors external to the genome, or a combination of genetic and environmental (i.e. not genetic) causes.

[139] Recombination: The rearrangement of genes that occurs when reproductive cells (gametes) are formed (in

reproduction).

[140] Mutation: A sudden random change in the genetic material of a cell that may cause it and all cells derived from it to differ in appearance or behavior from the normal type. The majority of mutations are harmful, but a very small proportion may increase an organism's fitness.

[141] D&MD (1999) p. 395.

[142] Diagnostics: Study related to identifying the nature of a problem, here an illness / disease.

[143] Pharmacogenomics can be defined as: 'genetic disaggregation of patient populations based on genetic indicators of their response to a pharmaceutical product'. Lehman Brothers (1997) p. 42.

[144] Genomics can be defined as: 'A scientific subdiscipline of molecular biology and computational science that studies the physical and informational structures of genomes'. Lehman Brothers (1997) p. 116.

[145] Bioinformatics as a term is constructed of 'bio' and 'informatics'. 'Bio' is naturally derived from the focus. Informatics is '(t)he study of the application of computer and statistical techniques to the management of information', and can be related to many different sciences. DOE (1992) p. 37.

[146] Lehman Brothers (1997) p. 55.

[147] Lehman Brothers (1997) p. 115.

[148] Gene therapy can be defined as: 'Insertion of normal DNA directly into cells to correct a genetic defect' - DOE (1992) p. 37.

[149] Forensic: 'relating to the scientific tests used to help with police investigations and legal problems' - Oxford Advanced Learner's Dictionary (1995).

[150] A more detailed introduction to the exciting perspectives in the recent advances in genetics combined with the application of biochips can be found in appendix 5.

[151] D&MD (1999) p. 395.

[152] NRC's Business Map on SMB.

[153] The availability of the reagents can be so limited and the costs so high that the biochip technology will make some experiments feasible that were too expensive using conventional techniques. Some reagents are even so scarce that the new biochip technology has made the experiments possible at all, given the constraints in availability. D&MD (1999) p. 395.

[154] Fortune (1999) p. 2.

[155] IPO is an abbreviation for 'initial public offering', meaning the point in time, when a company's stock is introduced commercially to the public. That is, the company's stock is sold publicly on an exchange.

[156] Other American companies in the industry: Cepheid (June 2000 - CPHD), Kiva Genetics, Micronics, Sequenom (February 2000 - SQNM), Orhid Biocomputer (May 2000 - ORCH). In parenthesis is indicated the months of the IPOs and the letter code, where relevant.

[157] NASDAQ abbreviation: AFFX. Revenues of USD 96.86 millions in 1999.

[158] NASDAQ abbreviation: INCY. Revenues of USD 264.78 millions in 1999.

[159] It has later been decided to establish the biotechnology laboratory in SMB, and not in NRC. This happened after the fixed date of analysis.

[160] Besanko (1996) pp. 276-285.

[161] Fortune (1999) p. 2.

[162] In vitro: 'Outside a living organism (generally in a test tube)' as opposed to in vivo: 'Inside a living organism'. Lehman Brothers (1997) p. 116.

[163] NIST (1998) p. 8 and Lehman Brothers (1997) p. 8.

[164] preceding footnote.

[165] US National Institute of Standards and Technology.

[166] NRC's Business Map on SMB.

[167] Ibid.

[168] Ibid.

164

[169] Ibid.

[170] Fortune (1997) p. 1.

[171] MST News (1999).

[172] Ibid. p. 4.

[173] The figure of merit in the microprocessor industry has been processing capacity at a more or less unchanged price level. This basically depends on how many transistors can be put on a chip, i.e. how close to each other they are.

[174] MST News (1999) p. 7. C.f. Moore's Law.

[175] Differences in packaging techniques may sound a little irrelevant, but refer to a critical component of an integrated, practical solution. E.g. Affymetrix has a cartridge solution, where disposable cartridges are put into more advanced and reusable equipment sold below costs to facilitate broader use (the so-called razor-blade model referring to Gilette) - Biospace.com (1999) p. 2. (www.biospace.com/articles - first posted July 6, 1999).

[176] MST News (1999) p. 6.

[177] Science (2000) p. 11.

[178] MST News (1999).

[179] Ibid. (1999) p. 6.

[180] District Court ruling as of July 20, 2000 - www.nasdaq.com.

[181] Commodification refers to the process some products go through from a differentiated product in terms of quality and price towards a commodity status, where quality is relatively undifferentiated and the good is traded based on price and quantity, in established qualities.

[182] Amram & Kulatilaka (1999) pp. 90 ff.

[183] Luehrman (1998a) pp. 51 ff.

[184] Amram & Kulatilaka (1999) p. 89.

[185] Luehrman (1998a) p. 51. See also section 4.3.

[186] This is a common perception among the contributors. E.g. Kester (1984) who was the first to treat real options on R&D - c.f. section 2.7.

[187] section 5.2.6.

[188] NRC Business Map on SMB.

[189] Trigeorgis (1996) pp. 2-3 & Amram & Kulatilaka (1999) p. 92. For a presentation, see section 4.3.1 Types of Real Options.

[190] section 3.5.

[191] Interview June 5, 2000 with Søren Isaksen, CTO, NKT Holding.

[192] section 5.2.2.

[193] Trigeorgis (1993) p. 6 & Trigeorgis (1996) p. 227.

[194] Trigeorgis (1996) p. 252.

[195] Amram & Kulatilaka (1999) p. 89.

[196] Amram & Kulatilaka (1999) state that option interactions may blur the analysis so much that, in practice, it is better to reframe the real option away from interactions in order not loose transparency and tractability. Amram & Kulatilaka (1999) p. 91.

[197] Amram & Kulatilaka (1999) pp. 97-98 & Luehrman (1998a) p. 51.

[198] Amram & Kulatilaka (1999) pp. 91-95.

[199] The project duration might be unknown due to internal factors in SMB that prolong the development (i.e. delays in the achievement of research targets or in the development of the required competencies). This, however, do not influence the calculation of the real option in this case, since it is specifically limited to looking at the option value three years ahead. If the developments that facilitate the option have not been

achieved after the three years, this is an inherent risk of the option, and whether the project can be prolonged or not, the three-year time horizon is considered known in the sense that it will not be shorter due to internal factors.

[200] section 5.6.1.

[201] section 5.1.

[202] Amram & Kulatilaka (1999) p. 96.

[203] Trigeorgis (1999) p. 118.

[204] Luehrman (1998a) p. 66.

[205] Faulkner (1996) p. 51.

[206] Ibid. p. 50.

CHAPTER 6

[207] Interview June 5, 2000 with Søren Isaksen, CTO, NKT Holding.

[208] In this rough and simplified projection accounting-wise and calculation of expected cash flows, net income, profits and cash flows are considered equal.

[209] Sales to profits ratio equals reported net income to net sales. The ratios are taken from www.nasdaq.com.

[210] Interests, taxes, depreciations and amortization are included in the calculation of net income. Particularly, the taxes paid by these companies cannot be expected to correspond to NKT's. Still, the estimated ratios will be upheld in the calculations for convenience and because it reflects not only Taiwanese taxes, but also the taxes levied on the companies internationally, and thus is hard to disaggregate and correct for.

[211] As such the early estimates may be seen as optimistic and the later as pessimistic.

[212] a perpetual annuity.

[213] Adapted from Copeland et.al (1996) p. 288. In the formula, anticipated growth, inflation, and drivers of growth can relatively unproblematic be incorporated, but this was not considered relevant for these projections.

[214] Dallocchio (1997) pp. 50-53 and Copeland et.al. (1996) pp. 266-274.

[215] Copeland et.al. (1996) p. 266.

[216] Dallocchio (1997) p. 48 and Copeland et.al. (1996) pp. 267-268.

[217] Copeland et.al. (1996) pp. 342-347.

[218] Definition: A measure of the volatility of a stock relative to the overall market. A beta of less than one indicates lower risk than the market; a beta of more than one indicates higher risk than the market. www.nasdaq.com uses the S&P 500 as the underlying index to measure the overall market for beta.

[219] Oxelheim et.al. (1998)

[220] Oxelheim et.al. (1998) and DAA (1999)

[221] Copeland et.al. (1996) p. 375.

[222] Homepage of the Copenhagen Stock Exchange - http://www.xcse.dk.

[223] Copeland et.al. (1996) p. 268-269.

[224] www.bondsonline.com, November 14, 2000.

[225] Copeland et.al. (1996) pp. 268-269.

[226] Ibid. p. 343.

[227] Definition: A measure of the volatility of a stock relative to the overall market. A beta of less than one indicates lower risk than the market; a beta of more than one indicates higher risk than the market. nasdaq.com uses the S&P 500 as the underlying index to measure the overall market for beta.

[228] '(T)he point on the average cost curve at which average costs are minimized is known as the minimum efficient scale' by definition - Besanko et al. (1996) pp. 77, 176-177. The use of the term minimum efficient scale is slightly different in this paper. By minimum efficient scale is here meant the minimum scale in terms

of investments in production facilities that is required to be competitive (i.e. produce competitively). In other words, in this paper it is the point where an increase in production scale does not lead to a competitively advantageous cost-reduction, and not at such an absolute level, as the above definition outlines it.

[229] Luehrman (1998a) pp. 60, 64.

[230] www.fondsborsen.dk under 'Statistik & Valuta'.

[231] Luehrman (1998a) p. 54.

[232] Trigeorgis (1999) pp. 120-121.

[233] Amram & Kulatilaka (1999) p. 100, Luehrman (1998a) p. 58, and Trigeorgis (1999) pp. 120-121.

[234] Amram & Kulatilaka (1999) p. 212.

[235] Amram & Kulatilaka (1999) p. 100, Luehrman (1998a) p. 58.

[236] Trigeorgis (1999) p. 121.

[237] Ibid.

[238] Both uncertainty marketwise and technologically.

[239] section 6.2.3.

[240] Caliper with the letter code CALP and ACLARA with ACLA.

[241] D&MD (1999) p. 393.

[242] Beta is: '(a) measure of the volatility of a stock relative to the overall market. A beta of less than one indicates lower risk than the market; a beta of more than one indicates higher risk than the market.' (source: www.nasdaq.com). Beta can take any positive value above zero, but rarely exceeds three. Beta is well-known from Discounted Cash Flow valuation, where it frequently is used to determine the investment-specific market risk premium through the use of the CAPM-model (c.f. section 4.3 and 7.2 for presentation).

[243] The beta values presented here are taken from the homepage of NASDAQ on July 20, 2000 (www.nasdaq.com).

[244] The market portfolio used in NASDAQ, AMEX and NYSE's beta calculations is S&P 500. S&P 500 is Standard and Poor's 500, a composite stock price index, which is weighted according to the market capitalization / market value (=shares outstanding multiplied by stock price) of 500 stocks that are traded on the three exchanges mentioned above.

[245] From the quotes on the exchanges and other financial sources, the price (i.e. value) of the option (C0), the current stock price (S0), the exercise price (Ex), the risk-free interest rate (rf), and the maturation (t) are all known.

[246] Hull (1997) p. 246. This procedure is known mathematically as an iteration.

[247] Ibid. p. 250. See also section 5.1.

[248] The dates of dividend payouts are known as ex-dividend dates in the financial jargon. Dividend payouts are distributed to the stock holders of record on the ex-dividend date. The ex-dividend dates and the dividend amounts are typically declared some time in advance; e.g. one to two months before.

[249] The stock price does not necessarily drop. This depends on the reaction of the stock market (c.f. Intel later).

[250] Hull (1997) pp. 249-250 & 269.

[251] Ibid. p. 250.

[252] Ibid. p. 249.

[253] Ibid. p. 250.

[254] The time horizon of the options traded on these two companies with the longest maturity - see later.

[255] Figures have been obtained as of July 19, 2000 at www.bondsonline.com.

[256] Hull (1997) p. 140.

[257] As all business men the market makers would like buy cheaply and sell expensively. There are regulations on upper limits for the bid-ask spread.

[258] The ITM, ATM, and OTM indications refer to the status of the options, if they were exercised immediately. Please refer to explanation in section 5.2.1. Hull (1997) p. 141.

[259] Hull (1997) p. 503.

[260] Assuming that the market is right.

[261] Hull (1997) pp. 498-499.

[262] Ibid.

[263] Hull (1997) p. 495.

[264] For an explanation of financial leverage see section 7.2.

[265] Hull (2000) p. 440.

[266] This behavioral explanation of the market is labeled 'crashofobia' - Hull (2000) p. 440.

[267] Hull (1997) p. 502.

[268] Ibid. p. 509.

[269] Amram & Kulatilaka (1999) p. 101.

[270] If the underlying asset is the only activity of the company or the option is on a stock, the jump diffusion outlined is similar to the risk of bankruptcy. This risk is presumably higher for biotech companies with no previous profits and no completely proven technology or market.

[271] Since the real option is a call option on introducing the technology to the market, it does not make sense to buy this underlying asset by initiating production and marketing, if the underlying asset is worthless, no matter what the price is.

[272] Hull (1997) pp. 246-247.

[273] The LEAPS options on Coca Cola and Intel are ignored here, since these two companies are included for comparison purposes.

[274] Hull (1997) pp. 246-247 & 505- see also later in the paper on the application of volatility matrices.

[275] Luehrman (1998a) p. 58.

[276] Hull (1997) p. 509.

[277] Ibid. p. 505.

[278] Fortune (1999) and D&MD (1999) pp. 392-395.

[279] section 6.2.6.

[280] Expiration date: January 19, 2002 and January 19, 2003.

[281] A simple 1-2 stock split leading to a halving of the stock price and a doubling of the number of shares.

[282] Expiration date: January 19, 2002 and January 19, 2003.

[283] Here, the ATM implied volatilities have not been calculated by interpolation, but taken at the exercise price closest to the current stock price. Furthermore, the implied volatilities have been taken from the longest maturity available, which January 2001 equal to 6 months.

[284] the development of the implied volatilities with changing maturities.

[285] Hull (1997) pp. 246-247.

[286] Hull (1997) p. 233 & Amram & Kulatilaka (1999) p. 213.

[287] Hull (1997) p. 233.

[288] Amram & Kulatilaka (1999) p. 213.

[289] Hull (1997) p. 233.

[290] Ibid. p. 235.

[291] Actually, it is the first trading day after the ex-dividend date that should be removed, since it is on this day that the decrease in value will occur.

[292] Hull (1997) p. 235.

[293] On the day of their introduction to NASDAQ ACLARA's stock price rose 71%, whereas Caliper's fell 11%.

[294] Hull (1997) pp. 233 & 248.

[295] Ibid.

[296] For the exact figures underlying the graphs, please refer to appendix 7.

[297] Hull (1997) p. 508.

[298] Ibid. p. 246.

CHAPTER 7

[299] Black & Scholes (1973) p. 644. See also section 4.2.

[300] section 6.2.

[301] Please note that the value changes of these percentage changes in the project duration, t also apply to the volatility as a variance (s2), and the interest rate, as mentioned before.

[302] Iteration in this case basically means that figures are processed in the formula until C0 is equal to the 'development costs' (sales and costs in the period from 2000 to time of the decision in 2003) or DKK 19 millions.

[303] Amram & Kulatilaka (1999) p. 69.

CHAPTER 8

[304] Beta is the covariance of the returns of the investment relative to the market portfolio, based on E(rm) = the expected rate of return on the overall market portfolio, E(rm) – rf = the market risk premium, and hence b = beta, the systematic risk of investment project.

[305] Luehrman (1998a) p. 60.

[306] section 5.3.

[307] Foss (1998) p. 12.

[308] Flyvbjerg (1991) p. 158. Own translation.

References

Literature

Akademiet for de tekniske Videnskaber (abbr. ATV): 'Den vanskelige balance: En bog om forskningsledelse', Grafodan Offset aps, 1997

Allison, Graham T.: 'Conceptual Models and the Cuban Missile Crisis' in American Political Science Review, vol. 63, no.3, pp. 689-718, 1969

Amram, Martha & Nalin Kulatilaka: 'Disciplined Decisions: Aligning Strategy with the Financial Markets', Harvard Business Review, January-February 1999

Amram, Martha & Nalin Kulatilaka: 'Real Options – Managing Strategic Investment in an Uncertain World', Harvard Business School Press, 1999

Andersen, Ib: 'Den skinbarlige virkelighed; om valg af samfundsvidenskabelig metode', Samfundslitteratur, 1999

Berk, Jonathan B., Richard C. Green & Vasant Naik: 'Valuation and Return Dynamics of New Ventures', National Bureau of Economic Research Working Paper 6745, 1998

Besanko, David, David Dranove & Mark Shanley: 'Economics of Strategy', John Wiley & Sons, 1996

BioInsights: 'Biochips: from Hype to Reality', www.bioresearchonline.com, 2000

Biospace.com: 'The Matrix; A Revolution in Array Technologies', www.biospace.com/articles/, June 7, 1999

Black, Fisher & Myron Scholes: 'The Pricing of Options and Corporate Liabilities', Journal of Political Economy no. 81 pp. 637-659, 1973

Boer, F. Peter: 'Traps, Pitfalls and Snares in the Valuation of Technology', Research Technology Management, pp. 45-54, September-October 1998

Brealey, Richard A. & Stewart C. Myers: 'Principles of Corporate Finance' 3rd Edition, McGraw-Hill Book Company, 1988

Buckley, Adrian: 'International Investment: Value Creation and Appraisal: A Real Options Approach', Handelshøjskolens Forlag, 1998

Business Week: 'Exploiting Uncertainty', June 7, 1999

Business Week: 'The Great DNA Chip Derby' by Ellen Licking, October 25, 1999

Børsen: 'Vurder e-business projekter som optioner', p. 19, March 21, 2000

Clinical Science: 'Science, Art and Drug Discovery; A Personal Perspective' by Simon F. Campbell, vol. 99, part 4, pp. 255-260, Portland Press, Published by the Biochemical Society and the Medical Research Society, October 2000

Copeland, Thomas E. & Philip T. Keenan: 'How Much is Flexibility Worth', McKinsey Quarterly, no. 2, 1998

Copeland, Thomas E. & Philip T. Keenan: 'Making Real Options Real', McKinsey Quarterly, no. 3, 1998

Copeland, Tom, Tim Koller & Jack Murrin: 'Valuation: Measuring and Managing the Value of Companies', 2nd Edition, Wiley Frontiers in Finance Series, 1996

Cox, John C., Stephen A. Ross & Mark Rubinstein: 'Option Pricing: A Simplified Approach', Journal of Financial Economics 7, pp. 229-263, 1979

Dallocchio, Maurizio: 'International Valuation of Firms: For M&A Value Management', Università Bocconi, October 1997

Dansk Aktie Analyse (abbr. DAA): 'Dansk Aktie Analyse', Quarterly Magazine, October 1999 (translation: Danish Stock Analysis)

Den store Danske Encyklopædi - Danmarks Nationalleksikon, Gyldendal

Dixit, Avinash K. & Robert S. Pindyck: 'Expandability, Reversibility, and Optimal Capacity Choice', National Bureau of Economic Research, NBER Working Paper Series 6373, 1998

Dixit, Avinash K. & Robert S. Pindyck: 'The Options Approach to Capital Investment', Harvard Business Review, May-June 1995

Drug & Market Development (D&MD): 'Technology & Strategy: The Current State of the Biochip Business', vol. 10, no. 11, November 1999

Eriksen, Bo & Nicolai J. Foss: 'Styring af strategiske optioner: Et redskab til dynamisk kompetenceudvikling', Odense Universitets Trykkeri, 1995

Ernst & Young: 'Bridging the Gap: Ernst & Young's 13th Biotechnology Industry Annual Report', December 1998

Faulkner, Terrence W.: 'Applying 'Options Thinking' to R&D Valuation', Research Technology Management, May-June 1996

Flyvbjerg, Bent: 'Case studiet som forskningsmetode', Institut for Samfundsudvikling og Planlægning, Aalborg Universitetscenter, 1988

Flyvbjerg, Bent: 'Rationalitet og magt; Det konkretes videnskab (bind 1)', Akademisk Forlag, 1991

Fortune: 'Gene Chip Breakthrough', March 31, 1997

Fortune: 'Good-Bye Test Tubes; Hello, Labs-on-a-Chip', October 11, 1999

Foss, Nicolai J.: 'Real Options and the Theory of the Firm', Copenhagen Business School, Department of Strategy and Industrial Economics, Series of Working Papers 98-3, 1998

Foss, Nicolai, J.: 'The Theory of the Firm: an Introduction to Themes and Contributions', Copenhagen Business School Working Paper, 1998

Frankfurter Allgemeine Zeitung: 'Die New Economy braucht neue Bewertungsverfahren' und 'Bei Realoptionen hinken europäische Manager der Realität hinterher', p. 30, May 8, 2000

Friedl, Anders L. & Thomas Gessø Hansen: 'Reale optioner: en revolution inden for kapitalbudgettering', Master's Thesis, Copenhagen Business School, 1998

Frost & Sullivan: ''Hairy Microchips': Mapping the Intricacies of the Genome, Decoding Mutations of Viruses', January 1998

Grant, Robert M.: 'Contemporary Strategic Analysis: Concepts, Techniques, Applications', 3rd. Edition, Blackwell Publishers, 1998

Hamel, Gary & C.K. Prahalad: 'Competing for the Future', Harvard Business School Press, 1996

Hamilton, William F. & Graham R. Mitchell: 'What is your R&D Worth', McKinsey Quarterly, no. 3, 1990

Herath, Hemantha S.B.& Chan S. Park: 'Economic Analysis of R&D Projects: An Options Approach', The Engineering Economist, Norcross, 1999

Hommel, Ulrich & Gunnar Pritsch: 'Investitionsbewertung und Unternehmensführung mit dem Realoptionsansatz« in Ann-Kristin Achleitner, Georg F. Thoma (editors), 'Handbuch Corporate Finance', pp. 1-65, Köln: Verlag Deutscher Wirtschaftsdienst, Supplement September 1999

Hommel, Ulrich & Gunnar Pritsch: 'Marktorientierte Investitionsbewertung mit dem Realoptionsansatz', in Finanzmarkt- und Portfoliomanagement, Vol. 13, No. 2, pp. 121-144, 1999

Huchzermeier, A. & C.H. Loch: 'Evaluating R&D Projects as Real Options: Why More Variability is not Always Better', INSEAD Working Papers Series 97/105/TM, 1997

Hull, John C.: 'Options, Futures, and Other Derivatives', 3rd Edition, Prentice Hall, 1997

Hull, John C.: 'Options, Futures, and Other Derivatives', 4th Edition, Prentice Hall, 200

Human Genome Program, U.S. Department of Energy, 'Primer on Molecular Genetics', Washington, D.C., 1992

Keil, Thomas: "External Corporate Venturing; Cognition, Speed, and Capability Development", short summary of a dissertation defended at Helsinki University of Technology handed out at REMAP seminar on Corporate Venturing, February 7, 2000, Copenhagen Business School

Kemna, Angelien: 'Case Studies on Real Options', Financial Management, Tampa, Autumn 1993

Kester, Carl W.: 'Today's Options for Tomorrow's Growth', Harvard Business Review, March-April 1984

Kogut, Bruce & Nalin Kulatilaka: 'Options Thinking and Platform Investments: Investing in Opportunity', California Management Review, Winter 1994

Kulatilaka, Nalin & Enrico C. Perotti: 'Strategic Growth Options', Management Science, vol. 44, no. 8, August 1998

Lehman Brothers: 'BioChips; Advances in DNA Array and Microfluidics Technologies', Lehman Brothers, November 1997

Leslie, Keith J. & Max P. Michaels: 'The Real Power of Real Options', McKinsey Quarterly, no. 3, 1997

Levy, Haim & Marshall Sarnat: 'Capital Investment & Financial Decisions', 4th. Edition, Prentice Hall, 1994

Lint, Onno & Enrico Pennings: 'A Business Shift Approach to R&D Option Valuation', in L. Trigeorgis (Ed): 'Real Options and Business Strategy: Applications to Decision Making', Risk Books, 1999

Luehrman, Timothy A.: 'Investment Opportunities as Real Options: Getting Started on the Numbers', Harvard Business Review, July-August 1998

Luehrman, Timothy A.: 'Using APV: A Better Tool for Valuing Operations', Harvard Business Review, May-June 1997

Luehrman, Timothy A.: 'What's It Worth? A General Manager's Guide to Valuation', Harvard Business Review, May-June 1997

Mantoni, Tue: 'A Real Options Perspective on R&D Investments', Master's Thesis, Copenhagen Business School, 1999

Mitchell, Graham R. & William F. Hamilton: 'Managing R&D As a Strategic Option', Research Technology Management vol. 31 no. 3 pp. 15-22, May-June 1988

Morris, Peter A., Elizabeth Olmsted Teisberg & Lawrence Kolbe: 'When Choosing R&D Projects, Go With Long Shots', Research Technology Management, January-February 1991

MST News: 'MEMS/MST Fabrication Technology based on Microbricks: A Strategy for Industry Growth', no. 1 (quarterly) March 1999

Myers, Stewart: 'Finance Theory and Financial Strategy', Interfaces vol. 14 pp. 126-137, January-February 1984

National Institute of Standards and Technology (abbr. NIST): 'Nano- and MEMS Technologies for Chemical Biosensors', 1998

National Institute of Standards and Technology (abbr. NIST): 'Tools for DNA Diagnostics 98-08', 1997

Nichols, Nancy A.: 'Scientific Management at Merck: An Interview with CFO Judy Lewent', Harvard Business Review, January-February, 1994

NKT 'Financial Statements 1992-1999', NKT, 1993-2000

NKT Research Center: 'NKT Research Center', NKT Research Center

NKT Research Center: 'Strategic Technologies. Business Development', NKT Research Center, 1999

NKT: 'A New Process for Treatment of PVC Waste, NKT

NKT: 'Focus: NKT's Integrated Approach to Transmission', NKT

NKT: 'Highlights 1999:1-4 & 2000:1', NKT 1999-2000

NKT: 'Midt i en fornyelsesprocess', NKT, 1996

NKT: 'NKT 100 år: Tusinder af flittige hænders værk', N. Olaf Møller, 1998

NKT: 'Superconductors in the Danish Energy Sector – Project Overview 1997-2001, NKT

NKT: 'Vision 2005: a New Way of Thinking', NKT, 1999

Oxelheim, Lars, Arthur Stonehill, Trond Randøy, Kaisa Vikkula, Kåre B. Dullum and Karl-Markus Modén: 'Corporate Strategies to Internationalise the Cost of Capital', Copenhagen Studies in Economics and Management, nr.A-12, Handelshøjskolens Forlag, København (translation: Business School Publishers, Copenhagen), 1998

Ridley, Matt: 'Genome: The Autobiography of a Species in 23 Chapters', Harpercollins, 2000

Robbins-Roth, Cynthia: 'From Alchemy to IPO: The Business of Biotechnology', Perseus Pr., 2000

Rumelt, Richard P.: 'Towards a Strategic Theory of the Firm', in Robert Boyden Lamb (Ed.): 'Competitive Strategic Management', Prentice Hall, 1984

Sanchez, Ron: 'Demand Uncertainty and Asset Flexibility: Incorporating Strategic Options in the Theory of the Firm', Copenhagen Business School, Department of Strategy and Industrial Economics, Series of Working Papers 99-6, 1999

Sanchez, Ron: 'Uncertainty, Flexibility, and Economic Organization: Foundations for an Options Theory of the Firm', Copenhagen Business School, Department of Strategy and Industrial Economics, Series of Working Papers 99-5, 1999

Schwartz, Eduardo S. & Mark Moon: 'Evaluating Research and Development Investments', in 'Project Flexibility, Agency and Competition; New Developments in the Theory and Application of Real Options' edited by M. Brennan and L. Trigeorgis, Oxford University Press, 2000

Sharp, David J.: 'Uncovering the Hidden Value in High-Risk Investments', Sloan Management Review, Summer 1991

Smit, Han T. & L.A. Ankum: 'A Real Options and Game-Theoretic Approach to Corporate Investment Strategy under Competition', Financial Management, Tampa, Autumn 1993

Smith, James E. & Robert F. Nau: 'Valuing Risky Projects: Option Pricing Theory and Decision Analysis', Management Science vol. 41 no. 5, May 1995

Springham, Derek G. (ed.): 'Biotechnology: The Science and the Business', 2nd Edition, Harwood Academic Publishers, 1991

Stevens, Tim: 'Picking the Winners' Industry Week, March 6, 2000

The Economist: 'Keeping All Options Open', p. 62, August 14, 1999

Trigeorgis, Lenos (Ed): 'Real Options and Business Strategy: Applications to Decision Making', Risk Books, 1999

Trigeorgis, Lenos (Editor): 'Real Options – Models, Strategies, and Applications', Praeger Publishers, 1995

Trigeorgis, Lenos: 'Real Options and Interactions with Financial Flexibility', Financial Management, Tampa, Autumn 1993

Trigeorgis, Lenos: 'Real Options: Managerial Flexibility and Strategy in Resource Allocation', The MIT Press, 1996

U.S. Department of Energy and The Human Genome Project: 'To Know Ourselves', Berkeley National Laboratory, California, July 1996

U.S. Department of Energy: 'Primer on Molecular Genetics', Human Genome Management Information System, June 1992 (http://www.ornl.gov/hgmis/publicat/primer/intro.html)

West, Thomas L. & Jeffrey D. Jones (Editors):'Handbook of Business Valuation', 2nd Edition, John Wiley & Sons, 1999

Internet Resources

US National Institute of Health - NIH National Center for Human Genome Research - http://www.nchgr.nih.gov

US Department of Energy - DOE Human Genome Program - http://www.er.doe.gov/production/oher/hug_top.html

US Oak Ridge National Laboratory - http://www.ornl.gov/TechResources/Human_Genome/home.html

Encyclopedia Britannica Online @ www.eb.com

MPP Working Paper Series

1/2001 **Marjatta Maula:**
High Tech High Touch. How Top Managers and Consultants Facilitate Organizational
Transformation by Improving Social Competencies and Total Quality

2/2001 **Peter Holdt Christensen:**
Jubii for vidensarbejderne? Om ledelsesudfordringer og ledelsesstrategier i en vidensvirksomhed

3/2001 **Niels Åkerstrøm Andersen:**
Beslutningens ubesluttelighed

4/2001 **Christian Frankel**
Fællesskabets markedsdannelse

5/2001 **Jon O. Pedersen og Christian Vintergaard**
Det danske venture capital marked - en oversigt anno 2000

6/2001 **Susanne Lamdahl Justesen**
Innoversity - a study of the dynamics inherent in the relationship between innovation and diversity (master thesis)

7/2001 **Nille Nolsø Skalts & Trine Brandt-Lassen**
chat - en sokratisk jordemoder - en afhandling om fænomenet dialog i chatmæssige sammenhænge (master thesis)

8/2001 **Philip Skjødt**
Bridging the gap between strategy & valuation - a real option approach to R&D valuation (master thesis)

9/2001 **Kim Gørtz**
Et spørgsmål om identitet. Filosofien om det samme og det andet

A list of working papers published in 1998-2000 can be found at MPP's homepage: http://www.cbs.dk/departments/mpp/working.shtml

www.ingramcontent.com/pod-product-compliance
Lightning Source LLC
Chambersburg PA
CBHW051213200326
41519CB00025B/7104